DEDICATION

Dedicated to my teachers who helped me at every step along the way on my journey of understanding the social order so that I might glorify God.

www.craigvincentmitchell.com

PREFACE

This book represents another step in a journey that began when I studied Christian Ethics/ Philosophy at Southwestern Baptist Theological Seminary. I did not fully understand what I was getting into, but the engineer in me had to get a complete understanding of the all the subject matter relating to the social order. How does it all fit together? I had to know. So when I finished my PhD in Christian Ethics/ Philosophy, I had to understand economics. So I went back to school and began my study of the social sciences. Once I got a grasp of economics, I had to get a grasp of politics/ government.

I have not arrived at my final destination, but I have learned enough to help others as they seek to put it all together. This book should help those in bachelors level philosophy, politics and economics programs. It should also help those in MPA and political science programs. Finally, this book should also prove helpful for those PhD students in public administration preparing to take their comprehensive exams.

I have had a lot of help along the way. Many more people than I could ever thank, but I must mention just a few of them. My teachers at Southwestern Baptist Theological Seminary who taught me Ethics/ Philosophy include: Ebbie Smith, Bob Bernard and Douglas K. Blount. My teachers at the Business School at University of Texas in Arlington (UTA) who taught me economics include: Roger Meiners, Michael Ward, C.Y. Choi and Mahmut Yashar. Finally my professors at the School of Urban and of Public Affairs at UTA include Colleen Casey, Enid Arvidson, and Andreshir Anjomani. Thanks for your patience and your great teaching.

Craig Vincent Mitchell, PhD

TABLE OF CONTENTS

Chapter 1: Philosophy

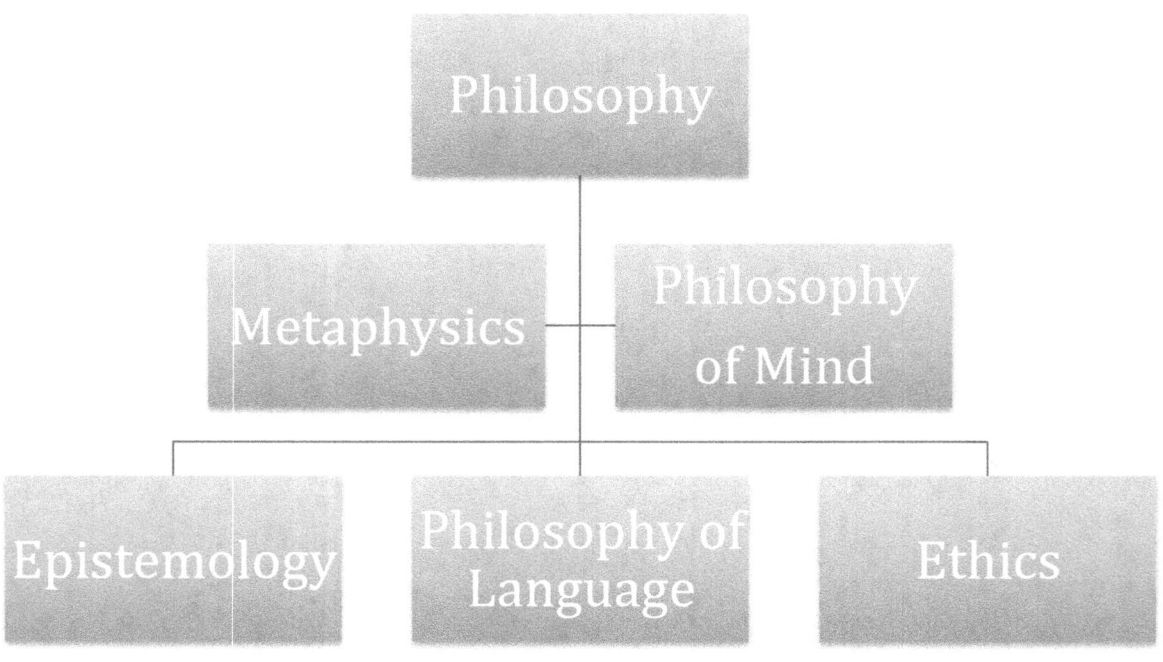

Chapter Outline

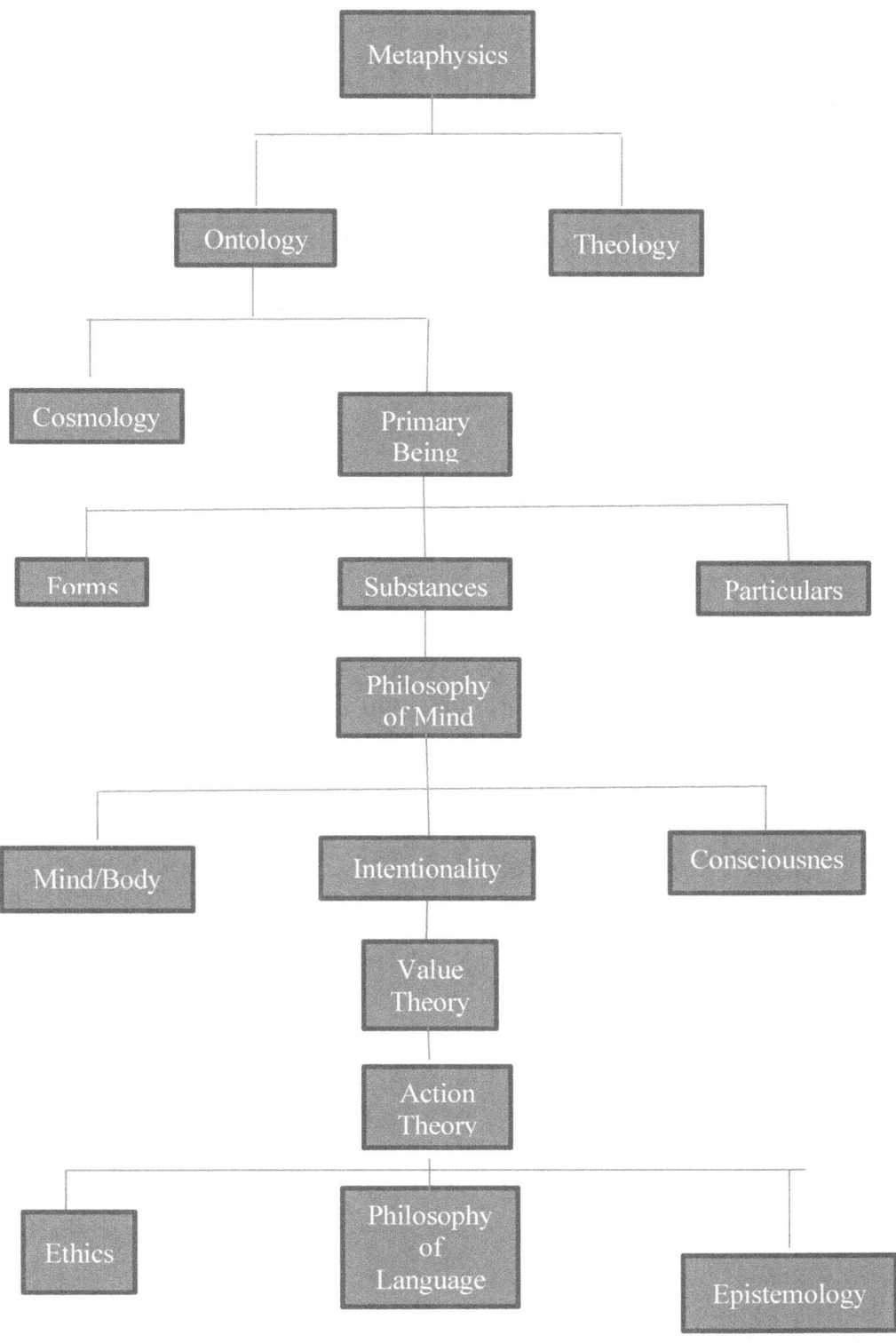

Plato's Philosophy

The starting point of Plato's philosophy is his metaphysics.

Metaphysics (ontology)		Epistemology	
Abstract Universals (the intelligible world) These exist in another world without space or time	**The Good** **Higher forms** Truth, beauty, and justice	**Dialectic** Pure reason	**Knowledge** (*scientia*) Reached via reason
	Lower forms Mathematics, geometry, class concepts	**Understanding** Makes use of hypotheses and images	
Concrete Particulars (the sensible world) These exist in this world of space and time	**Particular objects** Actual things	**Belief** Based on Reliable perception	**Opinion** (*opinio*) Reached via sensory experience
	Images Perception of things	**Conjecture** Based on unreliable perception	

Example of Plato's Metaphysics

Abstract Universals The world of the forms	**Higher forms**	**The Good**	This is the highest of the forms.	This is what is the most real of all things.
		The Form of Beauty	An objective, unchanging and eternal thing.	It is merely real.
	Lower Forms	**The Concept of Beauty**	Ideas of beauty accessible to human reason.	This is less real than the form of beauty because it can be misperceived
Concrete Particulars The world that we experience	**Particular objects**	**Individual beautiful things**	Anything that instantiates the property (or form) of beauty.	This is less real than the concept of beauty because it is a copy of what is real.
	Images	**Imitations of Beautiful things**	Includes things like art and representations of reality, like photographs, recordings etc.	This is the least real of all things because it is a copy of a copy.

Augustine's Philosophy

Augustine believed that all being and knowledge comes from God. He also believed that metaphysical forms are ideas in the mind of God.

Metaphysics (ontology)		Epistemology	
Abstract Universals The mind of God	**God** (truth itself, ultimate reality)	**Beatific Vision** (Requires faith)	**Divine Illumination** (this kind of knowledge is the most reliable)
	Eternal Truth (the true, the real, universals)	*Sapientia* Divine wisdom (Requires faith)	
Concrete Particulars This world	**Objects** Temporal truths, material things	*Scientia* Belief and understanding together (Requires faith)	**Knowledge** Sensory knowledge (This kind of knowledge is less reliable)
	Representations Temporal truths like history and empirical science	**Authority** (*Opinio*) No first hand knowledge	

Aristotle's Metaphysics

Andronicus of Rhodes placed Aristotle's writings in order. He took a number of related works and gave them the title *Metaphysics*. It means after the physics.

Ontology	**Primary Being** (*Prote Ousios*)	**Universals** - a concept of general application	
		Forms- ideas, blueprints or design of a thing	
		Essences- the necessary and intrinsic nature of a thing	
		Particulars- an instantiation of a form	
		Substances- the combination of form and matter	
	Cosmology	**Time**- where a thing exists	
		Space- where a thing exists	
		Causation Why a thing exists	**Formal Cause**
			Material Cause
			Efficient Cause
			Final Cause (*Telos*)
Theology	**The Prime Mover (God)**	His substance is immaterial, eternal and unchanging. He causes motion in the universe because everything is attracted to him. He is both beautiful and good. He thinks only of himself because there is nothing better to think about	
	Unmoved Mover	47-55 of these fill the outer void, beyond the sphere of the fixed stars. They are immaterial substance, having neither parts or magnitude.	
	Cosmic Order	is set in order and motion by the unmoved movers. These attract and are imitated by everything else.	

ONTOLOGY

	Nature of Universals	Type of ontology	States of Affairs	Bare particulars
Extreme Realism (Platonic Realism)	*Universalia ante res* (Universals before things)	Two or more world ontology, because more universals exist than are instantiated	Universals exist as state of affairs types.	Rejects the existence of bare particulars
Moderate Realism (Aristotelian Realism)	*Universalia in rebus* (Universals in things)	One world ontology. Only those universals that are instantiated in particulars exist	Universals and particulars exist as states of affairs.	Rejects the existence of bare particulars
Moderate Nominalism *Predicate nominalism-* or *Concept Nominalism-* (Conceptualism) Universals exist as concepts of the mind. Properties are created by the classifying mind	*Universalia post res* (Universals after things)	One world ontology	Universals and particulars exist as states of affairs.	Rejects the existence of bare particulars
Extreme Nominalism *Resemblance* or *Class Nominalism-* a particular is connected to other particulars because of their resemblance or they are in the same class. **See tropes**	Only things exist	One world ontology	States of affairs are not required.	Bare particulars exist.

Cosmology

Time	**Perceptual** - time as it appears to an observer	
The temporal aspect of reality	**Conceptual** - Time as it actually is.	A theory — A tensed view of time. This view allows for the past, present and future. The only aspect of time that exists is the present. Rejects the idea of a space-time continuum. Also known as presentism.
		B theory — A tenseless view of time. Relations of events are described as earlier than, or later than. Accepts idea of a space time continuum. Also known as eternalism.
Space	**Perceptual** - space as it is perceived by an observer	
The spatial aspect of reality	**Conceptual** - space as it actually is	
Causation	**First** – The cause of all other causes. Not Aristotle's idea	
What relates one event in reality to another temporally	**Formal** – the shape or "blueprint" to which an entity **conforms**.	
	Material - the physical "stuff" of which something is made.	
	Efficient – forces or activities/agents produce an entity.	
	Final – the purpose for which an entity exists.	
Space-time continuum—an idea explained in Einstein's special theory of revelation. It asserts that space and time are tied together as aspects of a four dimensional universe. There are three spatial dimensions and one temporal dimension.		

The Aristotelian Chain of Causes

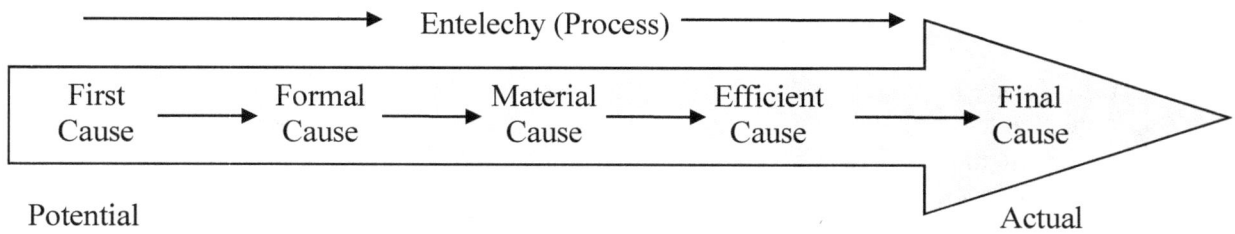

Potential   Actual

Causation

Only metaphysical realists accept all four causes. Most metaphysical nominalists reject all four causes. William of Ockham rejected the formal cause. George Berkeley rejected the material cause. David Hume rejected the efficient cause. Galileo Galilei rejected the final cause. Some contemporary nominalists accept the existence of the material and efficient causes.

First Cause	Not all realists accept this cause. This is Aquinas's idea	Aristotle did not have a first cause of any kind
Formal Cause	All realists accept this cause and all nominalists reject it	William of Ockham rejected this cause
Material Cause	All realists accept this cause and moderate nominalists	George Berkeley rejected this cause
Efficient Cause	All realists accept this cause and moderate nominalists	David Hume rejected this cause
Final Cause	All realists accept this cause and all nominalists reject it.	Galileo rejected this cause

Teleology

That branch of cosmology (metaphysics) that is concerned with final causes. The word "teleology" is based on the Greek root *telos* which means "achievement, power, completion as a state, or perfection." Teleology also refers to the appearance of purpose in nature. As a result, teleology is compatible with **naturalism**.

Metaphysics	Metaphysical realism	Teleology is compatible only with metaphysical realism
Axiology	Teleology in axiology requires metaphysical realism.	Teleology is compatible with value realism. Values are dependent upon metaphysics (ontology). The principle of organic unities is consistent with teleology. The principle of universality is also consistent with teleology.
Epistemology	Teleology in epistemology requires metaphysical realism	Teleology is compatible with epistemological realism as well as externalist approaches to epistemology. Only truth has intrinsic value in a teleological epistemology.
Ethics	Teleology in ethics requires metaphysical realism	Teleology is primarily concerned with the 'good,' rather than the 'right.' The 'good' (*summum bonum*) has intrinsic value instead of the 'right.' Teleology is consistent with moral realism. Virtue ethics and natural law are the only ethical theories compatible with teleology.
Aesthetics	Teleology in aesthetics requires metaphysical realism	Teleology is primarily concerned with beauty, because beauty is the only intrinsic value. Teleology is consistent with aesthetic realism.

Idealism

G.W. Liebniz coined the term "idealism" to explain that his metaphysical position was essentially the same as that held by Plato. It is difficult to define the term "idealism." Central to idealism is the thesis that reality depends upon the mind for its existence. Another idea associated with idealism is the rejection of materialism.

Type of idealism	Philosopher	Explanation
Objective idealism	**Plato** **Plotinus** **Liebniz**	What are most real are the forms. These forms are eternal, immutable, ontologically independent and immaterial. The forms are beyond sensory experience and are known only through reason. Some argue that this is just metaphysical realism.
Subjective idealism	**Bishop George Berkeley**	Berkeley rejected the existence of material bodies and believed that only minds exist. God's mind makes all things appear to human minds.
Absolute idealism	**G.W.F. Hegel**	This approach to idealism involves a subject-object dualism in which the subject is the ground of reality. Absolute idealists reduce material bodies to phenomenal states within the mind. The "mind" is a universal self-consciousness that exists behind or outside of nature. Reality is nothing more than a universal 'notion' (*Begriff*).
Transcendental idealism	**Immanuel Kant**	Kant believes that there is an external world (the noumenal world) that exists independently of the mind. His arguments against metaphysical speculation prevent one from actually knowing reality itself. All that one can actually know is the world of sensory appearances (the phenomenal world).
Critical idealism	**Gottlieb Fichte** **F.W.J. Schelling**	A negation of Kantian transcendental idealism which makes the distinction between self and non-self. It is a fore-runner to Hegel's absolute idealism. It asserts that the nature of reality is explained through mind derived principles of beauty and goodness. Like absolute idealism, the mind is a universal self-consciousness that exists behind or outside of nature.

Philosophy of the Mind

Philosophy of the mind is really a sub-discipline of metaphysics. It is a domain explored by both philosophers and by scientists. In the 21 century it has replaced philosophy of language as first philosophy. This came about when philosophers of language began to get stuck on a number of issues that can only be resolved in the philosophy of the mind.

Primary issues	1. What is the nature of the mind? 2. How does the mind relate to the brain and the rest of the body? 3. What are mental states? 4. How much can science tell us about the mind?
Cartesian dualism	Philosophy of the mind had its beginnings with Rene Descartes. He divided everything into either mind or body (spiritual or material). He argued that the mind and the body were united through the pineal gland. Cartesian dualism can take a number of different forms.
Materialism	This approach to philosophy of the mind assumes that the body or matter is all that exists. They assume that the mind is nothing more than the brain. There are a number of forms of materialism.
Functionalism	Functionalists allow for the possibility of immaterial substances, but are still committed to materialism. This is the dominant view in cognitive science and psychology.
Eliminativism	The view that there are no intentional states, such as: reasons for action, beliefs, desires, or intentions

Personal identity	**Personal identity and time** Does the self change with time, or does one become another person	
	The self Concerned with the nature of the self.	
	Agency Concerned with the will and how decisions are made.	
Cognitive science	**Cognition** What is consciousness? How does it work?	
	Emotion Concerned with the nature of the emotions and how they relate to cognition.	
	Action Concerned with individual acts and how they relate to cognition.	

Philosophy of Mind

Metaphysics	Consciousness	Intentionality	Personal Identity
Realism	Consciousness cannot be reduced to material/ physical processes	**Externalism** The content of the mind comes at least partially outside the individual. Compatible with a correspondence theory of truth.	**Externalism** What determines whether a person at one time and one at another are the same person depends on how the two are related physically, psychologically and how they relate to everything and everybody else.
Nominalism	**Reductionism or Eliminativism** Consciousness can be reduced to physical/ material processes	**Internalism** The contents of the mind come solely from within the individual. Not compatible with a correspondence theory of truth.	**Internalism** What determines whether a person at one time and one at another are the same person depends on how the two are related physically, psychologically

Contents of the Human Mind			
Metaphysics	**Rationality**	**Emotion**	**Volition**
Realism	Reason is what sets men apart from the animals and what makes man related to God. Reason is what allows men to act with purpose.	Emotions are not irrational. They are instead driven by reason. Emotions result from purpose. Emotions are bodily felt.	The will is normally driven by reason. It is only driven by emotion when it is weak. Men have wills that are in some sense free
Nominalism	Reason is and ought always be a slave of the passions	Emotions are irrational. Men are driven by their passions	Will is always driven by emotion. Men have wills that are not free in many senses.

The Mind/ Body Problem

Metaphysics	Type of combination	Substance	Mental states	Physical states
Realism	**Platonic Realism**	One substance	The mind acts causally on the body	The body acts causally on the mind
	Aristotelian Realism	One substance **Hylopmorphism** Psycho-somatic unity	The mind acts causally on the body and vice versa	The body acts causally on the mind and vice versa
		One substance **Supervenience**	**Teleological Functionalism** The mental supervenes on the physical	Physical facts govern all biological facts. The body acts causally on the mind and vice versa
Nominalism	Cartesian dualism	Two substances	The mind acts on the body through the pineal gland	The body acts on the mind through the pineal gland
	Parallelism/ occasionalism	Two substances	**Behaviorism** The mind does not act on the body	The body does not act on the mind
	Materialism/ epiphenomenalism	One substance	**Identity theory** The mind and mental states are just states of the brain	The body and physical states act on the body
	Subjective idealism	One substance	**Behaviorism** The mind is all that matters	The body does not act on the mind

Cartesian Dualism

Rene Descartes divided up the world between minds and material bodies.
Minds are: thinking substances which are, non-spatial, mental, and private.
Material bodies are: extended substances which are, spatial, have material properties and public.

Descartes believed that minds (or mental substances) can exist even after the demise of the body. He also believed that the mind and body interact and are united through the pinneal gland. In the modern period many philosophers attempted to explain how the mind and body interact.

Nicolas Malebranche	**Occassionalism**	The mind and body do not interact. Mental and physical states are coordinated by God.
Bishop George Berkeley	**Idealism**	Only the mind exists. All that exists are our minds and the mind of God. The world is apparent, and not actual.
Baruch Spinoza	**Panentheism**	There is only one substance, the divine substance.
G. W. Liebniz	**Parallelism**	The mind and body do not interact.
Contemporary ideas	**Epiphenomenalism**	The mind is a by-product of the body. The mind has no powers of causation over the body.
	Property dualism	Only material substances exist, but there are two types of properties. Spiritual and material properties.
Arguments against dualism	If the mind is immaterial, where is it located?	
	Mental causation- how does an immaterial object like the mind interact with a material object like the body?	

Materialism

This approach to philosophy of the mind assumes that the body or matter is all that exists. They assume that the mind is nothing more than the brain. There are a number of forms of materialism.

Behaviorism	**Philosophical**	This position assumes that Cartesian dualism is wrong because mental states are really to be understood in terms of behavior.	
	Psychological	An empirical approach to the study of the mind. It is the science of human behavior. Human behavior can be studied, but the mind cannot be. It assumes that Cartesian dualism is scientifically irrelevant	
	Radical	The position held by B.F. Skinner. It rejects the idea of psychological behaviorism.	
Identity theory or Physicalism	**Identity thesis**	Mental states are identical to brain states.	
	Type identity theory	Every type of mental state is identical to some type of physical state.	
	Token identity theory Not every mental state must has to be exemplified by a specific type of brain state.	**Anomalous monism**- a position held by Donald Davidson	
		Functionalism- allows for the possibility of immaterial substances, but is still committed to materialism. This is the dominant view in cognitive science and psychology.	**Black box**- the brain should be treated like a black box that responds to stimuli. The operation of the mind is not important to philosophers. The study of brain states should be left to psychologists and neurologists.
			Computer- assumes that the brain is a digital computer and that the mind is nothing more than a set of programs employed by the brain. The result is that mental states are nothing more than computational states of the brain. Some would argue that a computer with good artificial intelligence has a "mind."
Eliminativism	A kind of reductionism that there are no intentional states, such as: reasons for action, beliefs, desires, or intentions. The belief in such things amounts to "folk psychology."		
Arguments against materialism	Intentionality- materialism cannot explain intentionality		
	Consciousness- How can a material brain bring about consciousness?		
	Qualia- how can a material brain explain experiences like color, etc.		

Axiology: Value Theory

Value is concerned with what has worth and why. It is also concerned with how value motivates one to take action. Value theory has a history that goes back to Plato and Aristotle. Franz Brentano did much to explain value theory in the 19th century. His classic work in value theory is his *The Origin of Our Knowledge of Right and Wrong* (1889). His students, Oskar Kraus and Alexius Meinong added to his work. G.E. Moore employed these ideas in his *Principia Ethica* (1903). Contemporary work in this field has been continued by Roderick Chisholm (*Brentano and Intrinsic value*), Nicolas Rescher (*Introduction to Value* Theory), Noah Lemos (*Intrinsic Value*), Panayot Butchvarov (*Skepticism in Ethics*), Elizabeth Anderson (*Value in Ethics and Economics*).

Definition of Value	Value	A benefit oriented motivation for action. Values are ideals that have to do with the vision people have of the good life for the individual and his community. Values function both as constraints and as stimuli for action.
	Disvalue	A motivation for action that is not benefit oriented
	Intrinsic value	What something is valued as "an end" or "for itself." The ultimate end value of a thing
	Instrumental value	What is valued for the sake of something else. A value that is a "means" to an end.
Terminology of value	Value object	The object that is being evaluated
	Locus of value	An objective reason for value. Example: "Education is of great value for living the good life."
	Underlying value	Unstated values that are still important factors in decision making
	Value subscriber	A person who subscribes to a certain value or group of values
	Evaluation	A judgment regarding a value object
Value Experience	Brentano/Meinong value theory	Franz Brentano developed a theory of value that is based upon emotion. All valuation can be described in terms of love or hate. Love and hate can have different levels or degrees. His student Alexius Meinong refined Brentano's theory by explaining other aspects of value realism.
	Value subject	The value subscriber who experiences
	Emotion	A positive or negative emotion called the value feeling regarding the value object
	Value object	That which is being evaluated
	Existence judgment	A judgment about the realization or the existence of the value object

	Realism	Nominalism
Principle of organic unities The opposite of principle of summation	The value of a whole must not be assumed to be the identical as the sum of the values of its parts.	Rejects the principle of organic unities
Principle of summation The opposite of the principle of organic unities.	Rejects the principle of summation	The value of every whole is merely a sum of the value of its parts.
Principle of universality The opposite of the principle of conditionality	The part of a valuable whole retains exactly the same value when it is, as when it is not, a part of that whole.	Rejects the principle of universality
Principle of conditionality The opposite of the principle of universality	Rejects the principle of conditionality	The intrinsic value of a fact is conditional on what other states of affairs obtains, that is, the value of a part of one whole can be different when it is part of a different whole.
Principle of bonum variationis	Other things being equal, it is better to combine two dissimilar goods than to combine two similar goods. In other words, variety is intrinsically better than a lack of variety.	Rejects the principle of summation and supports the principle of organic unities.
Principle of bonum progressionis	Other things being equal, it is intrinsically better to begin badly and end well than to begin well and end badly.	Rejects the principle of summation and supports the principle of organic unities.
Principle of existence	The existence of an intrinsic good is itself a good and is preferable to its non-existence. The existence of an intrinsic evil is itself an evil.	
Principle of non-existence	The non- existence of an intrinsic good is not an evil and the non-existence of an intrinsic evil is preferable to its existence and is not a good.	

	Realism	Nominalism
Intrinsic Value An intrinsic value is something that is valued for its own sake.	Value monism- the idea that there is one primary value. Value supervenes on being. Only universals like properties, states of affairs, facts (states of affairs that obtain) intentional attitudes (like happiness) have intrinsic value.	Value pluralism, the idea that there is more than one intrinsic value of an object is an area of concern. Intentional attitudes like pleasure have intrinsic value
Extrinsic or Instrumental value An extrinsic value is something that is valued for the sake of something else.	Only concrete particulars have extrinsic value	Some concrete particulars have extrinsic value

	Definition	Value monism (Realism)	Value Pluralism (Nominalism)
Epistemology	The study or theory of knowledge. Knowledge is a universal.	Truth supervenes on being	Truth, belief, and justification
Morality	The study of the good or right action. The good is a universal.	Good supervenes on being	Consequences, rules
Aesthetic	The study of beauty, whether natural or artificial. Beauty is a universal.	Beauty supervenes on being	Beauty is subjective and is evaluated by some standard
Intentionality	A state of mind or special kind of belief that can be equated with a state of affairs.	Happiness (*eudaimonia*) supervenes on being	Happiness, Pleasure, and pain

Value Monism and Pluralism

(As explained by Elizabeth Anderson : *Value in Ethics and Economics*)

Value monism- only one thing can have intrinsic value

Value pluralism-many things can have intrinsic value

Agent neutral value- something that everyone has reason to value

Monism These theories assume that states of affairs do have intrinsic value.	**Naturalism**	'Good' can be compared to health or proper functioning. 'Goodness' supervenes upon empirical properties of an object. This position is teleological. It is compatible with an Aristotelian metaphysical realism or with a moderate nominalism. Proper function is the sole signifying response.
	G.E. Moore's Non-naturalism	'Good' is a simple and undefinable property that is known only by intuition. The 'good' can be compared with the object of aesthetic liking. Any attempt to explain value in terms of natural is committing the naturalistic fallacy. Moore is a metaphysical (platonic) realist who argues for the principle of organic unities.
	Hedonism	Only what is pleasant qualifies as 'good'. Pleasure is the sole value signifying response. This position is compatible only with metaphysical nominalism.
	Rational Desire Theory	'Good' is what is rationally desired. Desire is the sole value signifying response. This approach to value is compatible with an Aristotelian metaphysical realism or with a moderate metaphysical nominalism.
Pluralism These theories assume that state of affairs do not have intrinsic value.	**Consequentialism**	An egoistic moral theory that gives all agents the common aim of maximizing impersonal value. It assumes that all values are agent neutral. Practical reason demands that value be maximized. This is achieved by contrasting reason with emotions and social norms. This allows for a simple, precise and determinate procedure of justification that employs objective calculations to overcome disputes.
	Expressive theory of value	Action is guided by norms described in terms of ideals and evaluative concepts like virtues or vices.
	Pragmatic justification theory	This approach to value allows for the use of thick evaluative concepts which allows for a space of reasons, rather than thin concepts like good, bad, right, or wrong. This approach allows for commonsense, intuitive reasoning. Comparative value judgments are evaluated by considering their functions, why people care about them, and what practices of evaluation serve these functions.

The Fact/ Value Dichotomy

David Hume	*A Treatise of Human Nature*	• This dichotomy has its roots in Hume's fork. Truth is either analytic (necessary and deducible values) or synthetic (empirically verifiable facts). • It asserts that "One cannot derive ought from is." In other words, values (ethics and aesthetics) have nothing to do with metaphysics (ontology). • All supposed connections between ethics and metaphysics are based only upon induction. • Values are based solely upon emotions • This dichotomy rejects teleology, natural law and any idea of moral properties. • This implies that values have no significance for science, economics, law, political theory, or psychology.
G.E. Moore	*Principia Ethics*	He supported the fact/ value dichotomy. Many analytic philosophers followed after Moore's ideas. He argued that if one attempts to base morality upon nature then one has committed the naturalistic fallacy. The naturalistic fallacy is based on **the fact/ value dichotomy.**
W.V.O. Quine	**The Two Dogmas of Empiricism**	Quine argued against **the fact/ value dichotomy**. He asserted that the analytic/ synthetic distinction is the basis for the **fact/ value dichotomy**. He showed that the analytic synthetic dichotomy to be faulty. Consequently, the fact/value dichotomy collapsed with the analytic/ synthetic distinction.
Aristotle	*De Anima*	Aristotle's position is contrary to the **fact/ value dichotomy.** He argued that emotions are driven by reason. In other words, if one gets angry, he does so for a reason. Emotions, although sometimes faulty, are therefore judgments of value. Consequently, both facts and values are judged by reason.

Action Theory

Action theory has its origins in the writings of Aristotle. **Action theory** is often viewed as a sub-discipline of metaphysics. It is important for the study of **ethics** and for the study of **epistemology**			
Key Ideas	An **Event** is something that happens at a certain time and place An **Event** can be unintended	
	An **Agent** is something that can have intentions	
	An **Action** is an **event** with **agency.** Some actions are **intentional** and some are not	
Metaphysical Realism	**Teleology**	Actions are purposive and involve reason as a cause. Teleological views of action tell us the state of affairs toward which the behavior was directed.
	Parts and wholes	Metaphysical Realists believe that the whole has priority over the parts. In other words, the parts gain their identity from the whole of a thing. An action may have many parts, but the whole of an action is determined by the intention of the agent.
	Internalism	An *internal reason* is, roughly, something that one has in light of one's own "subjective motivational set"---one's own commitments, desires (or wants), goals, etc.
Metaphysical Nominalism	**Deontology**	David Hume argued for a **Belief/ Desire view of action.** Some Analytic Philosophers argued for a **Causal View of Action**
	Parts and Wholes	Metaphysical nominalists believe that the parts have priority over the whole. In other words, the parts have their own identities.
	Externalism	It is the view that there are external reasons for action; that is, there are reasons for action that one can have even if the action is not part of one's subjective motivational set.

Epistemology Overview of theories of knowledge		
Theories of knowledge	Internalism- Knowledge is justified true belief. The knower must know how he knows. Skepticism is a significant problem A deontological approach to knowledge	**Foundationalism** • suggests that knowledge is a structure, in which one piece of knowledge rests upon another • The foundation of this structure of knowledge must be properly basic • Compatible with the correspondence and coherence theories of truth
		Coherentism • Suggests that knowledge is a structure in which each piece of knowledge depends on each other • Compatible with correspondence and coherence theories of truth • Is actually another form of foundationalism
	Externalism- Knowledge is true belief produced by a reliable belief- forming process Does not require the knower to know how he knows Teleological approach to knowledge	**Naturalized epistemology** Knowledge results from natural processes. Reduces epistemology to psychology and cognitive science.
		Virtue epistemology Knowledge results from sensory experience, memory, and reason (both inductive and deductive). The intellectual virtues regulate belief-forming
		Proper functionalism Knowledge results from the sensory and intellectual faculties operating properly in the proper environment and in accordance with their design plan.
The Gettier Problem Edmund Gettier argued that knowledge is not **justified true belief.** He asserted that one can have a belief that is in fact true, in spite of the fact that he has sufficient but not the necessary justification. The result is that internalist epistemology has a difficulty that it has, as yet, not overcome. This is why externalist epistemology has gained more respectability.		

Meta- epistemology		
Metaphysics of Knowledge	**Sources of knowledge**	**Empiricism-** Knowledge results from sensory experience
		Rationalism- Reason is the primary source of knowledge
		Intuitionism-Knowledge results from feelings or some unknown means
		Memory-knowledge stored in the mind
		Testimony- knowledge received from other people
	Metaphysics	**Epistemic realism-** A position consistent with metaphysical realism and the correspondence theory of truth. Knowledge corresponds to the real world that exists independent of us.
		Epistemic Irrealism – A position consistent with metaphysical nominalism or idealism. It is also compatible with the coherence, pragmatic or semantic theories of truth. Knowledge is subjective and depends upon the observer
		Objects of Knowledge- what knowledge is supposed to be about
	Modal Epistemology	Considers what can be known from possible and actual worlds
Ethics of belief (also known as normative epistemology) It is concerned with one's responsibility for knowledge	**Virtue**	Knowledge is teleological and is regulated by intellectual virtues. Knowledge results in *eudaimonia.*
	Deontology	One must believe only when a high level of certainty exists. To believe otherwise is wrong.
	Consequentialism	Knowledge results in pleasure. Knowledge results when the amount of certainty is greater than the amount of doubt.
Value of knowledge Concerned with what and how one is motivated to know.	**Intrinsic Value of knowledge**	**Value Monists-** This position is consistent with the principle of organic unities and the principle of universality. Truth is the only intrinsic value of knowledge.
		Value pluralists-This position is consistent with the principle of summation and the principle of conditionality. Truth, belief, and justification all have intrinsic value.
	Instrumental value of knowledge	**Value monists** believe that individual bits of knowledge are instrumentally valuable
		Value pluralists believe that certain types of knowledge are more valuable than others.

Perception or Metaphysics of Epistemology				
	Source of knowledge	**Metaphysics**	**Theory of truth**	**Scepticism**
Extreme Realism (position held by Plato)	Rationalism	Extreme realism	Correspondence theory of truth. Truth corresponds to the world of the forms (universals)	Skepticism is high, because the senses cannot be trusted
Common Sense Realism (position held by Aristotle, Thomas Reid and G.E. Moore)	Combines empiricism with some rationalism	Moderate realism	Correspondence theory of truth	Skepticism is rejected because it conflicts with common sense.
Contemporary Realism (position held by David Hume)	Empiricism	Extreme nominalism	Semantic theory of truth	Results in extreme skepticsm
Epistemological Dualism (Position held by John Locke)	Empiricism	Moderate nominalism	Semantic theory of truth	Some skepticism must be accepted
Phenomenalism (Position held by Immanuel Kant)	Combines rationalism with some empiricism	Moderate nominalism	Coherence theory of truth	Mitigated skepticism
Subjective idealism (Position held by Bishop George Berkeley)	Empiricism	Moderate nominalism	Semantic theory of truth	Moderate skepticism
Relativistic Idealism (Position held by Friedrich Nietzsche)	Intuitionism	Extreme nominalism	Pragmatic theory of truth	Extreme skepticism

Internalist theories of knowledge

Knowledge is justified true belief. Internalist theories require that one know how he knows in order to know. All internalist theories fail to solve the Gettier problem.

Noetic Structure	Explanation	Metaphysics of knowledge	Ethic of Belief	Value of knowledge
Classic (or extreme) Foundationalism (Position held by Rene Descartes and John Locke)	Beliefs form the basis of the noetic structure **Problem:** Infinite regress problem	Metaphysical nominalism Semantic, pragmatic or coherence theory of truth	Deontological justification The knower has a responsibility to not believe something unless a high degree of certainty can be attained.	Value pluralism: justification, truth and belief all have intrinsic value
Moderate Foundationalism	Beliefs and sensory experience form the basis of the noetic structure	Metaphysical realism or nominalism Coherence, pragmatic or semantic theory of truth	Deontological or consequentialist Justification	Value pluralism
Wholistic (or moderate) Coherentism	Belief *A* receives positive epistemic status from playing an important role in a total system of beliefs.	Metaphysical nominalism Semantic or coherence theory of truth	Deontological or consequentialist justification	Value pluralism
Linear (or extreme) Coherentism An attempt to escape the infinite regress problem by using a circular structure.	Belief *A* gets it's justification from belief *B*. Belief *Z* gets its justification from belief *A*.	Coherence theory of truth	Consequentialist justification Justification is a matter of degrees. True beliefs are maximized and false ones are minimized.	Value pluralism

Externalist theories of knowledge

All externalist theories dismiss skepticism. All externalist theories emphasize the importance of reliabilism. Reliabilism is the idea that knowledge results from true belief formed by a reliable process.

	Explanation	Metaphysics of knowledge	Ethics of belief	Value of knowledge
Virtue Reliabilism Ernest Sosa, Jonathan Kvanvig, Hartry Field	Intellectual virtues a part of a reliable belief forming process	Metaphysical realism or nominalism Correspondence or semantic theory of truth	**Virtue Warrant** Intellectual virtues are necessary but are not sufficient habits for forming knowledge	Value pluralism (justification, truth, and belief, all have intrinsic value)
Naturalized Epistemology W.V.O. Quine Hilary Kornblith	Knowledge results from natural processes. Reduces epistemology to psychology and cognitive science	Metaphysical naturalism. Metaphysical realism or nominalism. Correspondence, Semantic or deflationary theories of truth	**Teleological justification** Intellectual virtues are not necessary but are sufficient habits for forming beliefs	Value monism or pluralism
Proper functionalism Alvin Plantinga	Knowledge results from the sensory and intellectual faculties operating properly in the proper environment and in accordance with their design plan.	Theistic or supernaturalist metaphysic Metaphysical realism Correspondence theory of truth	**Teleological warrant** Intellectual virtues are not necessary but are sufficient habits for proper functional belief forming processes.	Value monism (truth is the only intrinsic value)

Perception or Metaphysics of Epistemology				
	Source of knowledge	**Metaphysics**	**Theory of truth**	**Scepticism**
Extreme Realism (position held by Plato)	Rationalism	Extreme realism	Correspondence theory of truth. Truth corresponds to the world of the forms (universals)	Skepticism is high, because the senses cannot be trusted
Common Sense Realism (position held by Aristotle, Thomas Reid and G.E. Moore)	Combines empiricism with some rationalism	Moderate realism	Correspondence theory of truth	Skepticism is rejected because it conflicts with common sense.
Contemporary Realism (position held by David Hume)	Empiricism	Extreme nominalism	Semantic theory of truth	Results in extreme skepticsm
Epistemological Dualism (Position held by John Locke)	Empiricism	Moderate nominalism	Semantic theory of truth	Some skepticism must be accepted
Phenomenalism (Position held by Immanuel Kant)	Combines rationalism with some empiricism	Moderate nominalism	Coherence theory of truth	Mitigated skepticism
Subjective idealism (Position held by Bishop George Berkeley)	Empiricism	Moderate nominalism	Semantic theory of truth	Moderate skepticism
Relativistic Idealism (Position held by Friedrich Nietzsche)	Intuitionism	Extreme nominalism	Pragmatic theory of truth	Extreme skepticism

Philosophy of Language		
The nature of language	**Grammar**	Concerned with the forms and structures of words. This includes the arrangement of words in sentences and phrases
	Symbolic systems	Examines the range of things that can be communicated through symbols of various sorts
	Analyticity	Concerned with the priority of language to the mind (or vice versa)
	Theories of meaning	Concerned with what meaning is and what it is related to.
Language and the mind	**Innate ideas**	Concerned with whether or not innate ideas provide a foundation of language and communication
	Private language	Concerned with the existence of language internal to the individual
	Intensionality	Explores the relationship between communication and intension of the communicator.
Language and Metaphysics	**The world**	Concerned with how language represents the world and our thoughts about the world.
	Truth	What is the relationship between language and truth?
Semiotics	**Semantics**	The branch of linguistics concerned with the nature, structure and development of the meanings of signs and symbols. Focuses on epistemology, as well as semantic theories and mental states
	Pragmatics	The study of language which focuses attention on the users and the context of language use rather than on reference, truth or grammar.
	Hermeneutics	The art and science of interpretation
	Syntax	Concerned with the arrangement of words as elements in a sentence to show their relationship to one another.

Metaphysics of Language

Metaphysical Realism	**Semantic Externalism**	suggests that the content of our minds and languages is at least in part due to things external to the individual. An example of semantic externalism can be seen in the work of the Linguistic Essentialists. Semantic externalism is consistent with metaphysical realism and a correspondence theory of truth
		Causal Theory of Meaning-A theory of meaning based on the work of Saul Kripke (*Naming and Necessity*). This approach relates metaphysical essences, with intentions and meaning.
		Intension refers to the set of all *possible* things a word or phrase *could* describe. An intension is any property or quality connoted by a word, phrase or other symbol. **Intensionality** involves connotation
		Extension- refers to the set of all *actual* things the word describes. In other words, Extension concerns the denotation of a word. Extensionality involves denotation.
		Linguistic semantic externalism- the meaning of a word is environmentally determined.
		Cognitive semantic externalism- concepts (or contents) are available to a thinker are determined by their environment, or their relation to their environment.
Metaphysical Nominalism	**Semantic Internalism**	suggests that the contents of our minds is the only source for meaning and language.
		The British Empiricists held to a form of semantic internalism known as the **ideational theory of meaning**.

Substantive theories of truth			
Theory of Truth	**Universals**	**Descriptions**	**Comments**
Correspondence theory of truth	**Realist**: truth supervenes on being. This position was held by Plato and Aristotle	States of affairs are truth-makers. This theory is concerned with the metaphysics of truth.	Traditionalist approaches to the correspondence theory subscribe to metaphysical realism.
			Minimalist approaches to the correspondence theory of truth attempt to avoid the subjects of universals and particulars
Coherence theory of truth	**Nominalist, idealist:** This position was held by the Continental rationalists.	Truth results when there is a coherent set of beliefs. These beliefs may or may not have anything to do with reality. This theory of truth is primarily concerned with epistemology.	A coherence theory of justification (epistemology) is a necessary and sufficient condition for truth
			A coherence theory of justification is not a necessary and sufficient condition for truth
Pragmatic theory of truth	**Nominalist:** This position is held by pragmatists, who are radical empiricists and idealists. Some postmodernists hold this position	Truth is made and not found. Truth is what works. This theory of truth is primarily concerned with epistemology.	**Peirce-** truth is what is revealed at the end of scientific inquiry.
			James- truth is useful
			Putnam- attempts to reconcile pragmatism with realism
			Rorty- the pragmatist can see little difference between truth and justification.
Semantic theory of truth (Tarski's)	**Nominalist:** This position is consistent with the views of the British Empiricists and by some Analytic Philosophers.	This theory explains truth in a way that is consistent with science.	There are no variants for this theory. This theory of truth is primarily concerned with philosophy of language

Ethics		
Level	**Definition**	**Explanation**
Applied Ethics	**The use of ethics in different professions**	Examples include: business ethics, medical ethics, legal ethics, counseling ethics, etc.
Normative Ethics	**Ethical theories**	**Teleology-** ethics based on the nature and purpose of a thing
		Deontology- ethics based on rules or laws
Meta- ethics	**The foundations of morality**	**Metaphysics of Morality-** the nature of moral facts
		Moral Epistemology- how we know right and wrong
		Moral psychology- how we are motivated

Meta-ethics		
The foundations of morality		
Metaphysics of Ethics Investigates the nature of morality	**The status of moral facts**	Are there objective moral facts that exist independent of the observer? If not, then is there any objective value to morality?
	Free will/determinism	Concerned with moral culpability. Is man free to act on his own or is man's action predetermined by God? Is there a mediating position?
	Moral Language	Concerned with whether or not there is an objective moral reality and the nature of moral language.
	Moral properties	Explores the existence of moral properties. It is also concerned with the nature of moral properties.
Moral Epistemology Investigates how morality is known	**Cognitivism**	Moral knowledge is gained via a cognitive process
	Non-cognitivism	Moral knowledge is gained via a emotions. It assumes that there are no objective moral facts. None-the-less, this position asserts that morality is still useful.
Moral Psychology Investigates the nature of the moral self	**Moral Motivation**	Explores the relationship between moral facts and moral motivation
	Moral Development	Investigates how people develop morally
	Mental Health	Explores the relationship between morality and mental health

Metaphysics of Ethics Studies the nature of morality		
Moral Facts	**Realism**	Moral facts are found and not made by men. They exist independent of the observer.
	Irrealism (Anti-realism)	Moral facts are created and not found by men, but morality is useful for a successful society
	Nihilism	Moral facts do not exist, and morality is not even useful.
Moral Properties	**Naturalism**	Moral properties are identical to natural properties
	Eliminativism (ethical nominalism)	A reductionistic approach which asserts that science has no place at all for alleged moral properties or facts. It asserts that moral properties are nothing more than mythical entities.
	Supervenience	Moral properties are relationally dependent upon other properties
	Essentialism	A view of moral properties that is similar to naturalism, but it allows for the possibility of the supernatural. Moral properties depend upon the essence of a thing. It assumes that the essence of a thing carries an intrinsic and objective value.
Moral Language	**Emotivism**	A view of morality developed by the analytic philosopher A.J. Ayer. He asserted that moral statements are nothing more than primitive, emotional noise. Moral statements are meaningless because there is no such thing as morality. There are only emotions.
	Prescriptivism	A view developed by the analytic philosopher, Richard Hare. Moral language has a logic of its own. Moral language is more than just primitive emotions. It is instead more of a command. For example: To say that stealing is immoral means "don't steal." Morality is thus, about rules. These moral commands are universal, but they are not specific.
Moral Responsibility	**Freedom**	The moral agent is morally culpable for his actions because he is free to do as he wishes
	Compatibilism	The moral agent has limited moral culpability for his actions because his will is only partially free.
	Determinism	The moral agent does not have free will because of God, biology, or other external forces. Some hold that in this case, the moral agent is still morally culpable, others assert that the moral agent is not morally culpable

Moral Epistemology		
The study of how morality is known.		
Cognitivism Assumes that moral facts are found and not made. Morality is objective. Moral judgments express a belief. These beliefs can be true or false.	**Internalism** Moral knowledge is like other kinds of knowledge. Knowledge is justified true belief.	**Foundationalism** –moral knowledge is dependent upon a foundation of knowledge that is properly basic.
		Coherentism-moral knowledge relies upon a system of coherent beliefs.
	Externalism Moral knowledge is like other kinds of knowledge. Knowledge results from a reliable belief forming process or mechanism	**Naturalized epistemology**. Moral knowledge results from natural processes, perhaps a moral sense.
		Virtue epistemology-moral knowledge results from the use of virtues such as prudence
		Proper-functionalism-moral knowledge results when a normal healthy person functions as he should. This may involve the use of **naturalized epistemology or virtue epistemology.**
Non-Cognitivism Moral judgments do not express belief.	**Projectivism** Moral judgments are nothing more than our projecting emotions into the world	**Emotivism** (A. J. Ayer) There is no such thing as objective morality. Instead, morality is mere public opinion. To say that something is good is merely to mean that one likes that thing. To say that something is bad means that one dislikes that thing. Hence, morality is nothing more than emotional preference.
		Quasi-realism (Simon Blackburn) type of projectivism that seeks to explain and justify the realistic-seeming nature of our moral judgments
		Norm Expressivism (Allan Gibbard) A moral judgment expresses an agent's acceptance of norms.
Moral skepticism	Assumes that even if moral facts exist, that we cannot know them	**Pyrhonian skepticism**- you cannot even know that you cannot know anything
		Hard Empiricism- one cannot know morality because we have no moral sense
		The general belief that morality cannot be objectively known.

Moral Psychology		
Studies the nature of the moral self		
Principle of Minimal Psychological Realism-A good moral theory is one which explains the character, motivation and behavior of the average person.		
Moral Motivation	**Internalism** Assumes that there is a connection between moral judgment and motivation.	**Weak Internalism**- recognition of a moral fact or obligation provides some motivation for moral action
		Strong Internalism- recognition of a moral fact or obligation provides sufficient motivation for moral action.
	Externalism	The rejection of **internalism**
	Altruism	**Rational altruism**- for an agent to act altruistically is to act in a way that is beneficial to his own well being
		Psychological Altruism- Human nature is such that an agent acts to promote the interests of others
		Ethical Altruism- An agent ought to act in such a way as to promote the interest of others.
	Egoism	**Rational egoism**- a moral agent has reason to act in a way that is consistent with his own self-interest
		Psychological egoism-human nature is such that an agent acts only to promote his own self-interest
		Ethical egoism- An agent ought to act in such a way as to promote his own self-interest
	Welfarism	**Objectivism**-asserts that the well-being of an agent is not a matter of the agent's attitudes or preferences. Instead, well-being depends upon some external standard.
		Subjectivism-asserts that the well-being of an agent is a matter of the agent's attitudes or preferences
		Hybrid-asserts that some aspects of an agent's well-being depend upon the agent's attitudes or preferences and some do not.
Moral development	**Cognitivism**	An approach to moral development endorsed by **internalists** in which the moral agent regulates himself.
	Non-cognitivism	A view of moral development held by **externalists** in which the moral agent is regulated by others.
Moral health	**Welfarism**	Asserts that if one is healthy, he will recognize and be motivated by moral facts. It assumes that the moral man is a happy man
	Positivism	Asserts that there is no connection between recognition of moral facts and mental health.

Internalist moral development (cognitivism)

Aristotle		
Aristotle assumes that men have the ability to reason and communicate better than other creatures. He also assumes that man is a social creature. Aristotle thought that how one thinks determines how one feels and behaves. He assumes that children begin life as egoists and grow more towards altruism. To grow in character one must observe a person who has prudence (practical wisdom). As a result, the moral agent learns to decide how to act in different situations by using their virtues		
The Components of Character	**Desires**	**Sense Desires**- desire for pleasure through the senses. These desires involve some sort of belief.
		Passional Desires- evaluate the situation in terms of positive or negative desirability
		Rational Desires- provide motivation for action based on moral judgments
	Goods	*Summum Bonum*- the highest good
		Internal Goods- moral virtues
		Intrinsic external goods- these are goods to be pursued in and of themselves. For example, friendship
		Extrinsic external goods- these are not goods to be pursued for themselves. They are instrumentally useful.
	Reasons	**Practical reason** connects sense desires and the passional desires with the conception of the good life. It is also concerned with the totality of goods.
Stage 4 Virtue	The person normally acts virtuously because he has a firm and unchanging character.	
Stage 3 Self- control	The moral agent gains some control over his desires and sometimes acts in accordance with virtue. His character is still not firm and unchanging.	
Stage 2 *Akrasia*	After observing a virtuous person the moral agent becomes aware that he has vices and decides to become virtuous. This decision results partly to please himself, and partly to please others. The moral agent begins to exercise the virtues. Lack of power or knowledge prevent him from being virtuous.	
Stage 1 Vice	The moral agent must learn to be virtuous. He begins life concerned only with himself. His character is unformed.	

Ethical Theory

Teleology Term coined by Christian Wolff in 1748	1. The branch of cosmology concerned with final causes. 2. Ethics depends on metaphysics (metaphysical realism) 3. Goodness depends on being 4. Pursuit of the Good 5. The good depends on the nature of a thing 6. The good determines what is right
Deontology Term coined by Jeremy Bentham in 1834	1. The science of morality 2. Ethics has no relation to metaphysics (metaphysical nominalism) 3. Rules determine what is right 4. Right determines what is good 5. Ethics are only obligations to rules or laws 6. Rightness has priority over the good.
Consequentialism Term coined by GEM Anscombe in 1958	1. A type of deontology that seeks to maximize the good 2. Right action maximizes the good 3. British moral philosophy since the 17th century
Non Consequentialism	A rejection of consequentialism
Act	Rightness is determined by the action that one should take
Rule	Rightness is determined only by rules or laws

Teleology	Deontology	
	Act Consequentialism Contractarianism Act utilitarianism Virtue Consequentialism	**Rule Consequentialism** Contractualism Rule utilitarianism
Naturalism		
Virtue Ethics	**Act Non-Consequentialism** Existentialism Situational Ethics Moral Particularism Linguistic Virtue Ethics	**Rule Non-Consequentialism** Kantianism Rossian Intuitionism Divine Command Theory

Virtue Ethics		
Essential Components	**Natural law**	A kind of naturalism that suggests that ethical properties are identical to natural properties. Right and wrong are based upon the nature of a thing. **Virtues** are what make a thing good. **Virtue ethics** are based upon human nature. Aristotle argued that the **natural law** is universal, rational, and objective. **Natural law** points to the existence of God, who establishes the created order God also determines what is good and right.
	Doctrine of the Mean	The idea that there is a continuum of behavior. Virtue is in the middle of this continuum. A deficiency of a virtue is a vice. An excess of a virtue is a vice.
	Perfectionism	Virtues emphasize human excellences
	Welfarism	To act in accordance with virtue is in a moral agent's best interest. The virtuous person is a happier person.
Types of virtue ethics	**Aristotelian virtue ethics (classical)**	A premodern system of ethics focused upon character and **natural law**. The man of character acts in accordance with the natural law. The virtues of man are determined by this natural law (or the nature of a thing). The virtuous man gains happiness (*eudaimonia*—happiness gained by self effort**).** One gains character by watching some who already has character. One may also gain character by listening to or reading narratives
	Augustinian Virtue Ethics	A premodern system of Christian ethics**.** The natural (cardinal) virtues are insufficient to provide true happiness (beatitude-- happiness from God). Only the Christian can have hope of beatitude. The Holy Spirit infuses the theological virtues into the believer. The believer gains the cardinal virtues after the theological virtues.
	Agent Based	A non-teleological system of virtue ethics developed by analytic philosophers. It is a system that has no place for natural law.
	Linguistic Virtue ethics	A postmodern approach to virtue ethics developed by Alasdair MacIntyre and based upon the ideas of Ludwig Wittgenstein. It emphasizes the importance of narrative and community. It rejects moral, epistemological, and metaphysical realism

Internalist moral development (cognitivism)

Teleological Development

Aristotle		
Aristotle assumes that men have the ability to reason and communicate better than other creatures. He also assumes that man is a social creature. Aristotle thought that how one thinks determines how one feels and behaves. He assumes that children begin life as egoists and grow more towards altruism. To grow in character one must observe a person who has prudence (practical wisdom). As a result, the moral agent learns to decide how to act in different situations by using their virtues		
The Components of Character	**Desires**	**Sense Desires**- desire for pleasure through the senses. These desires involve some sort of belief.
		Passional Desires- evaluate the situation in terms of positive or negative desirability
		Rational Desires- provide motivation for action based on moral judgments
	Goods	*Summum Bonum*- the highest good
		Internal Goods- moral virtues
		Intrinsic external goods- these are goods to be pursued in and of themselves. For example, friendship
		Extrinsic external goods- these are not goods to be pursued for themselves. They are instrumentally useful.
	Reasons	**Practical reason** connects sense desires and the passional desires with the conception of the good life. It is also concerned with the totality of goods.
Stage 4 Virtue	The person normally acts virtuously because he has a firm and unchanging character.	
Stage 3 Self- control	The moral agent gains some control over his desires and sometimes acts in accordance with virtue. His character is still not firm and unchanging.	
Stage 2 *Akrasia*	After observing a virtuous person the moral agent becomes aware that he has vices and decides to become virtuous. This decision results partly to please himself, and partly to please others. The moral agent begins to exercise the virtues. Lack of power or knowledge prevent him from being virtuous.	
Stage 1 Vice	The moral agent must learn to be virtuous. He begins life concerned only with himself. His character is unformed.	

Linguistic Virtue Ethics

This postmodern approach to ethics was developed by Alasdair MacIntyre. His most siginificant works are *After Virtue, Whose Justice, Which Morality,* and *Three Rival Versions of Moral Inquiry.* MacIntyre subscribes to Thomas Aquinas's list of virtues because he combines the virtues of Augustine with the virtues of Aristotle. He was influenced by the thought of Ludwig Wittgenstein who rejected metaphysics and replaced it with linguistic analysis. Consequently, MacIntyre leaves no place for natural law or what he calls "metaphysical biology." Stanley Hauerwas has followed after MacIntyre's ethical theory. They are also metaphysical nominalists, rejecting the existence of universals.

Meta-ethical presuppositions	Metaphysics of morals	**Moral irrealism-** morality is important because of the community
		Free will- man is morally culpable because he is free
	Moral epistemology	**Cognitivism-** Moral knowledge is gained through the virtue prudence.
	Moral psychology	**Motivation internalism-** recognition of moral facts or obligation provides motivation for moral action
		Cognitivism- moral motivation comes from within the moral agent
		Welfarism- it is beneficial to the moral agent to act morally
Theological virtues Augustine	Love	The Love of God and the love of man for God's sake.
	Faith	Grows out of love and gives one spiritual knowledge
	Hope	Grows out of love and causes man to look at eternity
Cardinal Virtues Aristotle	Justice	The most important social virtue
	Prudence	Practical wisdom, a key to moral judgment
	Courage	The ability to overcome fear
	Temperance	Self-control
Community	The community is important because it determines meaning, truth, and morality. The individual must operate by the pre-established rules of the community.	
Narrative	Narrative is the key to learning of any type. Especially for learning moral character	
Language	We are surrounded by language and cannot understand without it.	

Non- Consequentialist Deontology	
Divine command Theory	This is a meta-ethical theory which argues that goodness is based upon God. It is also a normative ethical theory, in which the will of God determines what is right. It assumes that God's will is revealed. Some versions are compatible with only special revelation. Other versions are compatible with both special and general revelation.
Kantianism	This is a modern ethical theory that emphasizes universizability and equitability.
Rossian Intuitionism	An approach to ethics developed by the analytic philosopher, W.D. Ross. It posits a hierarchy of laws which must be obeyed.
Graded Absolutism	An approach developed by Norman Geisler which posits a hierarchy of laws that must be obeyed.
Existentialism	Existentialism has only one rule, be true to yourself. Act in accordance with who you are

Deontology arose in the modern period following the ideas of William of Ockham. Because of his metaphysical nominalism, Ockham was a proponent of a type of divine command theory, which separated God's will from God's nature. Thus Ockham separated ethics from metaphysics.

The Continental Rationalist were metaphysical nominalists whose approach to ethics was exemplified by Immanuel Kant. The Continental Philosophers were deontological as well.

The ethics of the British Empiricists (also metaphysical nominalists) was exemplified by David Hume who argued that "You cannot derive ought from is." (the fact/value dichotomy) The ethics of the British empiricists were deontological because it was divorced from metaphysics. Their ethics were also consequentialist.

Kantian Deontology

. This approach was developed by Immanuel Kant. It argues that morality is based on *a priori* principles. These ideas are expressed in his *Groundwork for a Metaphysics of Morals, Critique of Practical Reason,* and *Metaphysics of Morals*. Kant invented the idea of autonomy. Autonomy suggests that men do not need any external authority to do right because reason provides sufficient motivation for moral action.

Meta-ethical presuppositions	Metaphysics of morals	Moral irrealism-moral facts exist by reason. They are independent of the observer, but they have no metaphysical basis.
		The good- is an action done from a good will.
		Free will- man is morally culpable for his actions
	Moral epistemology	Cognitivism- moral judgments express a belief. Morality is known through the use of practical reason alone. The Bible is not needed.
	Moral psychology	Motivational internalism
		Cognitive moral development
		Positivism- virtue and happiness are not united in this life
Respect for Persons	Because every person is endowed with the ability to think and choose, all men should be treated with respect.	
Equality	Everyone should have an equal opportunity to attain whatever status they desire in a free society.	
Universality	The laws of society should apply to everyone.	
Hypothetical Imperative	Hypothetical imperatives concern instrumental or extrinsic goods. These goods are a means to some other good or end. Intrinsic goods in contrast are an end in and of themselves.	
Categorical Imperative These are concerned with intrinsic goods. It has two functions Function 1: to obligate the moral agent to obey. Function 2: to act as a test of moral maxims.	1. Autonomy	One should never to act in such a way that he could not also will that his maxim should be a universal law
	2. Respect for persons	Act so that you treat humanity, whether in your own person or in that of any other, always as an end and never as a means.
	3. Legislation for a moral community	All maxims that proceed from one's own making of law ought to harmonize with a possible moral community
Conclusions: Kant believed that virtue and happiness cannot be united in this life.	1. God exists and we should worship him 2. There is objective right and wrong 3. There is an afterlife 4. There is a postmortem judgment 5. God will reward the good and punish the evil in the next life.	

Deontological (Rossian) Intuitionism

W.D Ross is primarily concerned with meta-ethics. He explained what he thought was the dominat ethical theory of the 19th century in *The Right and the Good*

Meta-ethical presuppositions	Metaphysics of Morals	Moral realism- moral facts exist independent of the observer.
		Good is unexplained
		Free will- the moral agent has free will and is morally culpable
	Moral epistemology	Non- cognitivism- moral knowledge is intuited. Moral principles are self-evident.
	Moral psychology	Motivational internalism- recognition of moral facts provides motivation for moral action
		Cognitivism- moral motivation comes form within the moral agent.
Other presuppositions	Moral principles cannot be reduced or unified into general principles.	
	Moral principles are absolute	
	Ethics are deontological	
	Ethical conflicts are resolved through a hierarchy of laws	
7 Prima facie Duties	Promise keeping- one must always keep his promises under any condition	
	Fidelity- one should always be loyal and true to their family and friends	
	Gratitude- one should always be thankful for what others have done for them	
	Good will- one's actions should always be motivated out of good will	
	Justice- one should always strive to act justly and see that justice is carried out	
	Self-improvement-one should never be content with their character and should always strive to improve	
	Nonmalificence-one should always strive to control their actions so that they do not act out of evil intent.	

Act Utilitarianism

Jeremy Bentham took the utilitarianism of Frances Hutcheson and David Hume and modified it. It is a system that is teleological and consequentialist.. It is a hedonistic (focused on pleasure) approach to ethics. Bentham believed that it is better to be a satisfied pig than a dissatisfied Socrates. Utilitarianism seeks to maximize utility or the good.

Meta-ethical presuppositions	Metaphysics of Moral	Moral Irrealism- moral facts do not exist, but morality is useful
		The good is pleasure or happiness
		Free will- men have free will and are morally culpable
	Moral epistemology	Noncognitivism- the passions (emotions) act as a moral sense
	Moral psychology	Motivational externalism- recognition of moral facts or obligations do not provide motivation for moral action
		Noncognitivism- moral motivation comes from fear of punishment
		Positivism- happiness is equated with pleasure. There is no objective good to be united with virtue
Greatest happiness principle	Act utilitarianism provides the greatest amount of happiness for the greatest number of people.	
Explanation	An act is right if it results in as much good as any other alternative	
Calculus of happiness (hedonic calculus)	Decisions are based upon the total amount of pleasure to be gained minus the total amount of pain to be experienced	
	The number of people to experience the pleasure or pain	
	The certainty of the pleasure or pain	
	The intensity of the pleasure or pain	
	The duration of the pleasure or pain	
	The frequency of the pleasure or pain	
Political theory	A democracy is the best form of government because it is the most compatible to utilitarianism	

Virtue Consequentialism is a type of consequentialism. It argues that virtues help maximize the good.

Rule Utilitarianism

John Stuart Mill developed this ethical system in response to the weaknesses of act utilitarianism. Mill believed that it is better to be Socrates dissatisfied than a pig satisfied. This system is deontological and consequentialist. Utilitarianism seeks to maximize utlity or the good.

Meta-ethical presuppositions	Metaphysics of Morals	**Moral irrealism**- moral facts do not exist, but morality is useful
		Good is happiness (*eudaimonia*)
		Free will- moral agents have free will and are morally culpable
	Moral Epistemology	**Non-cognitivism**- moral judgments do not express belief
	Moral Psychology	**Motivational externalist**- recognition of moral obligation does not provide motivation for moral action.
		Non-cognitivism- moral motivation comes from fear of punishment
		Welfarism- to act morally is beneficial
Happiness		Is more than pleasure. Happiness (eudaimonia involves higher order pleasures such as intellectual and aesthetic enjoyments).
Definition of Rule utilitarianism		The rightness of an act does not depend upon its consequences. An act is right if and only if it is required by a code of rules whose acceptance would lead to the greater utility for society than any available alternative
Code of rules		These rules insure that a minimally correct behavior standard is enforced and encouraged.
Universality		The set of rules must apply to everyone

Social Contract Theory
(Contractarianism)

This approach was developed by Thomas Hobbes and, Jean Jacques Rousseau. Contractarianism is an ethical system that is deontological and consequentialist. It is both an ethical and a political theory.

Meta-ethical presuppositions	Metaphysics of Morals	**Irrealism-** moral facts do not exist but morality is useful.
		Good- whatever brings peace and order. What is right to do depends on what rules it would be in everyone's interest for all to accept.
		Free will- men are free moral agents who have free will. Consequently all men are morally culpable.
	Moral Epistemology	**Non-cognitivism-** moral judgments do not express belief.
	Moral Psychology	**Motivational externalism-** moral facts do not motivate a person to act morally
		Non-Cognitivism- people are motivated to act morally from fear of punishment
		Welfarism- to act morally is beneficial
Man's state of nature	According to Thomas Hobbes,"Man's natural state is a state of war of all against all." If left unto himself, man's life is "solitary, poor, nasty, brutish and short." Man is free, equal and rational, but he is also egoistic and anti-social.	
The Solution	The State	A strong state is the only way to protect men from each other. Every citizen owes total allegiance to the state because the state offers men protection from each other. The state is legitimate as long as it can demonstrate itself capable of exercising power.
	Social Contract	Men are born into society are automatically enrolled in the social contract. This contract is something that all rational and competent agents would agree to. Men have no way to get out of this contract. As such, they must obey the state
	Rights	Man has few rights and even these are subject to the needs of the state.
	Rules/ laws	People must forego the pursuit of their own interests to obey the rules that promote the interests of society as a whole.

Social Contract Theory
(Contractualism)

This position was developed by Immanuel Kant and most recently, by John Rawls. Like Contractarianism it is a deontological and consequentialist ethical and political theory.

Meta-ethical presuppositions	Metaphysics of morals	**Realist**-moral facts are found and not made.
		Good- is determined by what is right. All rational men can conclude what is right and will agree to it.
		Free will- men are free moral agents who are morally culpable.
	Moral epistemology	**Cognitivism-** moral judgments express belief.
	Moral Psychology	**Motivational internalism-** recognition of moral facts or obligation provides motivation for moral action.
		Cognitivism-moral motivation comes from within oneself.
		Welfarism- it is to one's best self-interest to act morally.
Man's state of nature	Men are rational and equal. At the same time, they are also anti-social and egoistic.	
	The state	The state is agreed to by all competent rational individuals for the good of all.
	The social contract	The social contract is a device used to reveal what is moral
	Rights	All men have equal rights
	Rules/ laws	Are understood as something that the rational individuals would agree to from a common perspective as one free and equal person among others.
	Virtue	According to John Rawls, **justice** is the primary virtue. He asserts that **justice** is fairness.

Philosophy of Science		
General Assumptions about science	**Science Involves**	1. Collection of data 2. Formulation of hypothesis 3. Testing of the hypothesis 4. Refining of hypothesis or 5. Elimination of the old hypothesis and reformulation of a new hypothesis
	Science Assumes	1. Regularity in nature 2. The results of tests are repeatable 3. Those who test and review tests will be objective and fair in their evaluations.
	Nature of Science	Science is an empirical inductive method for obtaining knowledge about the world.
	Logic of Science	**Abduction**- inference to the best explanation. An approach developed by Charles Sanders Peirce to explain a set of data.
	Naturalism	Assumes that everything that happens can be explained by natural phenomena. One can be a naturalist without being a **physicalist.**
	Physicalism	Only that which is physical exists. There is no spiritual or mental.
Limits of Science	**What science can and cannot do**	Science cannot claim to arrive at ultimate truth
		Science can provide confidence about a theory, but it cannot provide certainty
		Science requires testing
Scientific Realism	**Metaphysics**	Scientific theories accurately model reality
	Epistemology	One can know that a scientific theory is true.
	Axiology	Some argue that value has no place in science
		Others argue that science is value laden like all of reality
Scientific Anti-Realism	**Metaphysics**	Scientific theories cannot and do not model reality.
	Epistemology	One cannot know if a scientific theory is true
	Axiology	Some argue that science is as subjective as value

Scientific Method		
Some question the existence of a scientific method. If there is then science is a discipline. If there is not a scientific method, then science is a sham.		
Scientific Realism Scientific theories accurately model reality	**Assertion:** There is a scientific method based upon falsification and reason.	**Falsification-** Karl Popper argued that if science is an empirical-inductive activity, then scientific theories cannot be proven true, they can only be proven false through testing. When proven false, a theory must be discarded. With increased testing comes increased confidence in the truth of a theory. Scientific realists believe that there is a scientific method. Such as: **Hypothesis**-an unproved theory, proposition or supposition **Theory**-a hypothesis that has passed every objective test, thus yielding greater certainty that it is true. **Law**-a theory that passes every conceivable test, thus yielding the highest level of certainty that can be achieved
	Assertion: A scientific method is not needed for science to work	Some scientific realists argue that beauty is sufficient to prove the truth of a scientific theory. Hence, falsification is not necessary.
	Assertion: Scientific method does not need testing	**Bayes theory** is used to confirm a scientific theory based upon probability. It suggests that severe testing is a necessary but not a sufficient condition for achieving scientific knowledge.
Scientific Anti Realism Scientific theories cannot and do not model reality.	**Assertion**	There is not a scientific method because testing is not applied to all scientific ideas.
	Proof: There are many examples that science does not follow any method.	**Evolution-** evolution cannot be tested or falsified. Consequently it should not be treated as a theory, but only as a hypothesis
		Other minds- we cannot prove that other minds exist, but other minds are considered as a matter of fact.
		Psyco-therapy- there are at least 400 different approaches to psyco-therapy
		Superstring theory- there is no way to test this theory but many assume that it is true.
		Quantum theory- science cannot explain the behavior of sub-atomic particles

Scientific Realism

The metaphysics of science	**Semantic realism**	suggests that statements about theoretical entities are to be understood literally
	Reductionism	suggests that theoretical entities are constructions out of more familiar materials
The Epistemology of science	**Types of realism**	1. The best scientific theories are true 2. The best scientific theories are close to the truth. 3. We are rationally justified to believe that the best scientific theories are true or close to the truth. 4. **Minimal epistemic realism** asserts that it is logically possible to attain a state that warrants belief in a theory
The value theory of science	**Beauty**	A good scientific theory is beautiful
	Scientific virtues	A good theory must have scientific virtues in order to point to the truth. These include: simplicity, balance
Scientific method	**Scientific realism requires scientific method**	**Falsification**- Karl Popper argued that if science is an empirical-inductive activity, then scientific theories cannot be proven true, they can only be proven false through testing. When proven false, a theory must be discarded. With increased testing comes increased confidence in the truth of a theory. Scientific realists believe that there is a scientific method. Such as: **Hypothesis**-an unproved theory, proposition or supposition **Theory**-a hypothesis that has passed every objective test, thus yielding greater certainty that it is true. **Law**-a theory that passes every conceivable test, thus yielding the highest level of certainty that can be achieved
	Scientific realism does not require a scientific method	Some scientific realists argue that beauty is sufficient to prove the truth of a scientific theory. Hence, falsification via testing is not necessary.
Argument for Realism	**Success of science**	Applied science demonstrates the realism of scientific theories

Scientific Anti-Realism		
Metaphysics of science	**Instrumentalism**	Suggests that scientific theories are only useful, but do not accurately model reality
Epistemology of science	**Constructive empiricism**	Suggests that science does not aim at truth. Instead, science only aims at empirical adequacy. In other words, it provides information that meets the scientist's purposes
Value Theory of Science	**Pragmatism**	Science is not objective. Science is all about the subjective values of the scientific community.
Scientific method	There is not a scientific method because testing is not applied to all scientific ideas.	There are a number of examples that science does not follow any method. For example: evolution, psychotherapy, superstring theory chaos theory, complexity theory and others.
Other Arguments for Anti-Realism	**Theory of underdetermination**	Theory underdetermines data. In other words, for any given set of data, there are an infinite number of theories that can account for it.
	Thomas Kuhn *The Structure of Scientifc Revolutions*	Argues that scientists are not objective or fair. They operate out of self-interest by preserving the status quo. Younger scientists challenge the status quo through experimentation and demonstrate that the current paradigm is wrong. This results in a paradigm shift.
	Natural Ontological Attitude	Well confirmed scientific theories should be accepted as true. However, scientific realists make the mistake of adding metaphysical assumptions about the nature of truth.

American Pragmatism

American pragmatism is a mixture of empiricism and idealism. It holds that a theory is to be accounted true as long as it works. Pragmatists believe that all experience is value laden. Much of American Analytic philosophy was influenced by pragmatism. American Analytic philosophers who subscribed to pragmatism include such figures as W.V.O. Quine, Hilary Putnam, and Richard Rorty. Some types of pragmatism (like Rorty's) lead to postmodernity.

Charles Sanders Pierce (1839-1914)	Founded American pragmatism. The purpose of pragmatism is to make ideas clear. He coined the term "**pragmaticism**" to differentiate his views from William James. He subscribed to metaphysical realism. He rejects Cartesian certainty and methodological doubt. .
	3 kinds of truth **Transcendental truth**- the real character of a thing. What science attempts to ascertain **Complex truth**- the truth of propositions **Logical truth**- the conformity of a proposition to reality. Experience can refute or affirm this kind of truth. Every proposition is either true or false
	Pragmatic theory of meaning-the meaning of an idea is the sum of its practical consequences
William James (1842-1910)	James was influenced by Pierce. He viewed pragmatism as radical empiricism. Pragmatism is only a method to settle metaphysical disputes. He used pragmatism as a type of therapy.
	Pragmatic theory of truth- truth in our ideas means their ability to work. Truth is the "cash value" of an idea
	Pragmatic theory of meaning-the practical outcome of a belief is its true meaning
John Dewey (1859-1952)	Described his position as **empirical naturalism** or **naturalistic empiricism**.
	Pragmatic instrumentalism- knowledge is only for solving problems. This does not deny the objectivity of truth because it not made relative to any individual.

Positivism

Definition	The idea that something must be empirically or scientifically verifiable before it can be taken seriously.
	the theory that laws are to be understood as social rules. These rules are valid only because they are established by a human authority. As such, these rules or laws have no metaphysical basis. Consequently, morality should have nothing to do with law.
Scientism	**Scientism** is the belief that all that can be known, must be known through the scientific process. Anything that cannot be known through the scientific process is nonsense. Most who hold this position are not scientists at all. The scientists who hold this position are generally naturalists. Scientism is a view based on positivism.
David Hume	Hume was an empiricist who thought that facts should be separated from value. Facts are analyzed by reason, while values are understood via the passions. He argued that the connection of fact and value was based on nothing more than induction. As such, one cannot be certain of the connection.
Jeremy Bentham	Following Hume's fact/ value dichotomy, Bentham believed that morality was based on pleasure and pain, not reason. Further, he believed that rights are a fiction. Finally, he believed that natural law should be rejected. He argued that laws should be positivistic.
Auguste Comte	Comte's concept of positivism is a rejection of theology and moral philosophy so that science can be effective.

Major Movements in Analytic Philosophy

The "Linguistic turn" is about the movement from epistemology to philosophy of language. Philosophy of language is considered first philosophy in the study of Analytic Philosophy. The other branches of philosophy are understood in light of the changes in philosophy of language. According to Quentin Smith (in *Ethical and Religious thought in Analytic Philosophy of Language* for more in depth information read Scott Soames *Philosophical Analysis in the 20th Century*), there are five major movements in Analytic Philosophy.

Logical Realism	**G.E Moore and Bertrand Russell**	These philosophers are metaphysical realists who assert that every word in a sentence correlates to a sense or meaning.
Logical Positivism	**A.J. Ayer F.P. Ramsey Moritz Schlick Rudolf Carnap Otto Neurath**	Carnap defined philosophy as the analysis of the language of science. This language of science is concerned with both scientific uses and every day life. A key idea is the verification principle which argues that anything that is not empirically verifiable is meaningless. They also emphasized the fact/ value dichotomy.
Ordinary Language Analysis	**Ludwig Wittgenstein, J.L. Austin, Gilbert Ryle, R.M. Hare, P.F. Strawson, and John Searle**	Started by Ludwig Wittgenstein, Ordinary language analysts reject the verification principle because they argue that it is senseless by its own standard. These philosophers argue that philosophical statements are not tautologies or statements of equivalents. They are instead, empirical generalizations about how ordinary expressions are used. These philosophers deduce conclusions from the linguistic thesis that the sense of an expression is its ordinary use.
Post Positivists or Physicalists	**W.V.O. Quine Wilfrid Sellars D.M. Armstrong David Lewis Paul Churchland**	Started by Quine, this movement arose in response to both logical positivism and ordinary language analysis. Wilfrid Sellars is another leader in this approach to philosophy. These philosophers rejected the fact/ value dichotomy. They also believed that metaphysics is a legitimate field of study. Physical reality amounts to the referent of the theoretical sentences in the physical sciences.
Linguistic Essentialism	**Saul Kripke, Alvin Plantinga, Robert Adams, and David Brink**	This movement resulted from the ideas of Saul Kripke expressed in his work *Naming and Necessity*. By employing the use of possible worlds and necessity, the essentialists consider what is essential to trans-world identities. . The **Logical Essentialists (LE)** agree with the **PPP** that metaphysics is a legitimate field of study.

Logical Realism		
Correspondence theory of truth- a substantive theory that claims truth corresponds to reality		
Philosophers		
G.E Moore and Bertrand Russell and early Ludwig Wittgenstein		
Presupposition		
A logically perfect language free of the misleading tendencies of ordinary language is the goal of philosophy.		
Philosophy of Language	**Definite descriptions**	A name is really a description of the material object that we are discussing.
	Description theory	Sentences express thoughts, or propositions. Just as a sentence has a grammatical form, so the proposition expressed by the sentence has a logical form. Thus, a sentence can be represented logically.
	Semantic pragmatic minimalism	There is a minimal distance between what is said and the linguistic meaning of the utterance. Most hold that implicature is important but not part of what is said.
Epistemology	**Common sense Realism**	Some common sense propositions are known to be true
		Some common sense propositions are a matter of common knowledge
		Not everything that might be called a common sense belief or proposition is true or accepted.
		It is more reasonable to accept common sense propositions or beliefs than to accept a philosophical theory that implies that they are false
		Skepticism about the external world is to be rejected
		Some kind of **foundationalism** is essential to knowledge
		Epistemological particularism-particular instances of knowledge can be used as data to assess and develop epistemological theories.
Metaphysics	**Metaphysical realism**	Abstract universals as well as concrete particulars exist.
	Philosophy of religion	There is no God, so human life is meaningless
Axiology	**Value Realism**	Human life has an ethical meaning. Goodness and beauty have intrinsic value. We know of them through intuition.

Logical Positivism

Redundancy theory of truth- a deflationary theory which suggests that the ascription of truth to a proposition is apparent, but not actual. Ascribing truth to a proposition is actually doing nothing.

Philosophers
A.J. Ayer, F.P. Ramsey, Moritz Schlick, Rudolf Carnap, and Otto Neurath

Presuppositions
1. Philosophy is the logical analysis of sentences of the sciences.
2. One must study language to understand thought.
3. Ordinary language is deceptive so it must be translated into an ideal or artificial language to prevent confusion.
4. Something must be empirically verifiable for it to make any sense.

Philosophy of Language	**The function of language**	Language is used to express emotions about the arts or it is used to represent a scientific theory or proposition.
	Humean scepticism	**Hume's fork**- all knowledge is either a necessary truth or an empirical truth. All else is nonsense that must be rejected
		Hume's argument against causation- You cannot know that everything has a cause because knowledge of causation is only the result of empirical experience.
		Hume's argument against induction-Induction is based only upon probability of past occurrences. Events may or may not continue as they have in the past.
Epistemology	**Verification principle**	Knowledge is based on what is empirically verifiable
Metaphysics	**Metaphysical nominalism**	Only concrete particulars exist
	The function of metaphysics	According to Rudolf Carnap, metaphysics should be regarded as an art
	Philosophy of religion	The verification principle renders the concept of God as senseless. Since there is no God, human life has no meaning.
Axiology	**Emotivism**	Facts have nothing to do with value. Ethical sentences have no truth value. The only function of ethical sentences is to express moral emotions. "Good" only expresses approval. Human life is ethically meaningless.

Ordinary Language Analysis

.Wittgensteinian approaches to ordinary language analysis lead to postmodernity because of the focus on language and community.

Performative theory of truth- a deflationary theory that suggests to say that something is true is only to endorse a proposition

Philosophers

Ludwig Wittgenstein, J.L. Austin, Gilbert Ryle, R.M. Hare, P.F. Strawson, and John Searle

Presuppositions

1. Philosophical problems are due to the misuse of language.
2. Philosophers should focus on the subtleties of language use.

Philosophy of Language	Use theory of meaning- The meaning of a word is its ordinary usage	**Language games**- the context or the community determines the meaning of a word or sentence
		Speech act theory-speech acts express ideas and encourage certain types of behavior.
Epistemology		Philosophical theses are not empirical or synthetic, so they must be analytic (necessary and *a priori*).
Metaphysics	**Anti-metaphysical presupposition**	Ordinary language analysis seeks to rescue words from metaphysical usage and attempts to return them to ordinary usage.
	Philosophy of mind	Language depends on intention. Intentionality is an important component of philosophy of the mind.
	Philosophy of religion	Ordinary language analysis is poorly suited to the task of philosophy of religion, because it is self-referentially incoherent and it fails to accurately describe ordinary usage of religious sentences. Human life is religiously meaningless.
Axiology	Prescriptivism	Ethical sentences are like commands in that they influence the actions of another. They are different from commands because ethical sentences are universizable. We do not know if ethical sentences have truth value or not. Morals are relative. Human life is ethically meaningless.

Post Positivists or Physicalists

Philosophers include:

W.V.O. Quine, Wilfred Sellars, D.M. Armstrong, , David Lewis, Paul Churchland

Post-Postitivst analytic philosophy is said to go beyond rationalism and empiricism. This movement began in the 1950s. Many, but not all post-positivists are also physicalists. Two of the most significant works in this movement are WVO Quine's "Two Dogmas of Empiricism" and Wilfrid Sellar's "Empiricism and the Philosophy of the Mind."

Disquotational theory of truth- a deflationary theory which suggests that sentences rather than propositions are the primary bearers of truth.

Presuppositions

1. Physical reality is the microscopic or macroscopic referents of the theoretical sentences in the physical sciences.
2. Rejection of the views of the Logical positivists
3. Rejection of the views of the Ordinary Language Analysts

Philosophy of Language	**Underdetermination of Translation by Data**	The class of all possible data for an empirical theory, in which the notion of meaning plays a central role, radically undermines the claims about meaning that it makes
	Indeterminancy of Translation	The indeterminancy caused by an empirical theory, in which the notion of meaning plays a central role, cannot be resolved even if we have access to all of physical facts.
	Meaning	Meaning is not the center of philosophy. Donald Davidson developed a theory of meaning based on formal logic.
Epistemology	**Naturalized Epistemology**	By rejecting the analytic/ synthetic distinction Quine destroyed the rationalist form of foundationalism, while Sellars destroyed the empiricist form of foundationalism. Consequently, epistemology should be reduced to psychology or cognitive science.
Metaphysics	**Philosophy of mind**	The mind/ body dichotomy is rejected because the concept of mind or spirit is rejected. Identity theory or functionalism are preferred ways of thinking about the nature of the mind.
	Philosophy of religion	Physicalism assumes everything that exists is governed by the laws of physics. As such, it is poorly suited for philosophy of religion. Only atheists are comfortable with this position.
Axiology	**Pragmatism**	Quine destroyed the fact/ value dichotomy in his article "The Two Dogmas of Empiricism." Quine argued that all experience is value-laden. Ethics should be reduced to psychology or cognitive science.

Linguistic Essentialism

Saul Kripke, Ruth Marcus, Alvin Plantinga, Robert Adams, and David Owen Brink

Correspondence theory of truth- truth corresponds to reality

Presuppositions

1. Intentional and modal logics constitute the formal basis for linguistic essentialism
2. A precise formulation of the distinction between logically necessary attributes, nontrivial essences, and trivial essences is crucial to linguistic essentialism

Philosophy of language	**Rigid Designator Theory**	Many locutions are rigid designators. These rigid designators can be used for modal logic and possible world semantics.
Epistemology	**Naturalized Epistemology**	Knowledge results from natural processes
Metaphysics	**Philosophy of mind**	Allows for the existence of both the mind and the body.
	Ontology	**Essential properties-** a property is weakly essential just in case it is necessary to some object but not necessary to all objects. A property is strongly essential just in case it is necessary to some object but is contingently possessed by some other object
		Trivial and nontrivial essences- An Aristotelian essence is an example of a nontrivial essence. A trivial essence is one that is self-identical.
		Platonic realism- both abstract universals and concrete particulars exist. These concepts exist in different worlds.
	Philosophy of religion	Human life has religious meaning
Axiology	**Value realism**	Human life has ethical meaning

Types of Philosophy of History

Critical Philosophy of History	Speculative Philosophy of History
Also known as **"Historiography"**	• Deals with the metaphysics of history
Deals with questions like: • The nature of historical evidence • The degree to which objectivity is possible • Is there any significance to human history?	• The value of history • The meaning of history • The purpose of history • Is history cyclical? • Is history predetermined? • Is history teleological?

Historiography

Axes of Historiography	Nomothetic- Attempts to establish laws and generalities about people using the natural sciences-objective	Idiographic- Focus on the individual and recognition of uniqueness using the humanities- subjective
Synchronic- A specific moment in time	Sociological analysis	zeitgeist
Diachronic- Development and evolution through history	Big history, Evolution	Biography

Speculative Philosophy of History	
Speculative philosophy of history asks at least these basic questions:	
Unit of Study	• The individual • The family • The city • Sovereign territory • Civilization or culture
Patterns	Does history have any broad patterns?
	Is history deterministic?
	Does history have a direction?
	Does history have a cause?
Meaning	Does history have a meaning?
	How is the meaning of history known?

The Metaphysics of History	
Metaphysical Realism	**Metaphysical Nominalism**
History operates with a correspondence theory of truth	History can operate with any theory of truth
History is teleological	History has no value
History has a definitive meaning	History has no direction, since it is totally random
Value is imposed upon the process of writing history	History is meaningless
Pre-modern philosophers hold to this viewpoint	Modern and post-modern philosophers hold to this viewpoint

Pre- Modern History of Philosophy

Linear view of Time and History	The Judeo- Christian worldview is one in which there is a linear view of time. This view is often accompanied by theodicies and a strong view of eschatology
Cyclical view of Time and History	The ancient Greeks, the Norse, the Hindus, the Jains and the Chinese all hold to a cyclical view of time.
	The recent development of mathematical models of long- term secular socio- demographic cycles has revived interest in cyclical theories of history
Herodotus 484-425 B.C. The father of history	Here are presented the results of the enquiry carried out by Herodotus of Halicarnassus. The purpose is to prevent the traces of human events from being erased by time, and to preserve the fame of the important and remarkable achievements produced by both Greeks and non-Greeks; among the matters covered is, in particular, the cause of the hostilities between Greeks and non-Greeks. — *Herodotus, The Histories Robin Waterfield translation (2008)*
Aristotle 322 BC	Poetry is superior to history because poetry speaks of what must or should be true rather than what is true
Lucius Mestrius Plutarch 46-120 AD	Plutarch was a middle Platonist philosopher, who freely invented speeches for their historical figures and chose their historical subjects with an eye toward morally improving the reader.
Augustine of Hippo 354-430 AD	Christ died but once for our sins; now that he has risen from the dead, he will die no more (XII, 13, 2)." Time and history are teleological and linear, instead of cyclical. God providentially acts in the lives of men. This view is eschatological. Everything is understood in light of Salvation History
Ibn Khaldun, 1332-1406	introduced a scientific method to the philosophy of history, which was considered something "new to his age," and he often referred to it as his "new science," which is now associated with historiography. His historical method also laid the groundwork for the observation of the role of state, communication, propaganda, and systematic bias in history.
Jean Bodin 1530-1596	*Method for the Easy Knowledge of History* (1566) History is the true narration of things. There are three kinds of history: human, natural and divine.

Modern Philosophy of History

Modernity 1648-1960	Rene Descartes (1596-1650)- the father of Modernity	
	Metaphysical Nominalism- only concrete particulars exist	
	Epistemic Irrealism- There may or may not be a reality external to us. It cannot be known.	
	Epistemic Theories of Truth	Coherent theory of Truth- based on rationalism
		Pragmatic theory of Truth- based on empiricism
	Semantic Irrealism- Meaning is not tied to a correspondence theory of truth. Has a hermeneutic of doubt.	
	Semantic Theory of Truth- based on philosophy of language	

British Empiricists	Continental Philosophy
Exemplified by David Hume • An empiricist approach • Eschews any theological interpretations of the past • Explanations of the past are based on an assumed fixed human nature	**Exemplified by G.W.F. Hegel** • History is an intelligible process moving towards a specific condition- the realization of human freedom • The great man of history means that history is caused by "great men." • History is understood through dialectic
Analytic Philosophy of History • emphasizes the scientific status of historical knowledge • It emphasizes the empirically provable aspects of history • It is divorced from considerations of value	**Continental Philosophy of History** • The hermeneutical approach to the philosophy of history is exemplified in the writings of Heidegger, Gadamer, Ricouer and Foucault. • It involves existentialism and Marxism. • Historical knowledge depends on the interpretation of human actions and practices

Pre-modernity
Recorded History – 1648 AD

Discipline		Explanation
Metaphysical realism **(First Philosophy)**	**Ontology**	Both forms and concrete particulars exist.
	Theology	God is the **Prime Mover.** He is the first substance and cause of all motion in reality.
	Theory of Truth	Correspondence- Truth is based on reality
Epistemic Realism	**Externalism**	A **teleological** theory of knowledge. Reality exists independently of observers and it can be known.
Semantic Realism	**Externalism**	A **teleological** theory of meaning. Meaning is tied to the correspondence theory of truth
	Hermeneutics	The Bible is inerrant, sufficient and authoritative. **The *sensus plenior* requires metaphysical realism.
Moral Realism	**Moral Facts**	Moral facts have existence and are discovered. They are not man- made.
	Virtue Ethics	A **teleological** theory of ethics. Morality is based on the nature and purpose of a thing. Man is a rational creature and moral facts provide sufficient motivation for action.
Logical Realism	**Types of Logic**	**Deduction-** formal logics have existence like mathematics and numbers. This is a **teleological** approach to logic.
	Modal Forms	The subject matter of logic is modal fact

The Road to Modernity		
Event	**Cause**	**Date**
Nominalism	William of Ockham	1300-1980s
Renaissance	Francesco Petrarch	14-17th centuries
Protestant Reformation	Martin Luther	*95 Theses* 1517
Scientific Revolution	1. Nicolas Copernicus	*On the Revolutions of the Heavenly Spheres* 1543
	2. Galileo Galilei	*Dialogue Concerning the Two Chief World Systems* 1632
	3. Isaac Newton	*Principia* 1687
Enlightenment	Rene Decartes	*Discourse on Method* 1637
30 Years War	Treaty of Westphalia	Treaty of Osnabruck 1648
		Treaty of Munster 1648
Epistemological Turn	The switch from metaphysic to epistemology as first philosophy. From Rene Descartes to Immanuel Kant	1637- 1804

Modernity 1648-1950		
Metaphysical Nominalism	**Ontology**	Only concrete particulars exist
	Theology	There is no God. Atheism or agnosticism becomes the dominant position.
Epistemic Irrealism (First Philosophy)	**Internalism**	Our ideas arise only from within ourselves, independent of an external reality
	Theories of Truth	**Coherence Theory-** based on rationalism
		Pragmatic Theory- based on empiricism
Semantic Irrealism	**Internalism**	Our ideas and languages arise only from within ourselves independent of an external reality
	Hermeneutic	**Hermeneutic of Doubt-** the Bible is just a man made document that should be read like any other book
Moral Irrealism	**Deontology**	Morality is only about rules or laws.
	Moral facts	Moral facts do not exist. They are only man made
Logical Irrealism	**Logical Facts**	Logic is a tool of philosophy, and logical facts are only invented. Logical facts do not exist.
	Types of Logic	Deductive logic is a formal logic provides certainty, while inductive logic cannot.

The Road to Post-modernity

Romanticism	Started by musicians, poets, and artists who rejected Immanuel Kant's attempt to save the Enlightenment. Johann Fichte led the group that came to be known as the Continental Philosophers.	**1800**
Collapse of Cartesian Certainty	David Hume destroys both rationalism and empiricism	**1776**
	Friedrich Nietzsche Shows that we can know nothing. All that matters is power.	**1900**
Existentialism	Soren Kirkegaard developed a Christian version	**1850**
	Friedrich Nietzsche developed an atheistic version	**1900**
Phenomenology	Edmund Husserl and Martin Heidegger	
Structuralism	Ferdinand Saussure studied the relation of words to meaning	
Ordinary Language Philosophy	A movement within **Analytic Philosophy**, led by Ludwig Wittgenstein. They rejected the metaphysics of both the **Logical Positivists** and the **Logical Realists.**	**1945-1967**
The Linguistic Turn	Gustav Bergman explained that philosophy of language became first philosophy.	**1900-1960**

Post-modernity		
1960- present		
Discipline		**Explanation**
Metaphysical Nominalism	**Ontology**	Only concrete particulars exist
	Theology	The existence of God depends on the community
Epistemic Irrealism	**Internalism**	the contents of our minds arise independently of an external reality
Semantic Irrealism **(First Philosophy)**	**Internalism**	the contents of our minds and language arise independently of an external reality
	Theory of truth	**Tarsky**- semantic theory of Truth **Performative theory of truth**- truth is the endorsement of a proposition. **Structuralist Theory of truth**- truth is about power
	Hermeneutic	**Hermeneutic of suspicion**- the author is dead. Meaning is determined only by the reader and his community. Interpretation is only about power.
Moral Irrealism	**Moral Facts**	There are no moral facts except for those made by a community. Morality is determined by the community.
Logical Irrealism	**Logical Facts**	The are no objective logical facts. Logic is only a will to power used by a given community.

Chapter 2: Economics

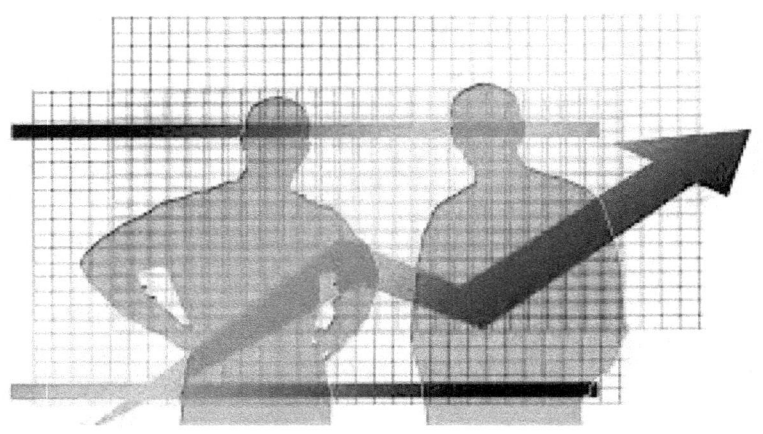

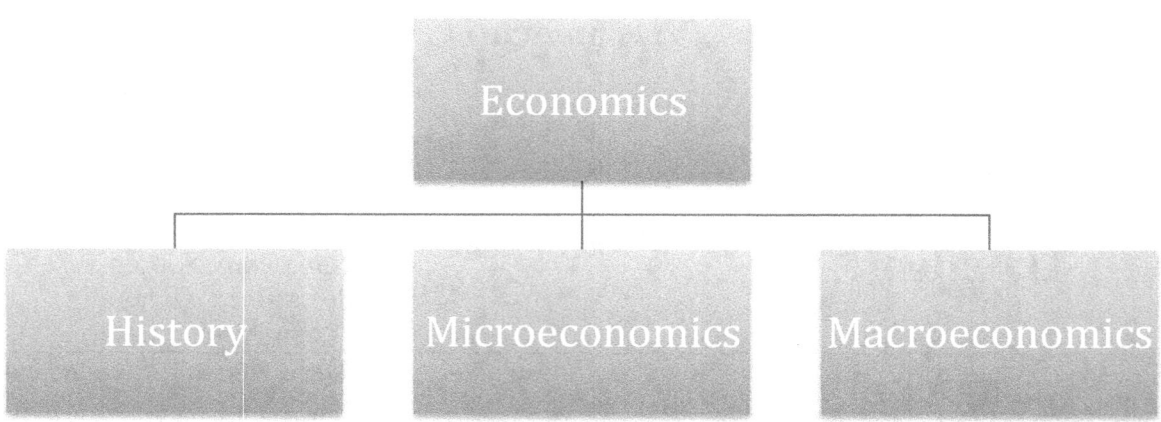

Periods of Economic History

Period	Name	Description
322 BC-1250 AD	Pre-Scholastic	From Aristotle to Thomas Aquinas
(1250-1776)	Scholastic	From the Salamanca School to Adam Smith
(1776-1871)	Classical	From Adam Smith to the marginalist revolution
(1871-2000)	Neoclassical	From the marginalist revolution to the present

Aristotle

- Politics is concerned with the city, which achieves autonomy and autarky
- Economics is about the household, which cannot achieve autonomy or autarky.
- Ethics is concerned with the individual, which does not achieve autonomy or autarky
- He viewed economic exchange as justice in distribution
- The household is a unit of production and consumption.
- The household has a hierarchy (Father, mother, children and slaves)
- The father relates to the wife in a political way.
- The father relates to the children and slaves in a kingly way.
- The household has a division of labor (men outside, women inside the home)
- There is *koinonia* between family members, but not between family and slaves..

Economics are Virtuous	Economic or natural transactions are concerned with the satisfaction of needs. Thus wealth is limited by purpose.	
Chrematistics (finance) is vicious.	*Chrematistic* or un-natural transactions, on the other hand are aimed at increasing wealth without limits. *Chrematistics* are vicious because wealth can become an end unto itself.	
Levels of Economy For all levels expenditure should not exceed income	Royal	Concerns a national economy. It includes coinage, exports, imports, and expenditure
	Satrapsy	A regional economy with six kinds of revenue, which include: land produce, peculiar products, merchandise, revenue from cultivation of soil and market dues, tax on animal produce and tax on artisans.
	City	Revenue comes from peculiar products of the country, merchandise and customs and ordinary taxes.
	Household	The least important economy. Revenue comes from land, other kinds of regular activity and investments of money

Augustine

- Augustine was the bishop of Hippo. He wrote about economic theory in his *City of God.*
- His theory of personal distribution explains how the tradesmen serves their customers and their families

Levels of the Economy	Personal	All men require some wealth to live. Only good men have their desires properly ordered. One should love his neighbor as himself.
	Domestic	A household or family should apply the same principles as the personal economy employs
	Political	This level of the economy concerns the whole social order. It is more complex than the other levels

Theory of Distribution	Augustine's theory of personal distribution explains how people are motivated by self-love and by the love for his neighbor
	The tradesman loves his customers with benevolence (wishing good to them) and not with beneficence because of scarcity.
	The tradesman loves his family with both benevolence and beneficence (doing good to them).
	The tradesman sells his product to customers to earn the means to provide for himself and his family.

Thomas Aquinas

- He was a priest of the Dominican Order
- Thomas Aquinas combined Aristotle's philosophy with Augustine's theology
- He wrote a commentary on Aristotle's *Politics*
- There are four types of economic actions associated with human and non-human goods

Economic Actions	Action	Description
	Production	Explains which goods are produced
	Exchange	How we are compensated through the sale of goods for our contributing to their production. Economic exchange is justice in distribution.
	Distribution	Determines who will consume goods
	Consumption	Or utility- which goods people prefer to consume

Salamanca School of Economics

This group of theologians developed political and economic thought based upon the work of Thomas Aquinas. There were some members of this school from the Augustinian and the Franciscan order, but they held a lesser influence on the development of these ideas.

Dominicans **University of Salamanca, Spain**	**Francisco de Vitoria (1480-1546)**	He was the founder of the Salamanca school. He wrote *De Indis et de Ivre Belli Relectione* which was concerned with international law as it related to commerce. He was an advocate of a worldwide free market. He also wrote *De Justitia*
	Domingo De Soto (1495-1560)	He wrote *De Iustitia et Iure* which was concerned with monetary theory. He thought that money should imitate the natural law, by being always firm and fixed. As such, the value of money should not be changed by governments
	Martin de Azpilcueta (1493-1586)	Also known as Navarrus, he wrote, *Manual de Confesores y Penitentes*. He was concerned with extreme need and held private property in high regard.
	Tomas de Mercado (1500-1575)	Emphasized the importance of private property. He noted that self interest cannot be separated from private property. He was also concerned with the theory of money.
Society of Jesus (Jesuits) **University of Coimbra Portugal**	**Luis de Molina (1535-1600)**	Wrote *De Iustitia et Iure* about private property. He argued that private property existed even before original sin. He also wrote *La Teoria del Justo Precio* which was concerned with prices and proper wages.
	Juan De Lugo (1583-1660)	He was concerned with private property and with commerce.
	Leonardo De Leys (1554-1623)	Also known as Lessius, his work influenced Hugo Grotius
	Francisco Suarez (1548-1617)	He emphasized the importance of natural law as it related to political and economic theory.
	Juan de Mariano (1535-1624)	His work focused on the government and monetary theory. He thinks that kings must act in such a way that he can damage the people without their consent. He also disapproved of currency debasement as a means of redistributing wealth.

Adam Smith
(The Wealth of Nations)

In 1776, Adam Smith published his *An Inquiry into the Nature and Causes of the Wealth of Nations.* Many consider him to be the father of modern economic theory. His economic/political theory is based upon his ethical thought (utilitarian) in his book *The Theory of Moral Senitments.* Adam Smith was primarily concerned with economic growth. Smith assumed that "men are not angels," that is that we act in our own self-interest, not for the common good. He was concerned to create an economic system wherein there were incentives to act for the common good, because it benefited oneself.

The results of Smith's system

Smith believed that a free market economy with a laissez faire government rewards the virtuous with wealth and punishes the vicious with poverty. Smith was a firm believer in free trade. He also believed that a free market economy with free trade between nations would result in the wealth of all the countries that participate in it. Thus making war less likely.

Laissez faire government	The government should not interfere with the market. The exception to this principle is that the government should take whatever measures are necessary to ensure a level playing field for all who participate in the marketplace.
Free market	The market is the most efficient way to allocate scarce resources. This is because the prices for a good or service are determined by the demand for it.
Property rights	Smith emphasizes the efficiency of privately owned property. Private ownership is thus, beneficial to society as a whole. He also makes clear the inefficiency of state owned property
Division of labor	Smith provides a systematic explanation of the division of labor and its consequences for a economy
Taxation	Smith asserts that taxation has a negative effect on the economy
	Tax money should only be spent on national defense, justice and public works

Neo- Classical Economics

Neoclassical economics is a term variously used for approaches to economics focusing on the determination of prices, outputs, and income distributions in markets through supply and demand, often mediated through a hypothesized maximization of utility by income-constrained individuals and of profits by cost-constrained firms employing available information and factors of production, in accordance with rational choice theory.

Marginalist Revolution	Marginalism as a formal theory can be attributed to the work of three economists, Jevons in England, Menger in Austria, and Walras in Switzerland. This occurred in the 1860-1870s.

Schools	People	Distinctives
Cambridge School	**Alfred Marshal** **William Stanley Jevons** **Francis Ysidro Edgeworth** **John Neville Keynes**	This school made economics a separate disciple from economics and politics. This occurred because they were heavily influenced by the positivism of Hume and Comte. John Neville Keynes separated economics into the practical, positive and normative domains. John Maynard Keynes developed the field of macroeconomics.
Austrian School	**Karl Menger** **Eugen von Bohm Bawerk** **Friedrich von Wieser** **Ludwig von Mises** **Freidrich von Hayek**	a school which bases its study of economics on the analysis of the actions of individual agents. Among the contributions of the Austrian School to economic theory are the subjective theory of value, marginalism in price theory, and the formulation of the economic calculation problem. This school never separated the positive aspects of economics from the normative.
Lausanne School	**Leon Walras** **Vito Volterra** **Vilfredo Pareto** **Leon Winiarski**	sometimes referred to as the *Mathematical School*, The central feature of the Lausanne School was its development of general equilibrium theory. In addition the development of Pareto optimality was another important development.

Austrian Economics

- Karl Menger started the Austrian School of Economics
- Most of its members assumed a causal realist approach to economics
- To the degree that it is realist it is also a teleological approach to economics
- It places little importance on mathematics because economics is a social science
- It combines law, politics, and economic theory
- It acknowledges the existence of macroeconomic problems, but rejects Keynesian macroeconomics.
- It focuses on microeconomics and political economy
- Macroeconomic problems are solved via microeconomic foundations.

	Definition	History
Praxeology	First discovered by the Greek philosophers, and used it as a foundation for a *eudaimonistic* ethics. The Scholastics extended **praxeological** analysis to the foundations of economics and other social sciences.	Ludwig von Mises coined the term *praxeology* and first applied to this approach. Von Mises and his followers employed **praxeology** to show that much existing economic and social theory was conceptually incoherent.
Essentials	**Methodological Individualism:** all economic phenomena can be traced back to the actions of individuals; thus individual actions must serve as the basic building blocks of economic theory.	
	Methodological Subjectivism: Economics takes man's ultimate ends and judgments of value as given. Questions of value, expectations, intent and knowledge are created in the minds of individuals and must be considered in this light	
	Marginalism: All economic decisions are made on the margin. All choices are choices regarding the last unit added or subtracted from a given stock.	
	Tastes and Preferences: Individuals' demands for goods and services are the result of their subjective valuations of the ability of such goods and services to satisfy their wants.	
	Opportunity Costs: All activities have a cost. This cost is the most highly valued alternative that is forgone because the means for its satisfaction have been devoted to some other (more highly valued) use.	
	Time Structure of Consumption and Production: All decisions take place in time. Decisions about how to allocate resources for the purposes of consumption and production across time are determined by individuals' time preference.	
	Consumer Sovereignty: In the marketplace consumers are king. Their demands drive the shape of the market and determine how resources are used. Intervention in the marketplace stifles this process.	
	Political Individualism: Political freedom is impossible without economic freedom	

Types of Political Economy

		Resource Allocation	
		Private	**Public**
Resource Ownership	**Private**	**Capitalism- Free Market Economics** (teleological, provides economic growth)	**Command Captialism-** (The Third Way) seeks a path between free market and socialist approaches to economic governance, but chiefly stresses technological development, education, and competitive mechanisms to pursue economic. (deontological, China?)
	Public	**Market Socialism-** Communism (deontological, provides no economic growth)	**Command Socialism-** economic systems where the means of production are publicly owned, managed and operated for a profit in a market economy. The profit generated in a market socialist system would be used to remunerate employees or go toward public finance. (deontological, France, Sweden)

Types of Political Economy II

	Liberty	Security
Efficiency	Market Capitalism	Command capitalism
Equity	Market Socialism	Command Socialism

Free Market Economics

- Free markets are teleological
- Free markets are consistent with natural law and virtue ethics
- Free markets emphasize property rights
- Free markets are most consistent with democratic republics
- Free markets are against government intervention
- Free markets are against inflation
- Free markets maximize freedom
- Free markets maximize economic growth

Human Nature	Free markets require rationality (teleological)
Markets	Markets clear (reach equilibrium) instantaneously
Walrasian Auctioneer	The *Walrasian auctioneer* is the presumed auctioneer that matches supply and demand in a market of perfect competition. The auctioneer provides for the features of perfect competition: perfect information and no transaction costs.
Classical Business Dichotomy	an increase in nominal factors, like wages, and prices have no impact on real factors like employment, economic growth and the interest rate
Perfect Competition Model	<ul><li>Everyone is a price taker (responds to price)</li><li>Ease of entry and exit into marketplace (there are many firms)</li><li>Perfect information (market failure results from asymmetrical information)</li><li>No transaction costs</li><li>No externalities (market failure caused by spillover effect)</li></ul>

The Circular Flow of the Economy

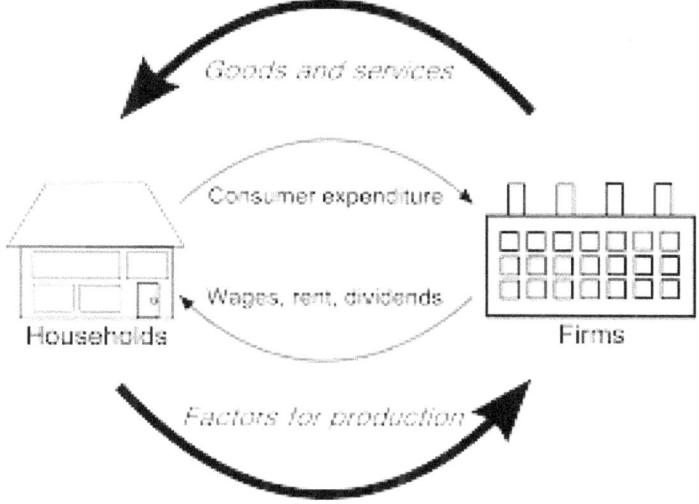

This is the basic model that explains how a free market economy works. It assumes that government upholds laws of commerce.			
Actors	**Businesses or Firms** Are profit maximizing	**Wages**	To households for labor
		Profits	To households that provided capital for firms (investment)
	Households Are utility maximizing	**Capital**	Supplied for investment in firms
		Labor	Supplied for firms
Markets	**Factor Market**	**Capital**	Needed for firms to produce
		Labor	Needed for firms to produce
	Product Market	**Goods and Services**	Provided for household consumption
		Revenue	Provided for firms

Primary Types of Goods

	Exclusive	Non-Exclusive
Private	**Private Goods** Owned and consumed by one person	**Club Goods** The kind of good where more than one person can pay for and benefit
Public	**Common Resources** This type of good is owned by no one. As a result, the tragedy of the Commons can result	**Public Goods** A type of good that results from a market failure. Government intervention is required to purchase this type of good

Other Types of Goods

Normal Goods	The more money that one makes, the more of the good that he will purchase
Inferior Goods	The more money that one makes, the less of that good that one will purchase
Substitute Goods	Goods **A** and **B** are substitutes if good **A**'s demand is increased, then the price of good **B** is increased. Conversely, the demand for good **A** is decreased when the price of good **B** is decreased.
Complementary Goods	Goods **A** and **B** are complements if good **A**'s demand is increased then the price of good **B** is decreased. Conversely, if the demand for good **B** is decreased, then the price of good **A** is increased.
Merit Goods	a commodity which is judged that an individual or society should have on the basis of some concept of need, rather than ability and willingness to pay.

Production Possibility Frontier

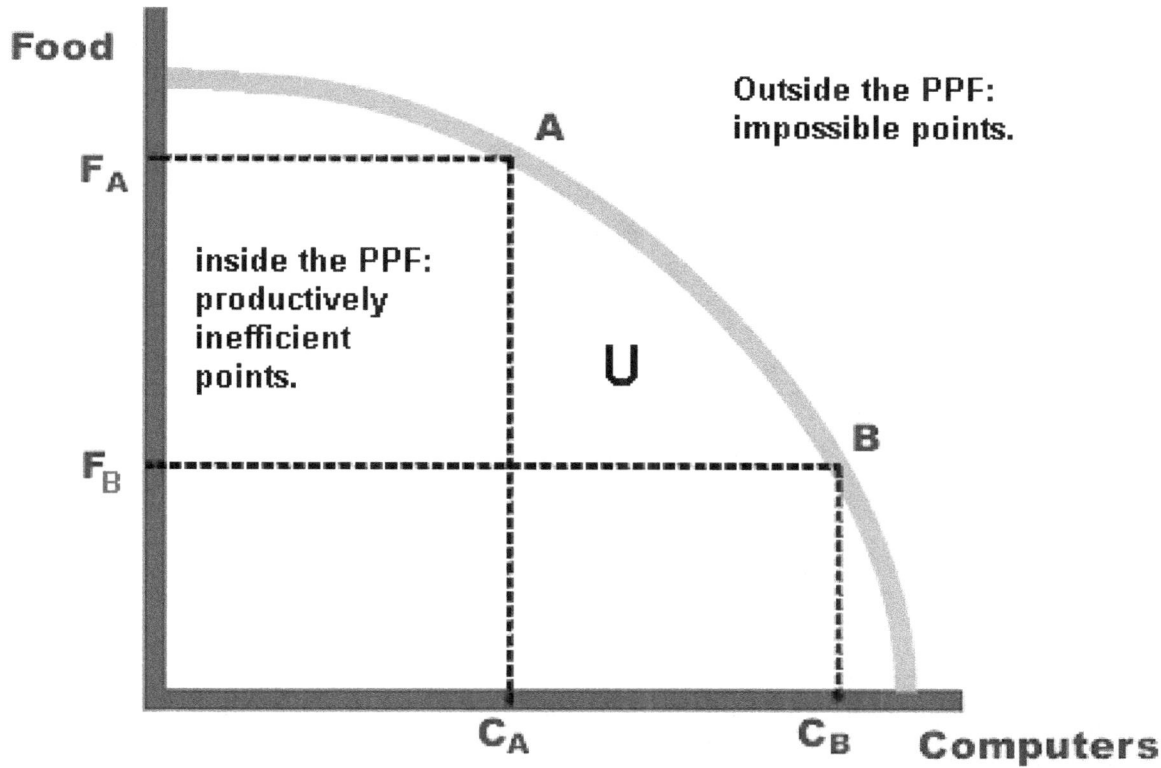

The PPF is a graphical representation of possible combinations of two goods that can be produced with constant resources and technology, such that more of one good could be produced only by diverting resources from the other good, resulting in less production of it.	
Microeconomics	This graph shows the various combinations of the amounts of two commodities that a economy can produce in a given amount of time.
Macroeconomics	This graph can be used to display the trade- offs of fixed capital versus the production of consumer goods

Indifference Curve

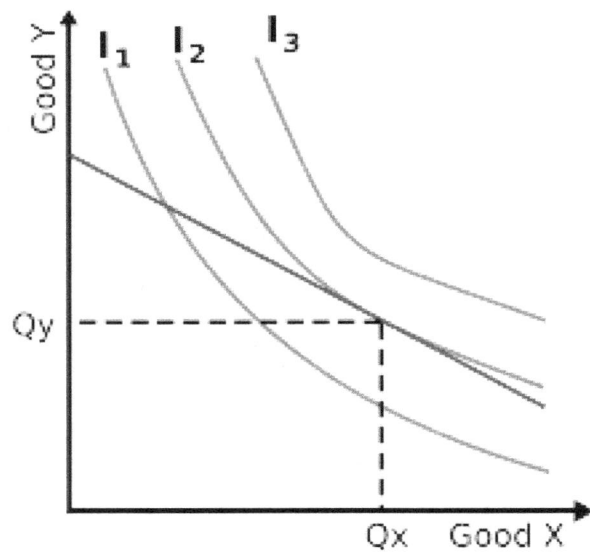

This graph displays a consumers preference for two goods when he is indifferent with the different amounts of each good. As such, it is a measure of the consumer's utility (happiness).	
Consumer Preference Theory uses indifference curves and budget constraints to develop demand curves. Assumptions of this theory are as follows:	
Preferences are complete	The consumer has ranked all available alternative combinations of commodities in terms of the satisfaction they provide him
Preferences are reflexive	The consumer will recognize when the two goods are identical in all respects
Preferences are transitive	Preferences are the same when three or more goods are similar
Preferences are continuous	These preferences are infinitely divisible
Preferences have strong monoticity	Assumes that more is better

Supply and Demand

The Neoclassical approach to economics is based upon the concept of marginality. This results in supply and demand curves. The *Walrasian auctioneer* is the presumed auctioneer that matches supply and demand in a market of perfect competition. The auctioneer provides for the features of perfect competition: perfect information and no transaction costs.

Demand	**Explanation**	Following the law of demand, the demand curve is almost always represented as downward-sloping, meaning that as price decreases, consumers will buy more of the good
	Determinants of Demand	the price of the good
		tastes and preferences
		the price of substitute goods
		the price of complementary goods
Supply	**Explanation**	A supply curve is a graph that illustrates that relationship between the price of a good and the quantity supplied .
	Determinants of Supply	Production costs, how much a good costs to be produced. Cost increases will move the curve to the left. Cost decreases will move the curve to the right
		Firms' expectations about future prices
		Technology advances will result in supply increases,which will move the curve to the right.
		Number of suppliers
Equilibrium	**Market Equilibrium**	A situation in a market when the price is such that the quantity that consumers demand is correctly balanced by the quantity that firms wish to supply.
	Partial Equilibrium	The supply-and-demand model is a **partial equilibrium** model, where the clearance on the market of some specific goods is obtained independently from prices and quantities in other markets.
	General Equilibrium	**General equilibrium theory** is a branch of theoretical economics. It seeks to explain the behavior of supply, demand, and prices in a whole economy with many interacting markets, by seeking to prove that a set of prices exists that will result in an overall equilibrium.

Supply and Demand
(Perfect Competitition Model)

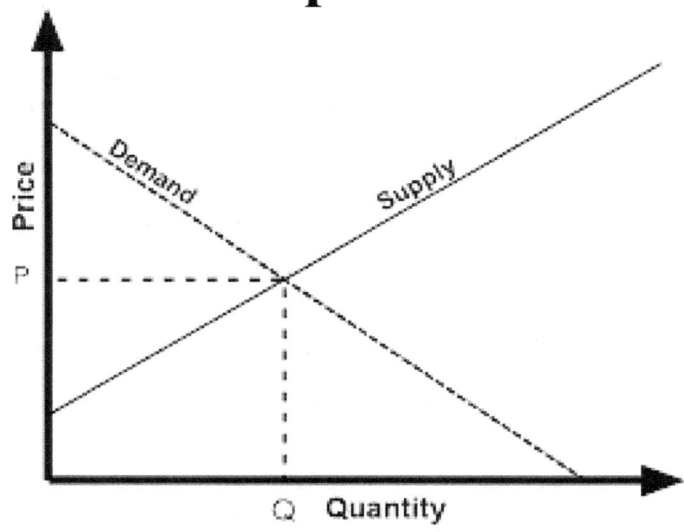

Changing Equilibria

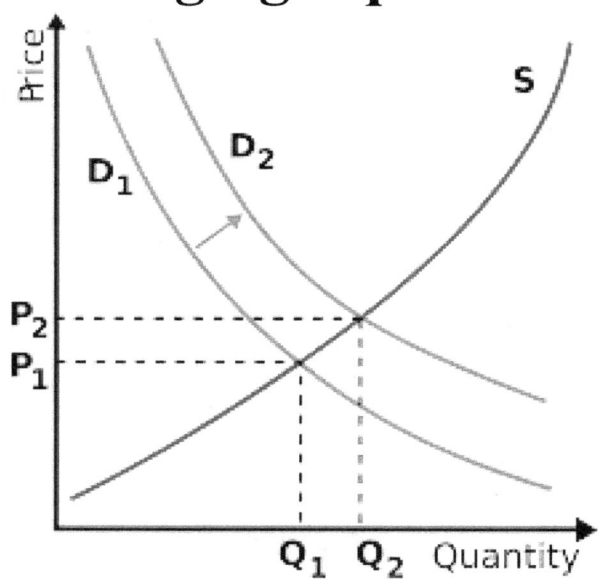

D1 represents the original demand
D2 represents an increase in demand
   Note the change in the equilibrium with each change of either supply or
demand

Supply Surplus and Shortage

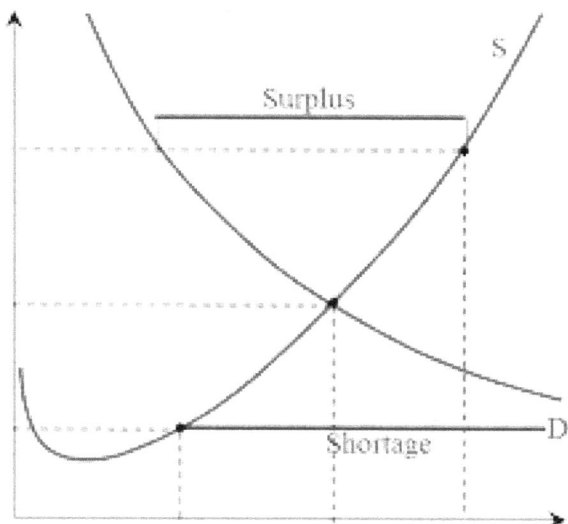

A surplus results from setting the price above equilibrium, like a minimum wage law.

A shortage results from setting the price below equilibrium, like a government placed price cap.

The equilibrium price is the best price

Consumer and Producer Surplus

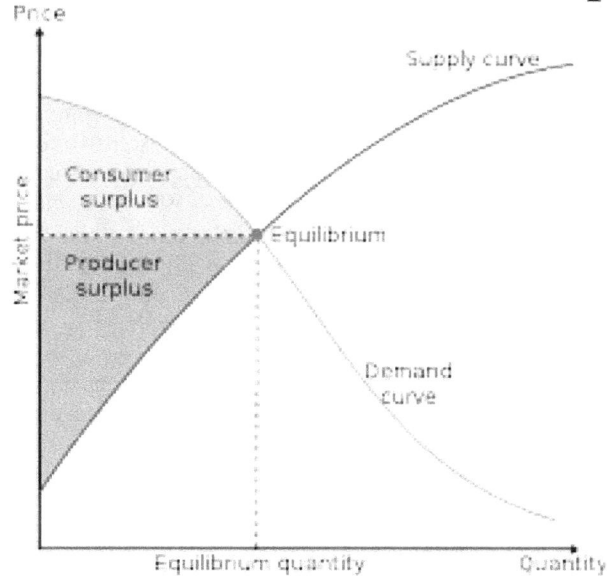

Consumer surplus is the benefit to the consumer. Producer surplus is the benefit to the producer.

Game Theory

Game theory is a method of studying strategic decision making. It was originally developed by Oskar Morgenstern and John von Neumann. More formally, it is "the study of mathematical models of conflict and cooperation between intelligent rational decision-makers." Game theory is mainly used in economics, political science, and psychology, as well as logic and biology.

Zero Sum Game	- a game such that one person's gains exactly equal the losses of the other participant(s). Most of these are two player games. This was the approach developed by von Neumann and Morgenstern.	
Cooperative Game	A game is *cooperative* if the players are able to form binding commitments. For instance the legal system requires them to adhere to their promises. In noncooperative games this is not possible.	
Non Cooperative Game	Often it is assumed that *communication* among players is allowed in cooperative games, but not in noncooperative ones. The work of John Forbes Nash assumes many of the cooperative solutions as noncooperative equilibria	
Multiple Player Game	When the game has three or more players. These type of games were made possible by the work of John Forbes Nash.	
Game Form	**Normal Form**	usually represented by a matrix which shows the players, strategies, and pay-offs . It is presumed that each player acts simultaneously, without knowing the actions of the other
	Extensive Form	The extensive form can be used to formalize games with a time sequencing of moves. Games here are played on trees . Here each node represents a point of choice for a player. The extensive form can be viewed as a multi-player generalization of a decision tree.
Nash Equilibrium	Named after John Forbes Nash. It is a solution concept of a game involving two or more players, in which each player is assumed to know the equilibrium strategies of the other players, and no player has anything to gain by changing only his own strategy unilaterally. If each player has chosen a strategy and no player can benefit by changing his or her strategy while the other players keep theirs unchanged, then the current set of strategy choices and the corresponding payoffs constitutea **Nash equilibrium.** The practical and general implication is that when players also act in the interests of the group, then they are better off than if they acted in their individual interests alone.	
	Subgame Perfect Equilibrium	**Reinhard Selten** developed this concept. It is a refinement of a **Nash Equilibrium** used in sequential games
	Bayesian Game.	**John Harsanyi** developed this concept. This is one in which information about characteristics of the other players (i.e. payoffs) is incomplete.

Normal Form Game

		Player 2	
		Compromise	Don't compromise
Player 1	Compromise	(0,0)	(-1,1)
	Don't compromise	(1,-1)	(-10,-10)

Extensive Form Game

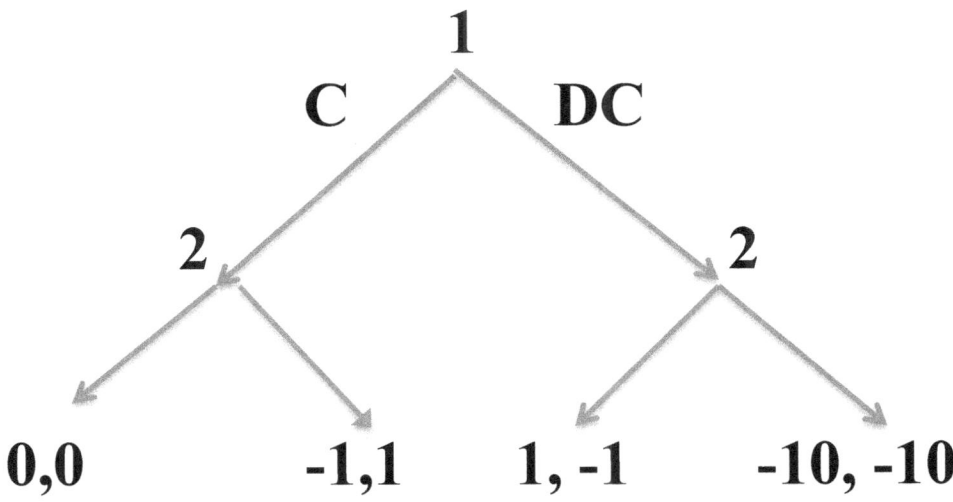

Moral Foundations for Social Welfare Economics

Philosopher	Concept	Implication
Vilfredo Pareto	**Pareto Optimality-** a policy improves social welfare only if every person either is made better off or left unaffected by the policy. That means that if even a single person is made worse off by the policy, it is not what economists call Pareto-improving.	Opposes income redistribution schemes to fund social programs like tax increases. A consumption tax is better because it taxes only voluntary transactions.
Nicholas Kaldor	a policy improves social welfare if those who gained were made enough better off that they could compensate the people harmed due to the policy change. In simple terms, policies that create winners and losers can be Kaldor-improving as long as winners win more than losers lose; that is, the aggregate gains must be larger than the aggregate losses.	Kaldor favors free trade, but Pareto would oppose free trade pacts. A similar divide would occur on large-scale public goods that require some people or businesses to be involuntarily relocated. All Pareto-improving policies are also Kaldor-improving, so Kaldor could support all the things that Pareto would support. Because Kaldor's condition for a policy being welfare-improving is weaker than Pareto's, more policies can pass Kaldor's test than Pareto's.
John Rawls	Rawls believed a policy improves social welfare if it benefitted those least well-off among the population. What happened to the rest of society did not matter to Rawls. For Only those at the bottom counted in determining whether a policy is a good one or not.	Redistributive policies fail both Pareto's and Kaldor's test for being welfare-improving, but pass Rawls' test.

Social Welfare Economics: Kenneth Arrow

Arrow's monograph *Social Choice and Individual Value* derives from his PhD thesis. In it he sets out a key result (in one final form).

In this work Arrow develops his **General impossibility Theorem**: It is impossible to formulate a social preference ordering that satisfies all of the following conditions. The theorem has tremendous implications for welfare economics and theories of justice. Amartya Sen extended the liberal paradox which argued that given a status of "Minimal Liberty" there was no way to obtain Pareto Optimality nor to avoid the problem of social choice of neutral but unequal results.

Arrow's work in Social welfare theory served as the basis for work in **Public Choice theory** and **New Institutional Economics**

Nondictatorship	1. : The preferences of an individual should not become the group ranking without considering the preferences of others.
Individual Sovereignty	2. : each individual should be able to order the choices in any way and indicate ties
Unanimity	3. : If every individual prefers one choice to another, then the group ranking should do the same.
Freedom From Irrelevant Alternatives	4. : If a choice is removed, then the others' order should not change.
Uniqueness of Group Rank	5. :The method should yield the same result whenever applied to a set of preferences. The group ranking should be transitive.

Social Welfare Economics

Term	Explanation
Perfectly Competitive Markets	Many firms and buyers
	Everyone is a price taker
	Free entry and exit
	Perfectly homogeneous products
	Perfect information- no asymmetrical information
	No spillovers on third parties or **Externalities.** Third parties are people who are neither buyers nor sellers
Efficiency and Welfare Analysis	An outcome is efficient or socially optimal if total gains from trade are maximized
	Efficient outcomes (quantities) are characterized as the quantity such that the **Marginal Social Benefit** (MSB) equals **Marginal Social Cost** (MSC)
First Welfare Theorem	Perfectly competitive markets (PCM) are efficient. In other words, the equilibrium quantity is the **Socially Optimal** quantity
The Second Welfare Theorem	Any socially optimal allocation of resources can be achieved by a perfectly competitive market, assuming that endowments can be redistributed
	Social Optimum= Marginal Private Benefit (MPB) = MSB = MSC = **Marginal External Costs + Marginal Private Cost** (MPC)

Externalities

Positive Externalities	If a positive externality exists, then MSB are greater than MPB. The difference between MSB and MPB is called **Marginal External Benefits** (MEB) MEB= MSB-MPB
Negative externalities	If a negative externality exists, then MSC are greater than MPC. The difference between MSC and MPC is called **Marginal External Costs** or Marginal Damages MEC= MSC-MPC

Market Failure

Asymmetrical Information	When both buyers and sellers enter into exchange without having sufficient information	**Adverse Selection**- when business is entered into without carefully selecting Partners/ customers
		Moral Hazard- bailing someone out will result in continued bad behavior
Externalities	An **externality** exists whenever one person's actions affect someone else's utility of some firms profits, other than through the price system If an externality exists, then there are side effects on third parties, thus violating our perfect competition requirements • **Equilibrium**= MPB+ MPC • **Social Optimum**= MSB+ MSC • Goods that generate negative externalities are overproduced relative to the social optimum • Goods that generate positive externalities are underproduced relative to the social optimum	**Positive Production Externalities**- production benefits parties other than the producer, yet the producer is not compensated
		Positive Consumption Externalities- when an individual's consumption increases the well- being of others, but the consumer is not compensated by others
		Negative Production Externalities- a company produces its goods and pollution
		Negative Consumption Externalities- After eating dinner, you begin to smoke cigarettes. The smoke from your cigarette affects my enjoyment of my meal.
	Public goods are a type of market failure because no one person can pay for the good, so government intervention is necessary to resolve the issue. • In general, the socially optimal quantity of a public good is Q0 such that • MSB (Q0)= sum MPB (Q0)= MSC	**Non Rival**- one person's consumption of a specific unit of a good does not rule out someone else consuming the same unit
		Non-Exclusive (or non-excludable) people who do not pay for a good cannot be prevented from consuming the good

Solutions for Externalities

Pigouvian Named after Arthur Cecil Pigou	**A taxation solution for externalities**	Pigouvian Tax (or subsidy) is a **price approach**. Tax per unit equal to marginal damages at the socially optimal quantity
Regulation	**A quantity solution for externalities**	Heterogeneity in the population of producers leads to different producers with different costs of reducing the negative externality • Set a target for reducing the externality, which may or may not be socially optimal • The social cost of externality reduction = private cost of externality reduction
Coasian Named after Ronald Coase	**A bargaining solution for externalities**	Establish property rights where they are missing. Then let people bargain over ownership of those rights
	The Coase Solution works when the agents are easy to identify The fewer the agents, the less the bargaining costs Enforcement costs are associated with rights	In law and economics, the **Coase theorem** describes the economic efficiency of an economic allocation or outcome in the presence of externalities. The theorem states that when trade in an externality is possible and there are no transaction costs, bargaining will lead to an efficient outcome regardless of the initial allocation of property rights. In practice, obstacles to bargaining or poorly defined property rights can prevent Coasian bargaining.

Public Goods

- In general, the socially optimal quantity of a public good is Q0 such that
- MSB (Q0) = sum MPB (Q0) = MSC
- Private provision of public goods is sub-optimal because of the free rider problem

Free Rider Problem-	someone who enjoys the benefits of consuming a good without contributing to the costs	
Private Provision	**Mechanisms for optimal provision of public goods includes:**	**Strong preferences**
		Altruism- someone is altruistic if other people's utility level enters his or her utility function
		"Warm Glow"- utility depends on their own consumption and level of contribution to the public good
Public Provision	**Issues include:**	**Crowd out-** individuals change behavior in response to government provision
		Measuring costs and benefits
		Determining the public preference

Taxation

- Wealth is a stock
- Taxes on consumption are indirect

Tax Efficiency	**Flat Tax-** a tax rate that everyone pays.	
	A lump sum tax is a fixed tax that must be paid by everyone and the amount a person is taxed remains constant regardless of income or owned assets.	
Tax Fairness	**Marginal Tax rate-** additional tax rate on a dollar of income	
	Average tax rate- equal to total tax paid as a fraction of total income	
	Statutory Tax Rate- tax rates specified in tax schedule	
	Effective Tax Rate- tax rates people actually pay	
Tax Equity	**Vertical Equity-** people with more income pay more taxes	**Progressive-** average tax rates increases with income
		Regressive- average effective tax rates decrease with income
		Proportional or Neutral- average effective tax rates are constant
	Horizontal Equity- similar individuals pay similar taxes, regardless of the economic choices that they make	
Income	**Haig Simons Comprehensive income-** taxable resources are equal to the change in an individual's power to consume during the year	Measures ability to pay regardless of savings choices consumption
		Improves vertical and horizontal equity
Externality and Public Goods	Derives from Haig- Simons Comprehensive Income Definition	
Tax Incidence	In economics, **tax incidence** is the analysis of the effect of a particular tax on the distribution of economic welfare. Tax incidence is said to "fall" upon the group that, at the end of the day, bears the burden of the tax. The key concept is that the tax incidence or tax burden does not depend on where the revenue is collected, but on the **price elasticity of demand** and **price elasticity of supply.** For example, a tax on apple farmers might actually be paid by owners of agricultural land or consumers of apples.	

Optimal Taxation

Ramsey Rule 1	Taxation and efficiency In general, deadweight loss (DWL) is approximately = ½ tax per unit x change in Q	
Income Tax	How do we choose tax rates for people with different income levels to raise a fixed amount of revenue when keeping DWL as low as possible?	
	Increase the tax rate	Raise more revenue
		People work less to avoid tax, tax base shrinks
		The Laffer Curve shows that increasing the tax rate will increase revenues for only a limited time
Solution to the optimal income tax problem	**Choose tax rate for each income group such that:**	MU_i= marginal utility of the income group
		MR_i= marginal revenue raised from taxing people in group I
		MU_i/MR_i = lambda • Lambda= marginal benefit of $1 in government hands instead of private hands

Taxation and Deadweight Loss

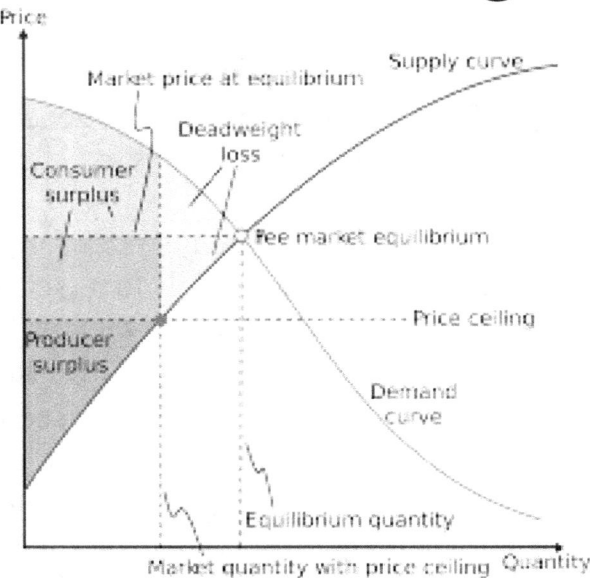

A tax on supply moves the supply curve to the left, thus deceasing supply. A taxation on supply raises the price of the good to the consumer. Regulations have the same effect as a tax, by placing a limit on either price or quantity.		
Consumer Surplus	is the difference between the maximum price a consumer is willing to pay and the actual price they do pay.	
Producer Surplus	is the amount that producers benefit by selling at a market price that is higher than the least that they would be willing to sell for; this is roughly equal to profit (since producers are not normally willing to sell at a loss, and are normally indifferent to selling at a breakeven price).	
Taxation: Revenue	**Total Revenue**	the part of consumer surplus lost to taxation and the part of producer surplus lost to taxation
Deadweight Loss	**Total Deadweight Loss**	the parts of consumer and producer surplus lost

Taxation and Deadweight Loss Continued

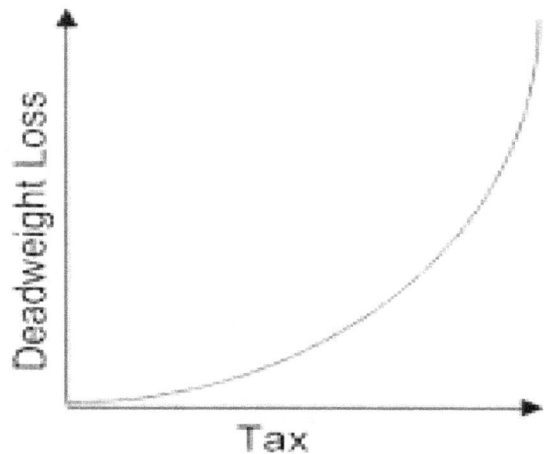

As taxes increase linearly, deadweight loss grows exponentially. Politicians need to be care about raising taxes.

The Laffer Curve

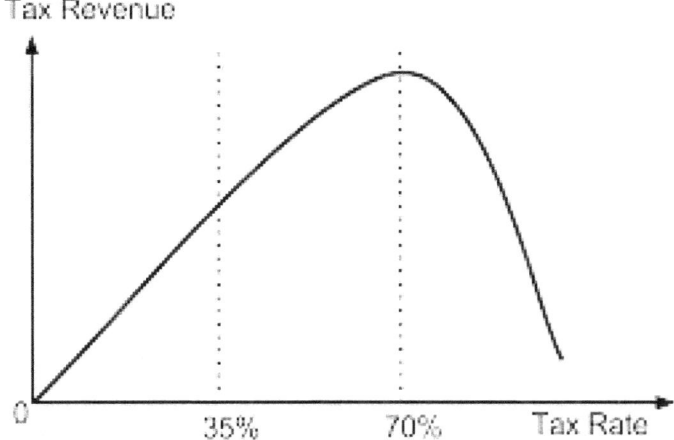

There is an optimal amount of taxation beyond which there is no more gain in revenue

Market Structures

Not all markets work the same. The market structure determines how a given market will work.

Perfect Competition Model	• Everyone is a price taker (responds to price) • Ease of entry and exit into marketplace (there are many firms) • Perfect information (market failure results from asymmetrical information) • Homogeneous goods • No externalities (market failure caused by spillover effect)
Monopolistic Competition	• many firms • Firms produce differentiated goods • Everyone is a price taker • Firms have ease of entry and exit • No spillover effects • Perfect information
Oligopoly	• Only a few firms • Everyone is a price taker • Danger of collusion or cartels
Monopoly	• Only one firm • Firms have barriers to entry • The government gives a single firm the exclusive right to produce some good or service • Firm is a price maker • A single firm can produce output at a lower cost than can a larger number of firms
Monopsony	• dictate terms to its suppliers, as the only purchaser of a good or service • a market with a single buyer • Examples include the military industry and the space industry

Monopolistic Competition

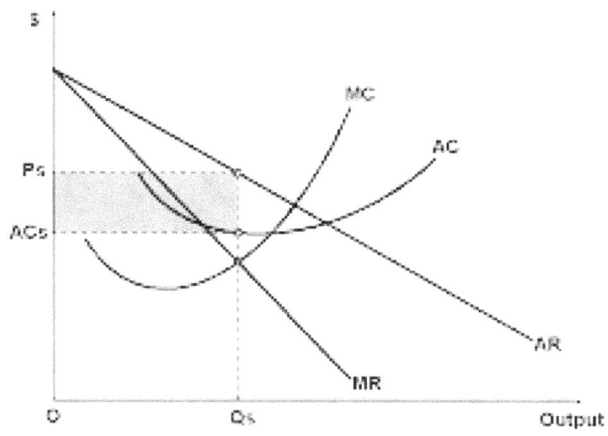

Monopolistic Competition is an Imperfect Competition Model	
In a monopolistically competitive market, firms can behave like monopolies in the short run, including by using market power to generate profit. In the long run, however, other firms enter the market and the benefits of differentiation decrease with competition; the market becomes more like a perfectly competitive one where firms cannot gain economic profit.	
Profit is maximized when Marginal Cost = Marginal Revenue	
Legend	**Ps**= the monopoly price **ACs**= the perfect competition price **Qs**= the perfect competition quantity **MC**= marginal cost **AC**= average cost **AR**= average revenue **MR**= marginal revenue
Description	• many firms • Firms produce differentiated goods • Everyone is a price taker • Firms have ease of entry and exit • No spillover effects • Perfect information

Oligopoly

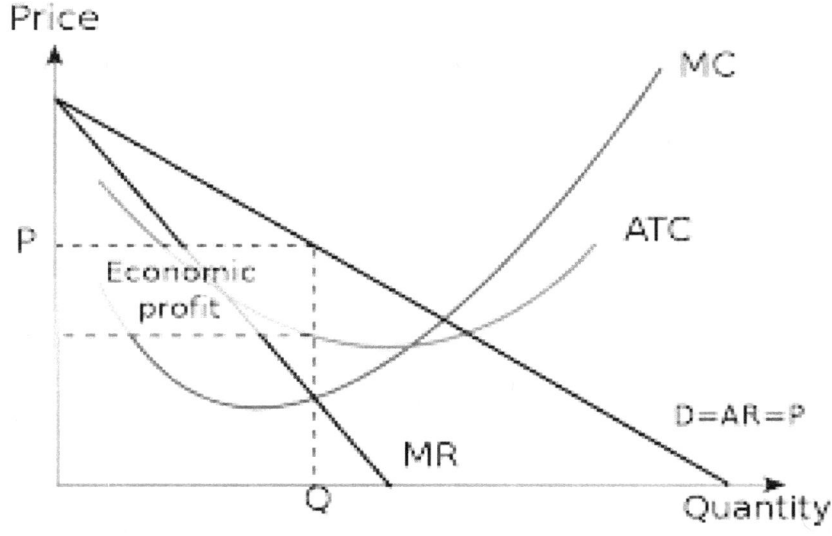

Oligopoly is an imperfect competition model		
This market only has a few firms and maximizes profit		
Types	**Stackelberg Duopoly-** the firms move sequentially in this model	
	Cournot Duopoly- The firms move simultaneously in this model.	
	Bertrand Oligopoly- The firms simultaneously choose prices in this model	
Legend	**P**= the monopoly price **Q**= the monopoly quantity **MC**= marginal cost **AC**= average cost **ATC**= average total cost **AR**= average revenue **MR**= marginal revenue	
Description	• Only a few firms • Barriers to entry are high • The firms are a price makers • Buyers have imperfect knowledge • Danger of collusion or cartels	

Monopoly

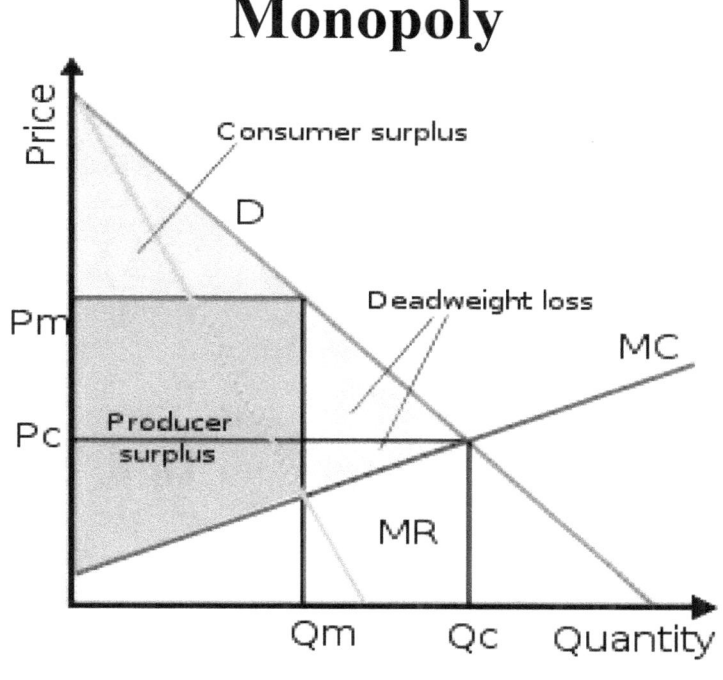

Monopoly is an imperfect competition model	
A single firm can produce output at a lower cost than can a larger number of firms. The monopoly price is always the highest price. It comes with considerable deadweight loss.	
The monopoly profit is maximized when **Marginal Revenue= Marginal Cost**	
Legend	**Supply**= Marginal Cost **Pm**= the monopoly price **Pc**= the perfect competition price **Qm**= the monopoly quantity **Qc**= the perfect competition quantity
Description	• Only one firm • Firms have barriers to entry • The government gives a single firm the exclusive right to produce some good or service • Firm is a price maker

Monopsony

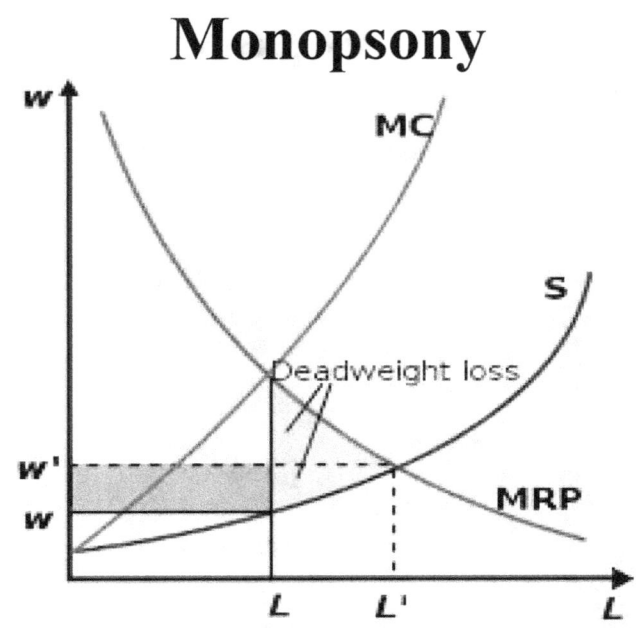

Monopsony is an imperfect competition model	
Monopsony- a market structure in which only one buyer interacts with many would-be sellers of a particular product.	
A monopsonist employer maximizes profits by choosing the employment level L, that equates the marginal revenue product (MRP) to the marginal cost MC	
Legend	**W= wage** **L= labor** **MC**= Marginal Cost **S**= supply **MRP**= Marginal revenue Product
Description	• dictate terms to its suppliers, as the only purchaser of a good or service • a market where a single buyer Examples include the military industry and the space industry

Organizational Economics

Transaction Costs	Ronald Coase was seeking to improve the efficiency of any transaction. Transaction costs are a measure of the inefficiency of any interaction between parties. If transaction costs are reduced, by either changing the organization or by changing the institutions then a better state of affairs is obtained.
Types of Transaction Costs	**Search and information costs**- the costs associated with gaining the right market information
	Bargaining costs- the costs of coming to an agreement
	Policing and enforcement costs- makes sure the other party fulfills his commitment
Transaction Cost Economics	According to Oliver Williamson, "In addition to being an interdisciplinary alliance of law, economics, and organization, I would describe transaction costs economics as (1) relentlessly comparative (organization forms are always examined in relation to alternative feasible forms), (2) microanalytic (the action resides in the details), (3) discrete structural (alternative forms of governance differ in kind, and so it is impossible to replicate markets by hierarchies or the reverse), and (4) preoccupied with economizing, principally with reference to organization rather than technology. Moreover, rather than being preoccupied with the imperative "This is the law here," the enterprise is inspired mainly by the question: "What's going on here?"
Main Propositions According to Oliver Williamson	The transaction is the basic unit of analysis
	Any problem that can be posed directly or indirectly as a contracting problem is usefully investigated in transaction cots economizing terms.
	Transaction cost economies are realized by assigning transactions to governance structures in a discriminating way.
	Although marginal analysis is sometimes employed, implementing transaction cost economics mainly involves a comparative institutional assessment of discrete alternatives—of which classical market contracting is located at one extreme, centralized, hierarchical organization is located at the other; and mixed modes of firm and market organization are located in between.
	Any attempt to deal seriously with the study of economic organization must come to terms with the combined ramifications of bounded rationality and opportunism in conjunction with a condition of asset specificity.
Major Areas of Study	**Organizational Structure** can increase or decrease costs
	Leadership- style can increase or decrease costs
	Corporate Culture- affects costs by changing preferences
	Personnel- human capital can make major cost differences

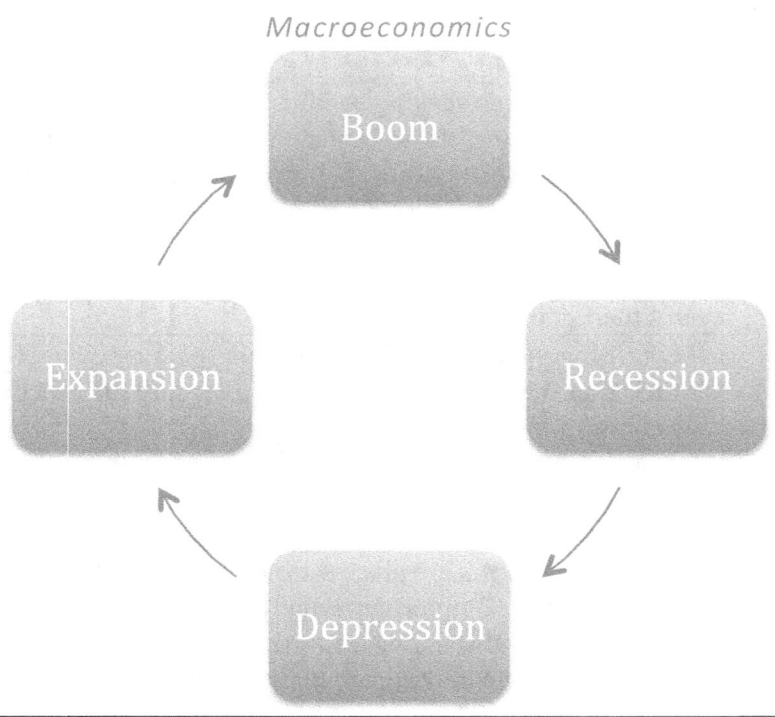

The Economic Cycle

The economy follows a four part economic cycle. Keynesians believe that this cycle can be controlled by fiscal and monetary policy. Free market economists like the University of Chicago or the Austrian School believe that the market should be set free from government intervention.

Indicators of Macro-economic Health	GDP	**Gross Domestic Product** is the market value of all goods and services produced within a country within a given time period.
	Growth	Measured in GDP
	Unemployment	The percentage of the labor force that is unemployed.
	Inflation	An increase in the overall level of prices in the economy.
Boom		The expansion and peak phase of the economic cycle. It is a period. It is sometimes accompanied with a rise in inflation.
Recession		A period of declining GDP and rising unemployment
Depression		Is a period of economic decline that lasts over 12 consecutive quarters
Expansion		A period of increasing GDP and declining unemployment

Macroeconomics

<ul><li>Macroeconomics is concerned with:</li><li>1. Long Range economic growth, measured in **Gross Domestic Product (GDP)**</li><li>2. Short run economic fluctuations in growth, inflation, and unemployment</li><li>3. Business cycles (boom, recession, depression, recovery)</li></ul>	
<ul><li>Macroeconomics can be viewed from three different lenses:</li><li>The **Short Run** is a one and a half to two year focus.</li><li>The **Medium Run** is concerned with a 2-10 year focus on the economy.</li><li>The **Long Run** is concerned with the economy over a generation.</li><li>**The Fresh Water School** is only concerned with the **Medium** and the **Long Run**</li></ul>	

Fluctuations	<ul><li>Macroeconomics is also concerned with short run fluctuations (business cycles).</li><li>What causes fluctuations and how to control them</li><li>There are fluctuations around the trend line</li><li>The trend line represents equilibrium or potential GDP when it has full employment</li><li>Investing is the driving force of fluctuation</li></ul> The **National Bureau of Economic Research** determines the date of U.S. business cycles
	<ul><li>**GDP** is measured quarterly</li><li>**Recession-** two consecutive terms (six months) of low economic growth</li><li>**Depression-** four terms (year) of low economic growth</li><li>**Great Depression-** 12 terms (three years) of low economic growth</li></ul>
Classical Economics	<ul><li>- Adam Smith, David Ricardo, John Stuart Mill, J.B. Say and the others . Assumes that the economy works the same at either the micro or macro level.</li></ul>
Macro economics-	<ul><li>John Maynard Keynes began this approach to economics during the **Great Depression**</li></ul>
Neo-Classical Synthesis	<ul><li>- the combination of microeconomics and macroeconomics</li></ul>
New Neo-Classical Synthesis	<ul><li>Combines aspects of each theory</li><li>From **New Classical Macroeconomics-** dynamic models (DSGE)</li><li>From **New Keynesian Macroeconomics-** wage and price rigidities</li><li>Quantitative models</li></ul>

Classical Macroeconomics

The classical economists assumed The Perfect Competition Model for all markets. This includes:

- Many firms
- Perfect Knowledge (no asymmetrical information)
- No spillovers (externalities)
- Everyone is a price taker
- Ease of entry and exit into market
- Homogenous products

Adam Smith	• was a moral philosopher who wrote ***An Inquiry into the Wealth of Nations*** • Assumes that people and markets are rational • Assumes perfect competition model • Government's only job is to ensure a level playing field
David Ricardo	• was a British business man and economist. He wrote ***Principles of Political Economy.*** • Ricardo taught the **Theory of Comparative Advantage**-Even if a country could produce everything more efficiently than another country, it would reap gains from specializing in what it was best at producing and trading with other nations. • Ricardo believed that wages should be left to free competition, so there should be no restrictions on the importation of agricultural products from abroad.

Jean Baptist Say	• a French economist known for free trade and reducing restraint on business
	• **Say's Law-**
	   • "Supply creates its own demand",
	   • "Supply constitutes its own demand",
	   • "If you build it, they will come",
	   • "Inherent in supply is the wherewithal for its own consumption"

John Stuart Mill	• ***Principles of Political Economy***, first published in 1848, was one of the most widely read of all books on economics in the period. • Mill's *Principles* dominated economics teaching. In the case of Oxford University it was the standard text until 1919 • Mill was for free trade. He also believed that a progressive income tax amounted to theft.

The Classical Business Dichotomy

The classical economists subscribed to the **Classical Business Dichotomy** and as a result, they held to the neutrality of money.

The **Classical Business Dichotomy** suggests that an increase in the money supply will affect **nominal**, but not **real** variables.

The **Classical Business Dichotomy** argues that changes in nominal variables have no impact upon real variables.

All Keynesians reject the **Classical Business Dichotomy**.

Real Variables	Nominal Variables
Y= Income, measured in GDP	Nominal wage- wage,
E= employment	not adjusted for inflation
I= interest	Nominal Interest- interest not adjusted for inflation

Major Macroeconomic Events/Periods

Great Depression	1930s- 1945 In this period, there was a labor surplus (25% unemployment) solved by increasing demand (supposedly) via government spending. Most economists today believed the issue was resolved by WWII.
Great Inflation	1970s-1981. This period was characterized by high inflation. It was resolved by Ronald Reagan and Paul Volker increasing the supply side. Increasing demand via fiscal policy could not solve the problem. Rational expectations replaced Keynesian macroeconomics.
Great Moderation	From the 1990s until 2008. The **New Neo Classical Synthesis** resulted from New Keynesian and some New Classical Macroeconomics approaches being combined by some economists
Great Recession	Current Crisis in 2008- present

Keynesian Economics

John Maynard Keynes was a student of Alfred Marshall. Operating with the belief that the laissez faire conditions that characterized the 19th century were dead, he created the field of macroeconomics and advocated a strong interventionist approach to the economy. As a professor of Cambridge University, he wrote, what many economist considered a work of genius, *The General Theory of Employment, Interest, and Money*. Keynes believed that the classical economic theory (Adam Smith) which served as the basis during the 19th century was a special case which fit within his larger, general theory of economics. As a tireless enemy of communism, Keynes desired the creation of more wealth.

Government	Keynes believed that the economy was like a machine that can be controlled by the government. Consequently the four part economic cycle can be stopped if the government takes the right approach. Keynes's system is compatible with socialism and with dependency theory (protectionism). It advocates government intervention to stimulate the level of demand. It also asserts that a small amount of inflation is acceptable to maintain full employment
Monetary Policy	The government can stimulate the economy by increasing or decreasing spending and by raising or lowering taxes when the economy slows down.
The Market	Keynes viewed the market as dangerous. As such, it should not run free. Instead, the government needs to intervene in the market to ensure stability.
John Kenneth Galbraith	The popularizer of Keynes views in the United States. As a professor of Harvard University he wrote three books that challenged the ideas of the neo-classicalist economists. These books include: *The affluent Society, The New industrial State,* and *Economics and the Public Purpose.* He also led Harvard University to become the main proponent of Keynes's ideas in the US.

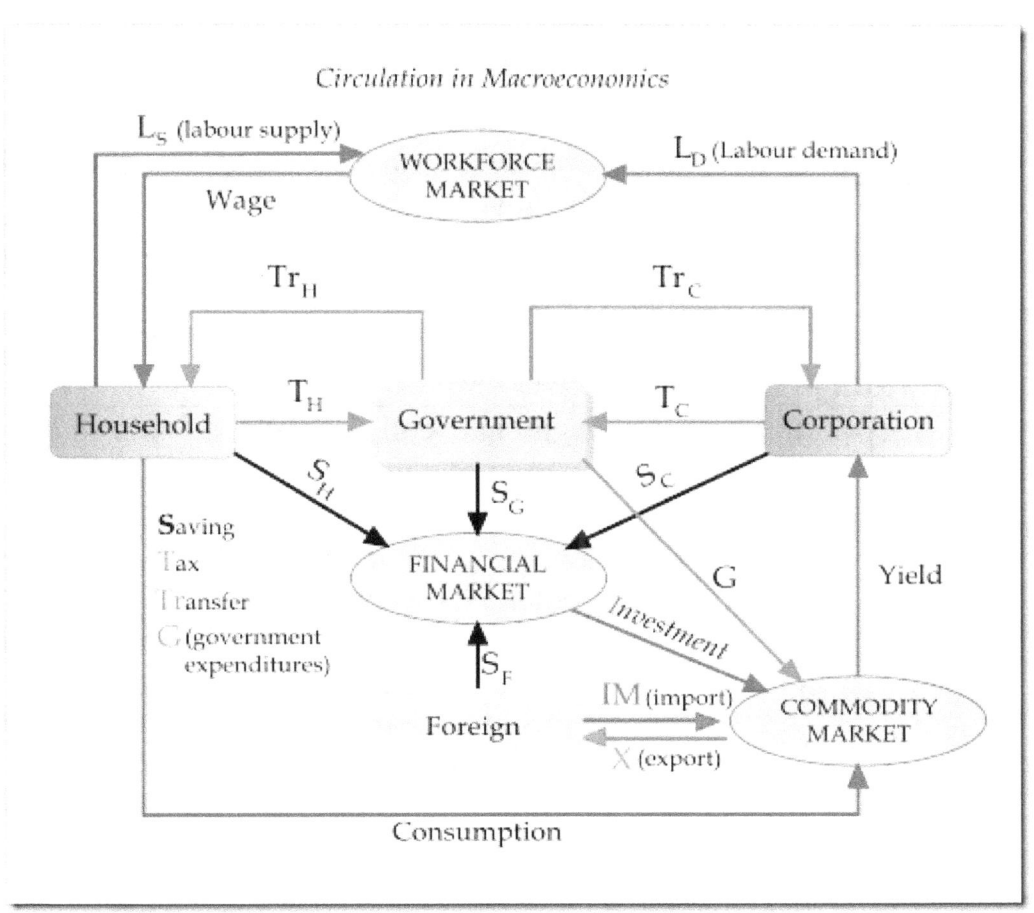

Macroeconomic Circular Flow of Money

Four Actors	**Households**	Are utility maximizing
	Firms	Are profit maximizing
	Government	Receives taxes to provide public goods
	Foreign Investment	Provide investment from outside of the country
Three Markets	**Labor Market**	Comes from households and receives wages
	Financial Market	Investment comes from households and provides profits
	Commodity Market	Goods and services produced by firms

Keynesian Macroeconomics

John Maynard Keynes wrote *The General Theory of Employment, Interest and Money*

The Nature of the Market	• He argued that markets are irrational and sometimes provide undesirable results. So the government must intervene
Labor Markets	• Because of wage stickiness, he thought that labor markets are different.
Classical Business Dichotomy	• Keynes rejected the Classical Business Dichotomy
Consumption	• Aggregate consumption depends on the amount of aggregate income.
Say's law	• Keynes rejected Say's Law and emphasized that the government should drive aggregate demand by fiscal policy

Monopolistic Competition	• Because of the labor surplus of the Great Depression, he assumed a **monopolistic competition model**
	• Keynes assumed that the **Monopolistic Competition** model best described a macro-economy. This includes:
	  • Many firms
	  • Ease of entry and exit
	  • Product differentiation
	  • Firms are price makers (setters)

Circular Flow of Income	• **Y=C+I+G+(X-M)**
	  • **Y**= **income**, measured in **GDP**
	  • **C**= **consumption**- spending by households
	  • **I**= **investment**- accumulated investment
	  • **G**= **government spending**
	  • **X**= **exports**
	  • **M**= **imports**
	• **Y=C+S+T**
	  • **C**= **consumption**
	  • **S**= **savings**
	  • **T**= **taxes**

IS/ LM Curves

(The Short Run Model)

Policy	**Fiscal policy** involves changes in government spending and the level of taxation. Fiscal policy moves the **IS (Investment Savings)** curve on the IS/LM charts The flatter the LM curve is, the more effective that fiscal policy is. **Ricardian Equivalence**- Because of regime changes, a tax cut today means a tax raise tomorrow If you have a balanced budget, then budget deficits do not matter because deficits are offset by savings	When the central bank (aka "the fed") performs **monetary policy** by increasing or decreasing the amount of money in the market. It results in the movement of the **LM (liquidity Money)** curve in the IS/LM model. The flatter the IS curve is the more effective monetary policy will be

	Crowding out- Results from government spending too much and not leaving any room for investment.
	
	I= S + (T-G), or when increased government spending results in both investment and savings being minimized
	
	Fiscal Policy makes sense until crowding out occurs
		The Federal Reserve achieves its goals by
		  1. **Open market purchases and sales**
		  2. **Reserve Rate**- how much banks must keep on hand
		Federal Interest Rate- the rate that banks can loan to each other. Also known as the discount rate. Banks can also borrow from the Federal Reserve

Curves	**IS (investment/ savings)**- Goods and Services **Fiscal policy** involves moving the IS curve. **Fiscal policy** results from changing government spending or the level of taxation	**LM** (liquidity/ money)- Financial markets **Monetary policy** results from changing the interest rate that the Federal reserve charges banks
Schools	**The Salt Water school**- employs the use of the IS/LM model	**The Fresh Water School**- rejects the IS/ LM model because it is short run. They believe that both fiscal and monetary policy should be avoided because we do not know the long term effects of short run government intervention.

IS/LM Model
AKA Fleming- Mundell Model

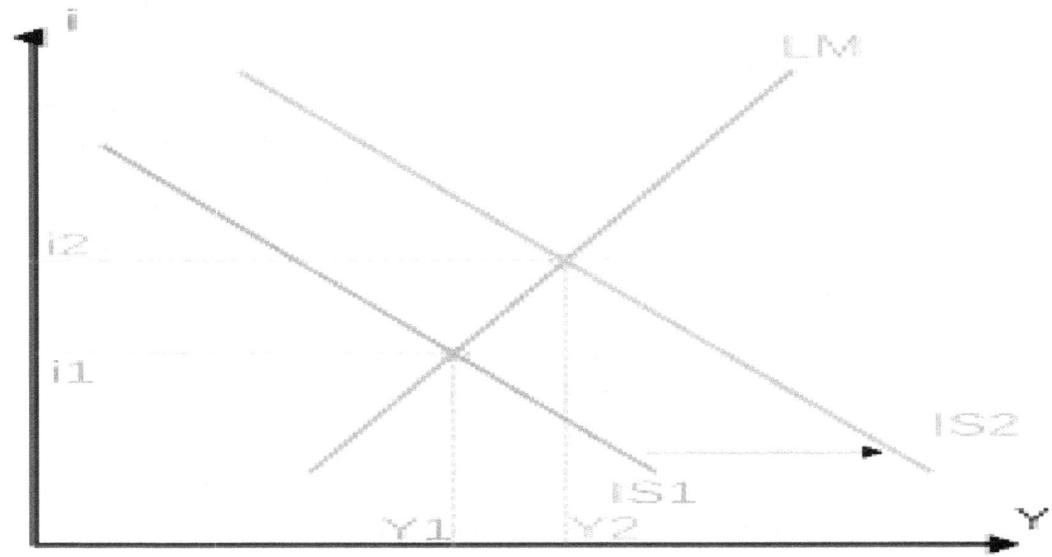

The Fleming Mundell Model explains the economy in the short run (2 years or less).	
Fiscal Policy	The legislative and executive branches of government determine the amount of taxation and spendiing
	The flatter the IS curve the more effective monetary policy is.
Monetary Policy	The Federal Reserve Bank raises or lowers the interest rate by printing money or refusing to do so.
	The Flatter the LM curve is the more effective fiscal policy is.

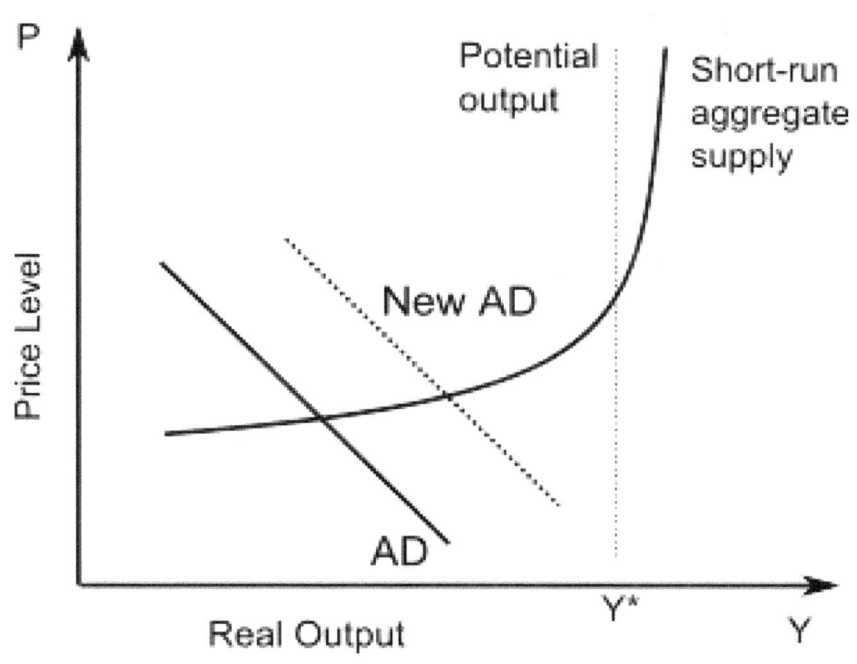

AD/ AS Model		
As a medium range model, the AD/ AS looks 10 as far as 10 years down the road.		
	Aggregate Demand	**Aggregate Supply**
	The aggregate demand curve has a negative slope.	**Long run aggregate supply (LRAS)** is vertical because a change in the price level does not affect the quantity supplied in the long run.
	Reasons that a lower price will increase aggregate demand: 1. **increases purchasing power of money** 2. **a lower price reduces the demandfor money** 3. **domestic goods will be less expensive relative to foreign goods**	**Short run aggregate supply (SRAS)** is has a positive slope because in the short run firms will expand output as the price level rises.
Markets	Goods and Services- **IS** (investment/ savings)	**Factors Market** • Capital • labor
	Financial markets- **LM** (liquidity/ money)	

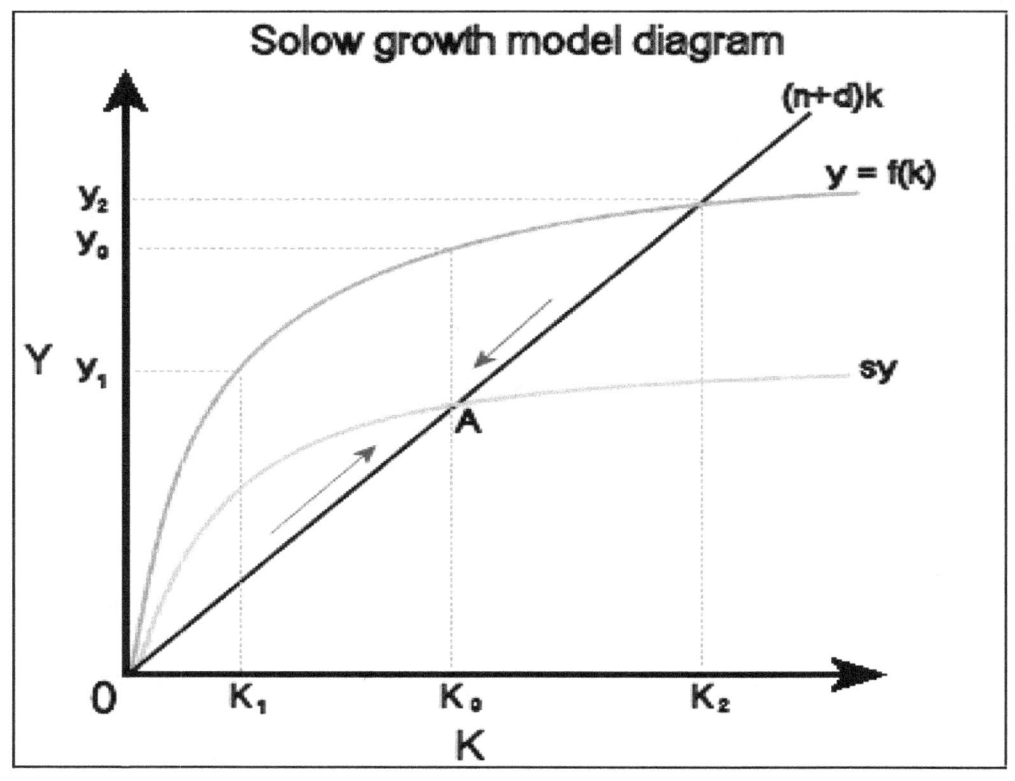

Solow growth model diagram

Long Run Growth Model

Salt Water	Fresh Water
Solow Exogenous Growth	**Endogenous Growth**
The **neoclassical growth model**, also known as the **Solow–Swan growth model** or **exogenous growth model**, is a class of economic models of long-run economic growth set within the framework of neoclassical economics. Neoclassical growth models attempt to explain long run economic growth by looking at productivity, capital accumulation, population growth, and technological progress.	**Endogenous growth theory** holds that economic growth is primarily the result of endogenous and not external forces. Endogenous growth theory holds that investment in human capital, innovation, and knowledge are significant contributors to economic growth. The theory also focuses on positive externalities and spillover effects of a knowledge-based economy which will lead to economic development. The endogenous growth theory also holds that policy measures can have an impact on the long-run growth rate of an economy. For example, subsidies for research and development or education increase the growth rate in some endogenous growth models by increasing the incentive for innovation.

The Phillips Curve

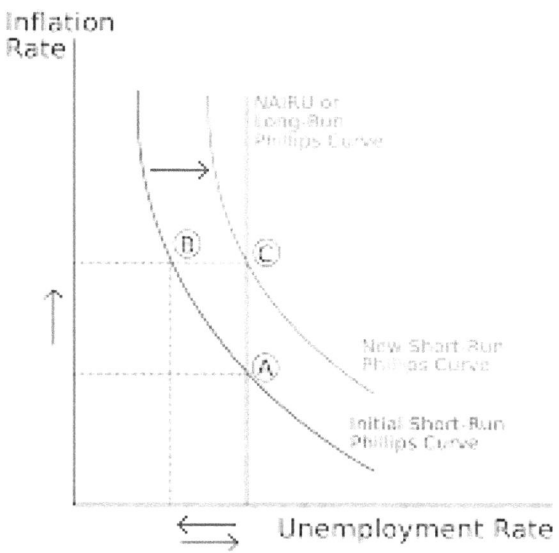

Named after A. William Phillips, the Phillips Curve relates inflation to unemployment. It is no longer used today because it is seen as being too simplistic. Some modified forms of it are still in use	
Keynesians	They believed that government through fiscal policy could make trade offs between these factors.
Short Run	This relationship between inflation and unemployment is true only in the short run
Long Run	Milton Friedman was the first to argue that in the long run, the Phillips Curve does not hold
NAIRU	Non- Accelerating Inflation Rate of Unemployment- also known as the natural rate of unemployment.

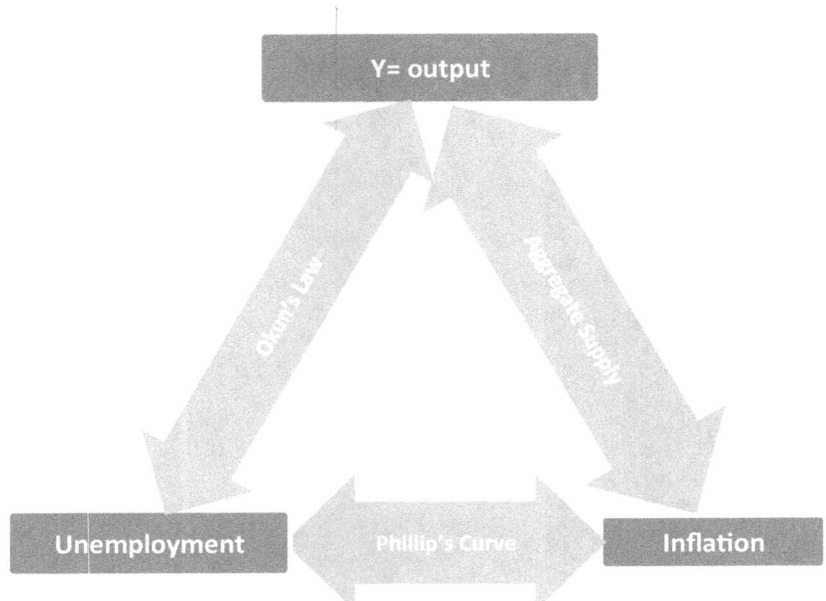

Macroeconomic Principles

Principle	Explanation
Phillip's Curve	<ul><li>Relates inflation to unemployment</li><li>Keynesians believe that **inflation** can be reduced at the cost of increased **unemployment** (and vice versa)</li><li>The Phillips curve is useful in the short run, but is not stable over time</li></ul>
	<ul><li>Over the last thirty years, the curve has flattened out.</li><li>This is partially due to the weakening of trade unions</li><li>This is also due to globalization.</li></ul>As a result, Keynesians cannot easily make adjustments
Okun's Law	<ul><li>Relates unemployment to output</li><li>Keynesians believe that the government should attempt to make trade offs between these two factors</li><li>**Sacrifice ratio-** the amount of output lost when inflation is reduced one percentage point</li></ul>
Aggregate Supply Relation	<ul><li>Relates output to price and inflation</li><li>Wage setting is related to labor supply</li><li>Price setting is related to labor demand</li><li>Labor accounts for lions share of production and consumption</li><li>Policy makers affect Aggregate Demand via fiscal or monetary policy</li></ul>

Two Schools of Macroeconomic Thought

Salt Water Macroeconomics	Fresh Water Macroeconomics
Keynesian approaches. Most of these schools are located along the coasts. They are for activist government intervention in the market place, because people and markets are irrational.	**Non Keynesian approaches**. Most of these schools are located near the great lakes. They reject government intervention in the marketplace because they believe that people and markets are rational.
Classical Keynesians- these held to Keynes original ideas	**Monetarists-** Friedman, Brunner, Meltzer and Laidler argued that monetary policy should be employed rather than fiscal policy. Fiscal stimulus results in permanent inflation and only a temporary rise in employment Assumes the neutrality of money (money matters in the short run, but not in the long run) This movement dies in the 1970s because they did not develop new intricate model
Neo- Keynesians- Tobin, Hicks, Modigliani, Solow and Samuelson argued that macroeconomics needed microeconomic foundations. Known as the **Neo- Classical Synthesis** it includes Keynesian theory for the short run and Walrasian theory for the long run Hicks provided the IS/LM model for short run analysis	**New Classical Macroeconomics-** Lucas, Barro and Sargeant argued that macroeconomics should be based on classical microeconomic theory. Employed dynamic optimization models (**Inter temporal General Equilibrium).** Assumes perfect competition Assumes that markets clear instantaneously Assumes super-neutrality of money (monetary policy matters only if it is unexpected)
New Keynesians- Taylor, Phelps, Fischer, Blanchard, and Mankiw considered the criticisms of the **New Classical Macroeconomics**. • Developed Dynamic Stochastic General Equilibrium (**DSGE**) • Assumes wage and price stickiness. • Assumes monopolistic competition • Employs both fiscal and monetary policy	**Real Business Cycles- (a separate movement within NCM)** Kydland, Prescott and Plosser argued that business cycles are not the result of market failure, but the result of efficient response to production shocks. • Real disturbances are the cause of economic instability • Quantitative models that are forward looking • Actual output is always the same as potential output • Monetary policy does not matter at all

New Classical Macroeconomics	
Principles	**Explanation**
The Lucas Critique	• Lucas argued that people are rational and forward looking (**Real Expectations**) • Econometric methods are backward looking and do not help in predicting the impact of economic policy changes • Game Theory should be employed
Efficient Market Hypothesis (Eugene Fama)	• All prices in financial markets are correct and reflect market fundamentals • The market is efficient if security prices fully reflect all relevant information that is available about the value of securities • Prices of financial instruments follow random walk The results in the market being hard to beat
Policy Ineffectiveness Principle	• -governments should not interfere with the economy because people will rationally expect changes and take it into account. • Governments do not know exactly where they are because it takes so long to get economic data • Governments may make a situation worse by acting • Policies may not have the desired effect
The Permanent Income Hypothesis (PIH)	• is a theory of consumption that was developed by the American economist Milton Friedman. • The key conclusion of this theory is that transitory, short-term changes in income have little effect on consumer spending behavior.

Different Schools of Macroeconomics

Schools	Sub-group	Market Structure	Fiscal Policy	Monetary Policy
Salt Water Schools	Keynesians	Monopolistic Competition	Provides short run solution to labor surplus	Monetary policy does not matter
	Neo-Keynesians	Monopolistic Competition	Provides short run solution to labor surplus	Monetary policy does not matter
	New Keynesians	Monopolistic Competition	Provides short run solution to labor surplus	Monetary policy matters in the short run and should be used.
Fresh Water Schools	Monetarists	Perfect Competition	It only matters in the short run and it causes permanent inflation.	**Neutrality of money-** monetary policy does not matter in the long run. Should not be overused
	New Classical Macro-economists	Perfect Competition	Causes permanent inflation and it should be avoided	**Super Neutrality of Money-** monetary policy does not matter in the long or short run. Should be avoided.
	Real Business Cycles	Perfect Competition	Causes permanent inflation and it should be avoided	Monetary policy is totally ineffective. Should not be used at all.

Consumption

	People	Group	Definition
Keynesian Consumption Model	John Maynard Keynes	Keynesians	**Average Propensity to Consume (APC)** falls as income rises. Saving is luxury
Life Cycle Hypothesis	Franco Modigliani	Neo-Keynesian	Assumes consumption on lifetime income. Savings allow consumers to move income from those times when income is high to those times when it is low
Inter-Temporal Choice Hypothesis	Irving Fischer	New Keynesian	Budget constraints and preferences together determine choices about consumption **(C)** and savings **(S)**
Permanent Income Hypothesis	Milton Friedman	Monetarist and New Classical Macroeconomics	short-term changes in income have little effect on consumer spending behavior.

Macroeconomic Equilibrium

Term	Explanation
General Equilibrium	**General Equilibrium** includes all three markets
	Aggregate Demand Goods and Services markets- **IS** (investment/ savings) Financial markets- **LM** (liquidity/ money)
	Aggregate Supply- Factors Market
	Aggregate Demand and Aggregate supply are used to find **DSGE**
Inter- Temporal General Equilibrium	**Households** choose consumption and labor on the basis of wages, prices, utility, and wealth over their whole lifetimes, instead of considering these quantities at just one point in time.
	Firms choose hiring, investment, and output on the basis of productivity and demand over the foreseeable future, instead of considering these quantities at just one point in time.
Dynamic Stochastic General Equilibrium	**Dynamic-** changing **Stochastic-** over time (inter- temporal) **General Equilibrium-** equilibrium between the financial, goods and factor markets.

	New Keynesian DSGE models build on a structure similar to RBC models, but instead assume that prices are set by monopolistically competitive firms, and cannot be instantaneously and costlessly adjusted.	**Real Business Cycles** (RBC) theory builds on the neoclassical growth model, under the assumption of flexible prices, to study how real shocks to the economy might cause business cycle fluctuations.
	Saltwater **DSGE** models are backward looking (**Adaptive Expectations**)	Freshwater **DSGE** models are forward looking (**Real Expectations**)
	None of these models predicted the crisis in 2007/8. Consequently, the efficacy of these models is in question.	

Chapter 3: Politics

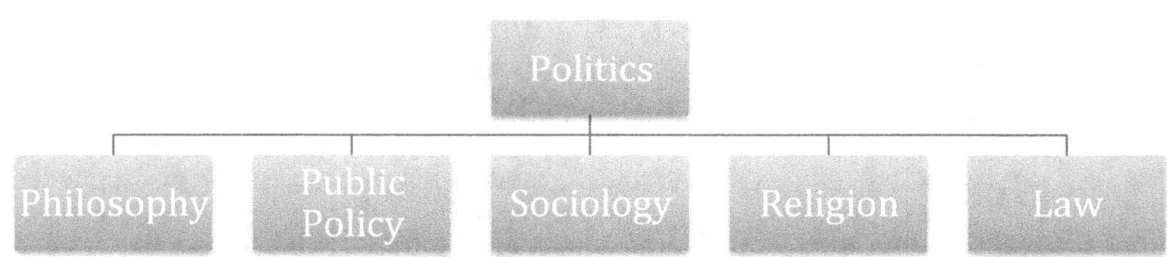

Political Philosophy		
Morality and the state	**Welfarism**	The state has the function of looking after the welfare of its people
	Perfectionism	The promotion of human excellence is a primary factor in the evaluation of the political and social worth of a society. This assumes that there is a distinctive human nature.
	Positivism	Political philosophy has nothing to do with morality
Types of Government (According to Aristotle)	**Benevolent monarchy**	According to Aristotle, this is the best kind of government
	Aristocracy	This is the rule of the best.
	Polity	The rule of citizens
	Democracy	The rule of the many
	Oligarchy	The rule of the few
	Tyranny	The worst kind of government
Political Spectrum	**Liberal**	**Classical liberal** emphasize personal freedom and individual rights. These rights include the right to life, liberty and property. They desire to limit the power of the state.
		Modern liberal emphasize the freedoms of the French revolution, specifically; liberty, equality and fraternity. This position rejects social morality
		Radical desire dramatic and immediate change
	Moderate	Believe that the best position is one that avoids extremes
	Conservative	**Libertarian** is fiscally conservative but desires no interference from the government.
		Communitarian emphasizes the individual's duties to society
		Reactionary believes that things have changed too much and desires to change things back

Plato's Ranking of Government		
1	**Monarchy**	Rule of the one. This ruler is concerned with the good of the people
2	**Aristocracy**	Rule of the best, only a few
3	**Democracy**	Rule of the many. All of the people vote
4	**Tyranny**	Rule of the one. This ruler is selfish and self-centered.

Plato's Republic		
Level of Government	**Function**	**Explanation**
Philosopher Kings	**Ruling Class**	These come from the best of the guardians. They are sent to study philosophy for a number of years before they can begin to rule. After studying they know the world of the forms. Consequently, they understand the nature of the good and the nature of justice. They will know what should be done for the city and why.
Guardians	**Soldier/ Policeman**	These are the strongest and most intelligent of the people. They are both men and women. They have the job of executing justice as dictated by the philosopher kings and defending the city-state
People	**Artisan, Farmers, Workers**	These are involved in producing for the needs of the city state.

Aristotle's Assumptions

Subject	Explanation
God	**Prime Mover-** His actuality is the final cause. He is the ultimate first cause. The end which all things desire and to which they are ordered.
Teleology	*Telos-* the final cause. Beings fulfill their nature and are oriented towards the supreme good when they pursue their *Telos.*
Nature	*Phusis-* Nature is both ethical and political because it is structured by a hierarchy of goods and virtues.
Unity	**Unity** is essential, not accidental, because essence is one, not many. The supreme goal of all beings is unitary because it is to attain **autarky.**
Autarky	Self- sufficiency. The activity that secures autarky is **unity,** the contemplative understanding of the divine. This is the highest intellectual virtue.

Aristotle on Action

Subject	Discipline	Books by Aristotle
Cosmos- The ultimate order of things	**Theology**-God is the ultimate end to which everything is ordered	*The Metaphysics* Book lambda
City-State The *cosmos* frames the operation of the *Polis*	**Politics (*Politike*)**- the study of the city-state	*The Politics*
Household- The *Oikos* is a part of the *Polis*	Economics (*oikonomike*) the art of household management	*The Politics* *The Economics*
Individual Man- Oriented towards marriage, the *Oikos* and the *Polis*	Ethics (*ethika*) is the science of character	*The Nicomachean Ethics* *The Eudomean Ethics* *The Magna Moralia*

Aristotle's Levels of Society

Community	Explanation
City-State	*Polis* is the most complete or perfect type of natural community. This type of community achieves autarky and exists for the sake of the good life..
Village	*Kome* is a natural association of households existing for the fulfillment of economic needs and for protection against animals and hostile people.
Household	*Oikos* is the most basic of the natural social units.

Aristotle's Rankings of Government

The bottom half of government types is the corruption of the first half of government types. This ranking is based on the idea that the best government is most capable of doing the common good, which is justice.

	Rule of the One	Rule of the Few	Rule of the Many
Best	**(1)** **Benevolent Monarchy**		
Better		**(2)** **Aristocracy** Rule of the best	
Good			**(3)** **Polity or Timocracy** Vote of the land owners. A combination of the polity and the oligarchy.
Bad			**(4)** **Democracy** Vote of all people
Worse		**(5)** **Oligarchy**	
Worst	**(6)** **Tyranny**		

Aristotle on Virtue

Aristotle believed that every person needs the moral and intellectual virtues. Only statesmen needed the political virtues.

Type of Virtue	Specific Virtue	Explanation
Political	**Justice**	To give what one deserves
	Magnaminity	The magnanimous man needs no one. He is autonomous, self-sufficient and confident. He will help others but does not need help.
Moral	**Justice**	To give each one as he deserves
	Wisdom (*phronesis*)	This is both a moral and an intellectual virtue. This is practical judgment/ reason
	Courage	The ability to do what one should in spite of danger
	Temperance	Self control
Intellectual	**Wisdom** (**Sophia**)	Philosophical reason
	Wisdom (*phronesis*)	This is both a moral and an intellectual virtue. This is practical judgment/ reason.
	Reason (*nous*)	Rational intuition
	Science (*Episteme*)	Knowledge of the forms
	Craft (*Techne*)	Art, skill

Aristotle's Politics

Group	Requirements	Explanation
Politicians/ statesmen	**Virtues**	• The most virtuous have the strongest claim to rule • Because of the different types of regimes, one can be a good politician without being a good man • **Prudence-** practical wisdom • **Justice-** giving others their due • **Magnanimity-** great souled one, he does great things because he should. The magnanimous man needs no one, but helps others.
	Knowledge	• **Constitutions-** — For the city — For the tribe • **Economics-** — Sources of revenue — expenditures — Sources of food
	Skills	• Rhetoric is a skill that must be learned by effective leaders • The purpose of rhetoric is to persuade the citizens • Rhetoric should be used to get people to act virtuously
	Primary Concern	• The legislator must make education of the young his object above all else • Common education shapes citizens to enable him to serve the common good of the city • Education includes physical education, reading, writing, and the arts

Aristotle's Politics Continued

Citizens	The Ideal	<ul><li>If a regime is to endure, it must educate all citizens in such a way that they support the kind of regime that it is and the principles that legitimate it</li></ul><ul><li>The ideal citizen follows the laws and supports the principle of the regime</li></ul><ul><li>Depending on the type of regime, one can be a good citizen without being a good man</li></ul>
	Paterfamilias	<ul><li>The male head of the household</li><li>He is the head magistrate in the home</li><li>He is the high priest in the home</li><li>He has the ability to reason</li><li>He has the right to vote</li></ul>
	Middle Class	<ul><li>A middle class is more virtuous than the others</li></ul><ul><li>Free from the arrogance of the rich</li><li>Free from the envy of the poor</li><li>Ready to obey reason</li></ul><ul><li>"A political community that has extremes of wealth and poverty is not a city of free persons, but one of slaves and masters, the ones consumed by envy, the others by contempt"</li></ul>

Aristotle's Rhetoric

- Rhetoric is "the faculty of observing in any given case the available means of persuasion.
- Rhetoric is the counterpart of dialectic.
- While dialectical methods are necessary to find truth in theoretical matters, rhetorical methods are required in practical matters such as adjudicating somebody's guilt or innocence, or adjudicating a prudent course of action to be taken in a deliberative assembly

The Art of Rhetoric: Outline	
Book I: **Logic**	**Sections on logic are closely connected with dialectic**
	While knowledge is primarily concerned with truth, rhetoric is primarily concerned with statements and their effects on the audience.
	The word "rhetoric" may also refer to "empty speak", which reflects an indifference to truth, and in this sense rhetoric is adversarial to knowledge.
	Rhetorical proofs include: *ethos*, *pathos* and *logos*
	Chapters 1-3 are general remarks
	Chapters 4-14 focus on propositions
	Chapter 15 is concerned with means of persuasion
Book II: **Emotion** **(Or Moral** **Psychology)**	**This section shares subject matter with Aristotle's ethical writings and his *Psychology***
	the orator must not only try to make the argument of his speech demonstrative and worthy of belief; he must also make his own character look right and put his hearers, who are to decide, in the right frame of mind.
	Chapters 1-11 deal with emotions
	Chapters 12-19 focus on character traits
	Chapters 20-26 focus on logic
Book III: **Language**	**Shares subject matter with *The Poetics***
	The parts of a speech include: introduction, statement, argument and epilogue
	Chapters 1-5 of the book is focused on language
	Chapters 6-18 of the book is focused on the arrangement of a speech

Augustine's Politics

- Most of Augustine's political thought can be found in his largest work ***The City of God.***
- He explains how man's love of self results in the temporal city of man
- He then explains how the love of God moves the believer to the eternal city of God.
- He does not believe that the state can instill virtue

The nature of Kingdoms	What are kingdoms but great robbers? For what are gangs themselves but little kingdoms? The gang itself is made up of men, it is ruled by the authority of a prince, it is knit together by the pact of a confederacy: the booty is divided by the law agreed upon…It was an apt and true answer given to Alexander the Great by a pirate who had been seized. For when that king had asked the man what he meant by keeping hostile possession of the sea, he answered with bold pride, "What do you mean by seizing the whole earth; but because I do it with a petty ship, I am called a robber, while you who does it with a great fleet are styled emperor. Book IV, chapter 4
Christians in Government	Christ's servants, whether they are kings, or princes, or judges, or soldiers are bidden, if need be, to endure the wickedness of an utterly corrupt state, and by that endurance to win for themselves a place of glory in the Heavenly Commonwealth, whose law is the will of God
Patriotism	Augustine argues that "Christianity does not destroy patriotism but reinforces it by making of it a religious duty. The Old Testament prophets and the New Testament writers alike command obedience to civil authority and to the laws of the city. To resist these laws is to defy God's own ordinance, inasmuch as civil society is intended by God himself as a remedy for evil and is used by him as an instrument of mercy in the midst of a sinful world, as St Paul teaches in Romans 13."

Augustine's Politics Continued

Public Policy	Were our religion listened to as it deserves, it would establish, consecrate, strengthen, and enlarge the commonwealth in a way beyond all that Romulus, Numa, Brutus, and all the other men of renown in Roman history achieved
Justice	<ul><li>Justice is loving and serving God only, and therefore ruling well all else</li><li>There is no just state because men reject the teachings of Christ</li><li>The state is a divine gift that is imposed on fallen man for his temporal benefit</li></ul>
Law	<ul><li>Augustine believed that there were two types of law</li><li>The Eternal law is the law of God. It is made by God and it exists eternally. It includes the natural law.</li><li>Temporal law is law made by men</li></ul>
Human Nature	<ul><li>Men have free will</li><li>Men are moved by loves which can be sinful (more often than not)</li><li>Men ultimate crave peace</li></ul>

Thomas Aquinas on Politics

- Aquinas employed the philosophy of Aristotle with the theology of Augustine
- Aquinas is not as optimistic as Aristotle
- Aquinas is not as negative about politics as Augustine
- He believed that the best form of government is a monarchy, advised by an aristocracy

Political Virtues	<ul><li>The political virtues are aimed at the common good</li><li>He changes the definition of the virtue **magnanimity**</li><li>The magnanimous man is a politician who is a great- souled man and thus, does great things</li><li>The magnanimous man has the theological virtues and is led by God</li><li>He also emphasizes **legal justice** as a political virtue</li></ul>
Cardinal Virtues	<ul><li>Justice</li><li>Wisdom</li><li>Courage</li><li>temperance</li></ul>
Theological Virtues	<ul><li>faith</li><li>hope</li><li>love</li></ul>
Justice	<ul><li>Legal justice- The political virtue *par excellence*</li><li>It is aimed at the **common good**</li></ul>
---	---	---
Justice	**Particular justice**	**Commutative justice**
		Distributive justice

Law	<ul><li>**Eternal Law**- the laws of God (we do not know what else is here)</li></ul>
	<ul><li>**Divine Law**- the Old and the New Testaments</li></ul>
	<ul><li>**Natural Law**- human participation in the Eternal law</li></ul>
	<ul><li>**Civil Law**- the temporal, man made law</li><li>The civil law should be in line with the natural law</li><li>Bad civil law is contrary to the natural law</li><li>Human law cannot regulate every aspect of human life</li></ul>

Metaphysics and the Social Order

General Position	Specific Position	Priority	Social Order
Realism	**Extreme Realism** (Plato)	The whole comes before the **parts**. **Relationality** is a metaphysical property.	The **community** comes before the **individual**. Responsibilities come before rights.
	Moderate Realism (Aristotle) **Moderate**	The **whole** comes before the **parts** in natural things.	The **community** comes before the **individual**. Responsibilities come before rights
Nominalism	**Nominalism** (Conceptualists)	Can take either position	Can take either position
	Extreme Nominalists	The **parts** come before the **whole**	The **individual** comes before the **community**. Rights come before responsibilities.

Metaphysics and the social Order
(Part II)

Metaphysical Position	Individual (Ethics)	Household (Economics)	City (Politics)
Extreme Realism (Plato)	Only a part of a whole. The whole can be a **household** or the **city.** The **individual** is only a part.	Only a part of a whole. The city is the whole.	The whole has priority over the parts. The **city** has priority over everything. The whole is more than the sum of its parts.
Moderate Realism (Aristotle)	A part cannot achieve autonomy or autarky. The **individual** is only a part.	A part cannot achieve autonomy or autarky. The **household** has priority over the **individual.**	Achieves autonomy and autarky. The **city** has priority over the household and the individual. The whole is more than the sum of its parts.
Nominalism	The part has priority over the whole. The **individual** is a part.	The **individual** has priority over the household. The **household** can be a part or a whole.	The whole is only the sum of its parts. The **individual** and the household have priority over the city.

The Individual and the Community

Ontology	Parts and Wholes	Epistemology	Ethics
Realism	The Whole comes before the parts	**Teleology** The **community** is a legitimate source of knowledge. Traditions and creeds are important	**Teleology** What is good is good for the **community**. Responsibilities come before rights.
Nominalism	The **Parts** come before the **whole**	**Deontology** The **individual** is a better source of knowledge than the community. Traditions and creeds are rejected	**Deontology** What is good is good for the **individual**. Rights come before responsibilities.

The Pre- Modern State	
Plato's Republic	**Feudal State**
1. Philosopher kings 2. Guardians 3. Workers	1. First Estate- prayors- clergy 2. Second Estate- fighters- nobility 3. Third Estate- laborers- general estate
Centralized, territory- wide administrative apparatus that allows the medieval king to supervise their realm down to the local level The medieval monarchy became the individual's primary membership association Legal systems were established based on the rediscovery of Roman law Medieval monarchs became the head of state State sovereignty unified political rule within a territory	

Steps to Modern Political Philosophy	
Niccolo Machiavelli 1469- 1527	• He wrote *The Prince* • He was not a Christian and believed that Christianity was responsible for the loss of Italian power. • Machiavelli believed that public and private morality had to be understood as two different things in order to rule well. • A ruler must be concerned with reputation, but must also be willing to act immorally at the right times.
Jean Bodin 1530- 1596	• He wrote *The Divine Right of Kings* • A political and religious doctrine of royal and political legitimacy • A monarch is subject to no earthly rule • A monarch derives his right to rule directly from God • The state does not have a responsibility to enforce doctrine
The Formation of the Modern Territorial State	1. The Protestant reformation 2. The Thirty years war 3. The Treaty of Westphalia (1648)

Thomas Hobbes: Leviathan

Thomas Hobbes- 1588- 1679	*Leviathan* is published in 1651. It argues for a social contract and the rule of an absolute sovereign.	
Leviathan	**Part I: of man**	Hobbes gives an account of human nature. He asserts that man's state of nature is of war: of every man against every other man. If left to himself, man will live a life that is short, nasty, pitiable and Brutish.
	Part II: of the Common Wealth	The common wealth is established by men (not God). All agree to give up the right to govern themselves and give this authority to the king or an assembly of men. There are three types of commonwealths: monarchy, aristocracy and democracy. The best of these is the monarchy.
	Part III: Of a Christian Common Wealth	Hobbes argues that religious power is subordinate to civil power.
	Part IV: Of the Kingdom of Darkness	Hobbes is concerned with the darkness of ignorance, as opposed to the light of true knowledge. The causes of this darkness include: 1. misinterpretation of scripture 2. demonology of heathens 3. the mixing of religion with Aristotle's philosophy 4. Only churchmen benefit from the darkness of ignorance.

Modern Political Philosophies

All modern political philosophy is in response to Hobbe's *Leviathan*

Liberalism	Conservativism
• is a political philosophy founded on ideas of liberty and equality. Liberals generally support ideas and programs such as • freedom of speech • freedom of the press • freedom of religion • free markets • civil rights	**is a political philosophy emphasizing:** • Natural law and transcendent moral order • Religion precedes civilization • Tradition and culture guide man and his worldview • Western Culture must be defended • Patriotism is encouraged
Liberalism is started by John Locke (1632- 1704)	Conservativism is started by Edmund Burke (1729- 1797)

Liberalism

John Locke (1632-1704) He wrote*:* ***Two treatises on Government***	Government acquires consent from the governed which has to be constantly present for a government to remain legitimate. Lawful government does not have a supernatural basis. Locke defined the concept of the separation of church and state Locke explained natural rights, based on natural law that government cannot violate because of the social contract.
Montesquieu Charles-Louis de Secondat, Baron de La Brède et de Montesquieu (1689-1755) He wrote ***The Spirit of the Laws***	Montesquieu pleaded in favor of a constitutional system of government, the preservation of civil liberties and the law, and the idea that political institutions ought to reflect the social and geographical aspects of each community. In particular, he argued that political liberty required the separation of the powers of government
Classical Liberalism	is a political ideology, a branch of liberalism which emphasizes liberty and advocates: civil liberties, political freedom with representative democracy under the rule of law and economic freedom
Social Liberalism	is a political ideology, a branch of liberalism which emphasizes equality and advocates: Social justice and • A strong, welfare oriented and interventionist state

Social Liberalism

is a political ideology, a branch of liberalism which emphasizes equality over liberty and advocates:

- Social justice
- A strong, welfare oriented and interventionist state

Jean Jacques Rousseau 1712- 1778	Man in his state of nature is a noble savage until he is corrupted by society. When men give up their self -rule and submit to authority via a social contract, individuals can preserve themselves and remain free. The general will of the people is better than being submitted to the individual will of others. Sovereignty is in the hand s of the people, rather than the government.	
French Revolution: Influenced by Jean Jacques Rousseau. It is based on Social Liberalism. It emphasized equality over liberty.	Nicholas Babuef	Utopian socialism
	Charles Fourier	Utopian socialism
	Henri de Saint Simon 1760-1825	Father of scientific socialism. He influenced both Karl Marx and Friedrich Engels. He argued that the needs of the working class must be fulfilled to have a successful society and an efficient economy.
Georg Wilhelm Friedrich Hegel 1770- 1831	He argues for the dialectic of the macro-community of the state versus the micro community of the family. The state subsumes family and civil society and fulfills them. The individual's supreme duty is to be a member of the state. The constitution is the spirit of the people.	
Ludwig Feuerbach 1804- 1872	A left Hegelian who advocated social liberalism, atheism and materialism. His works serve as a bridge between Hegel and Marx	
Marx and Engels	They combined the ideas of Rousseau, Saint-Simon, Hegel and Feuerbach. They helped developed modern sociology and communism.	
The Frankfurt School	A school critical of both capitalism and Soviet socialism. Dedicated to a Marxist view of political economy and social theory.	

Conservativism

Edmund Burke	<ul><li>Natural law and transcendent moral order</li><li>Religion precedes civilization</li><li>Tradition and culture guide man and his worldview</li><li>Western Culture must be defended</li><li>Patriotism is encouraged</li><li>Natural rights are human customs conforming to divine intent</li><li>Man's rights exist only when man obeys God's law, for right is the child of law</li><li>God has given men law and with that law rights</li><li>Men do not make law, they merely ratify or distort the laws of God</li></ul>
Libertarianism	an extreme laissez-faire political philosophy advocating only minimal state intervention in the lives of citizens.
Cultural Conservativism	described as the preservation of the heritage of one nation, or of a shared culture that is not defined by national boundaries
Neo-Conservativism	the anti-Stalinist left of the camp of American conservatism. Neoconservatives frequently advocate the promotion of democracy and promotion of American national interest in international affairs, including by means of military force
Paleo-conservativism	combines right-libertarian politics and conservative values.

	Marxism
Karl Marx and Frederick Engels wrote the *Communist Manifesto* and *Das Kapital*. These works explain a political-economic philosophy that have held much of the world in slavery for the better part of the last century. There is no one agreed to system, but rather a family of theories associated with Marxism. Today, these theories are viewed as a failure. There are a number of significant components to this family of theories. They are:	
Atheism	Marxism subscribes to a metaphysical materialist viewpoint. In this position there is no God and religion is only an opiate of the masses
Class struggle	Marx saw class struggle as an ongoing problem throughout history. Because he was influenced by Hegelian thought, he held a teleological view of history. He believed that history would culminate with the working class overthrowing the ruling class. This socialist revolution results in the complete liberation of man.
Theory of society	Marx provided a critical analysis of society. He concluded that economics is the foundation of society, and all else is superstructure. He believed that society would evolve from the primitive commune to the social class with a capitalist economy. The last stage of this evolution is a socialist revolution resulting in the elimination of private property and the division of labor.
Science	Marx claimed that this theory is scientific. That is, he believed that history progressed based on an inexorable law. The end of history, the socialist utopia was inevitable. It is as certain as the laws of gravity or the laws of motion.

Western Followers of Marx

Critical Theory	The Frankfurt School (Germany)	Critical theorists recognize Freud, as well as Marx, as a conceptual revolutionary. They attempt to combine the ideas of both as a means of understanding and changing society. The Frankfurt school includes philosophers such as Max Horkheimer, Theodore Adorno, Herbert Marcuse, and Jurgen Habermas
Marxist Anti-humanism	France	This approach to Marxism involves a reaffirmation of the classical Marxism as well as a refusal of the problematic aspects of human nature (economic) or essence of man. It is a reaction to both critical theory as well as Sartre's Marxist humanism. This movement includes philosophers like Althusser, Balibar, Pecheaux, Poulantzas, Hindness, and Hirst.
Marxist Humanism	France, Britain, North America	An attempt to modify Marxism along the lines of a Sartrean existentialism.
Analytic Marxism	Britain/ North America	An attempt to employ the methods of Anglo-American Analytic Philosophy to Marxist analysis of society. Analytic Marxism includes philosophers like J. Elster, and A. Przeworski.

The Progressive Movement

- They were economists, sociologists, ministers of the social gospel, municipal reformers, efficiency experts, journalists and reform minded politicians.
- The first generation progressives were born between 1850-1870. (too young for the Civil War)
- Mostly descended from families from the Massachusetts Bay area.
- Mostly the children of ministers or missionaries. They wanted to redeem America.
- They were nationalists to the core
- They emphasized the primacy of the collective over the individual

Left Progressives	Right Progressives
- They rejected Classical Liberalism - They identified more with Hamilton, because he believed that too much liberty leads to anarchy. - Woodrow Wilson and Franklin Delano Roosevelt are examples	- American Conservative thinking was not always anti-statist. - They rejected Classical Liberalism - They identified more with Jefferson, who was more for liberty than for a strong government. Theodore Roosevelt

Economic Progressives	- The social gospel reformers believed that a Kingdom of Heaven could be built on earth without the return of Christ. - Christian men and women, providentially equipped with science and the state would build it with their own hands. - The economic reformer consciously adopts an ethical ideal, shows how it is to be attained, and encourages people to strive for it. - "The expert economist is like a priest, with priestly functions. He first acquainted the people on what they should want and only then acquainted them with the means of their satisfaction." Edwin R.A. Seligman

The Progressive Movement Continued

The goals of progressives	<ul><li>To make government less corrupt.</li><li>To make government more democratic</li><li>To give government a far bigger role in the economy.</li><li>To re-shape society through a large administrative state.</li><li>To emphasize the collective and to reduce the individual.</li></ul>
Government	They believed that America needed a new government which was non-partisan, scientific and had the discretionary powers required to control the world's largest economy.
	The U.S. Constitution was antiquated and tied the hands of the president.
	Government should be run by people who were disinterested experts, university educated and credentialed.
	They believed in the application of science to achieve efficiency. Thus they were supporters of the social engineer to improve life. They also emphasized efficiency in business and public administration.
Professional Economics	In 1880 there were three faculty members at the leading universities who focused on political economy.
	The industrial revolution resulted in a geyser of money that flowed into American universities.
	Brand new universities included: Ezra Cornell (1868), Cornelius **Vanderbilt** (1871), **John Hopkins** (1876), Jonas Clark (1889), Leland **Stanford** (1891), John D Rockefeller (University of Chicago 1891).
	Between 1870 and 1900 American university students quadrupled, as did the ranks of faculty members
Public Administration	Woodrow Wilson created the field of public administration in the U.S.A.. This would become the fourth branch of government. These agencies were chartered to be independent of their creators

Progressive Leaders

Ministers	Walter Rauschenbush (1861- 1918)	Baptist pastor who taught at Rochester Theological Seminary
	Washington Gladden (1836- 1918)	Condemned individual liberty as an unsound basis for democratic government.
	Josiah Strong (1847- 1916)	Protestant clergyman, organizer , editor and author. He argued that Anglo- Saxons are the superior race who must Christianize and civilize the "savage" races.
Economists	Richard T. Ely (1854- 1943)	He was a political economist and a leader in the Social gospel Movement
	John R. Commons (1865- 1947)	Originally intended to be a minister, but became an economist
	John Bates Clark 1847- 1938	Intended to become a minister, but he became an economist and taught a Columbia University.
Politicians	Theodore Roosevelt (1858- 1919)	First Republic progressive president of the U.S.A.
	Woodrow Wilson	First Democrat Progressive President of the U.S.A. Former president of Princeton University. He developed the field of public administration
Lawyers	Learned Hand (	Legal Realist who rejected natural rights. Moral values are only a matter of taste and of their times. The U.S. Constitution should be understood in light of historical analysis
	Louis Brandeis (1856-1941)	Nominated by Woodrow Wilson to the U.S. Supreme Court
Journalists	Herbert David Croly (1896- 1930)	Co- founder and editor of the *New Republic,* which became the voice of the Progressive Movement
	Walter Lippmann	Co- founder of the *New Republic*
	Walter Weyl	Co- founder of the *New Republic*

Progressive Leaders Continued

| Philosophers | William James (1842-1910) | The father of American psychology and pragmatic philosopher |
| | John Dewey (1859- 1952 | Pragmatic philosopher and educator. He believed that education is a social process and a institution for social reform. Civil society should be reformed around a strong state Journalism should shape public opinion for collectivism and a strong state. Experts and politicians should communicate the right ideas and values. |

Sociological Power Structures

Structure	Theorists	Explanation
Elitism	**C. Wright Mills**	The theory posits that a small minority, consisting of members of the economic elite and policy-planning networks, holds the most power and that this power is independent of a state's democratic elections process.
Pluralist Theory	**Robert Dahl**	politics and decision making are located mostly in the framework of government, but that many non-governmental groups use their resources to exert influence. Groups of individuals try to maximize their interests. Lines of conflict are multiple and shifting as power is a continuous bargaining process between competing groups. Any change under this view will be slow and incremental
Multiple Elite Theory	**T.J. Lowi** **Mancur Olson**	Oligarchical coalitions tend to control a particular are of policy making
Neo-pluralism	**Charles Lindblom** **Hugh Heclo** **John Kingdon** **Baumgartner** **Clarence Stone** **Sabatier**	attributes primacy to the competition between interest groups in the policy process but recognized the disproportionate influence business interests have in the policy process.
Corporatism	**Schmitter**	The socio-political organization of a society by major interest groups, or corporate groups, such as agricultural, business, ethnic, labour, military, patronage, or scientific affiliations, on the basis of common interests. Corporatism is theoretically based upon the interpretation of a community as an organic body
Statism		is the belief that the state should control either economic or social policy, or both, to some degree
Consociation	**Arend Lijphart** **John McGarry** **Brendan O'Leary**	often viewed as synonymous with **power-sharing**, although it is technically only one form of power-sharing. Some consider it to be a form of corporatism while others claim that economic corporatism was designed to regulate class conflict, while consociationalism developed on the basis of reconciling societal fragmentation along ethnic and religious lines

Political Power Structures

Structure	Explanation
Anarchy	A stateless form of society which employs the use of voluntary institutions. Some assert that it advocates more specific institutions based on non- hierarchical free associations. Anarchism holds the state to be undesirable, unnecessary, or harmful
Minarchy	The belief that states ought to exist (as opposed to anarchy), but that their only legitimate function is the protection of individuals from aggression, theft, breach of contract and fraud. Consequently, the only legitimate governmental institutions are the military, police and courts. In the broadest sense, it also includes fire departments, the executive and legislatures as legitimate government function.
Monarchy	a form of government in which sovereignty is actually or nominally embodied in a single individual (the monarch).
Republic	a form of government in which power is held by the people and representatives they elect, and affairs of state are a "public matter", rather than privately accommodated (such as through inheritance or divine mandate).
Democracy	A form of government in which all eligible citizens participate equally—either directly or through elected representatives—in the proposal, development, and creation of laws. It encompasses social, economic and cultural conditions that enable the free and equal practice of political self- determination..
Oligarchy	a form of power structure in which power effectively rests with a small number of people. These people could be distinguished by royalty, wealth, family ties, education, corporate, or military control.
Anocracy	a regime-type where power is not vested in public institutions but spread amongst elite groups who are constantly competing with each other for power
Totalitarianism	a term used to describe a political system in which the state holds total authority over the society and seeks to control all aspects of public and private life wherever possible.

Karl Popper on the Nature of Society

The Open Society and Its Enemies is Popper's two-volume work on political philosophy first printed in London by Routledge in 1945. The work criticizes theories of teleological historicism in which history unfolds inexorably according to universal laws, and indicts as totalitarian Plato, Hegel and Marx for relying on historicism to underpin their political philosophies.

Volume 1 **The Spell of Plato**	Popper argued that most Plato interpreters viewed his political philosophy through a benign lens, without taking into account its dangerous tendencies toward totalitarian ideology. Popper divorced Plato's ideas from those of Socrates, claiming that the former in his later years expressed none of the humanitarian and democratic tendencies of his teacher. In particular, he accuses Plato of betraying Socrates in the *Republic*, wherein Plato portrays Socrates sympathizing with totalitarianism.
Volume 2 **The High Tide of Prophecy: Hegel, Marx, and the Aftermath**	Popper moves on to criticize Hegel and Marx, tracing back their ideas to Aristotle, and arguing that the two were at the root of 20th century totalitarianism.

Closed Society	Based on tradition and archaic rules. Static religion is an essential aspect of a closed society.	
	Socialism	Both Nazism and Communism are manifestations of a closed society

Open Society	The type of society in which the human drive for change can be fulfilled. It is based on ideals and aspirations. It is free of the effects of religion.	
	Free Markets	Popper had began to consider that the power of the law and the market is conditions of prosperity of the West therefore those prophets were mistaken which proclaimed that the property is a theft, and merchants are parasites. If law guarantees implementation of contracts that protection of the law is necessary for the free market. Free markets are both a product and a motor for an open society

The Common Good

Political Philosopher	Explanation
Plato	Unity is the common good
Aristotle	Justice is the common good
Augustine	human well-being found in the good of the whole society is the common good
Thomas Aquinas	Justice, which is human well-being found in the good of the whole society is the common good
Thomas Hobbes	Peace is the common good
Adam Smith	Self-interest serves the common good
Karl Marx	The common good is achieved when the state is the owner of all property, resulting in the equality of all
Alexis de Tocqueville	The common good is independence found in a democratic society. It is found in the absence of a monarchy
John Maynard Keynes	The common good is full unemployment. The political problem of mankind is to combine three things: economic efficiency, social justice and individual liberty
John Rawls	The common good consists of certain general conditions that are equally advantageous to everyone
Robert Nozick	The common good is achieved with a minimal state that respects individual rights which could foster a framework for a constellation of communities constituting a sort of utopia.
Milton Friedman	The common good is achieved when businesses strive to maximize profits. Corporate Social responsibility is contrary to a common good.
Neo-liberalism	Rejects the concept of a common good

The Public Policy Process

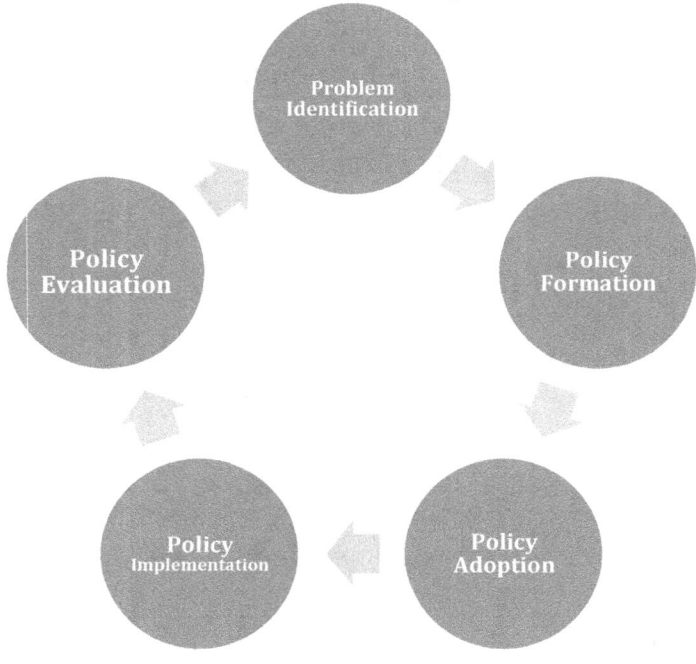

Policy Phase	Explanation
Policy Identification	The framing of a problem begins with the perception of a wrong. Problem definition is a subjective thing, but it is also an iterative process.
Policy Formation	Choosing between different policies
Policy Adoption	Once a policy solution is chosen, it must then be championed throughout the policy process
Policy Implementation	When a policy solution has been selected and officially adopted, it must then be implemented with the appropriate parts of government and infused with the appropriate level of funding.
Policy Evaluation	After the policy solution has been implemented, it must be evaluated to determine if it has accomplished the purposes for which it was implemented.

Policy Analysis

According to William N. Dunn, author of *Public Policy Analysis,* "policy analysis is partly descriptive, but it is also partly normative. To investigate problems of efficiency and fairness, policy analysis draws on normative economics and decision analysis as well as ethics and other branches of social and political philosophy- all of which are about what ought to be.

Policy Relevant Information	**Policy Problems**	It is an unrealized need, value, or opportunity for improvement attainable through public action.
	Expected policy Outcomes	Likely consequences of one or more policy alternatives designed to solve a problem.
	Preferred Policies	Potential solutions to a problem
	Observed Policy Outcomes	A present or past consequence of implementing a preferred policy
	Policy Performance	The degree to which an observed policy outcome contributes to the solution of a problem.
Policy Analytic Methods	**Problem Structuring**	These methods are employed to produce information about which problem to solve.
	Forecasting	These methods are employed to produce information about expected policy outcomes
	Prescription	Methods of prescription are employed to create information about preferred policies.
	Monitoring	Employed to produce information about observed policy outcomes.
	Evaluation	Employed to produce information about the value or utility of observed policy outcomes and their contributions to policy performance.
Strategies of Analysis	**Prospective and Retrospective Analysis**	**Prospective policy analysis** involves the use of information before policy actions are taken.
		Retrospective policy analysis characterizes the operating styles of: **Discipline Oriented Analysts, Problem Oriented Analysts and Applications Oriented Analysts**
	Descriptive and Normative Analysis	**Descriptive Policy Analysis** parallels descriptive decision theory
		Normative Policy Analysis parallels normative decision theory
	Problem Finding and Solving	Problem solving methods like econometrics are technical in nature while problem finding methods are conceptual
	Segmented and Integrated Analysis	**Integrated Policy Analysis** links the four strategies, while **Segmented Analysis** remains specialized social science disciplines

Policy Data Analysis

Policy analysis has traditionally been dominated by a positivist- rationalist approach. The positivist- rationalist approach views policy analysis as a linear problem solving process. Post- positivists argue that it is impossible for policy analysis to inoculate itself against the normative value of answering the key question.

Period	Epistemology	Methods	Examples
Pre-modern	**Epistemic realism-** there is a real, objective world that can be known. This world includes facts and values	Quantitiative and qualitative methods are used	
Modern	**Positivism-** value free, empirical, scientific approaches are the only ways to obtain knowledge	Quantitative methods are superior	Welfare economics
	Post- positivism- all experience is value laden. Scientific approaches include facts and values	Mixed methods: quantitative and some qualitative	Welfare economics Focus groups, interviews
Post-modern	**Epistemic irrealism-** All knowledge is perspectival.	Qualitative methods are superior to quantitative	Feminist, Marxist and perspectival approaches to analysis

Theories of Decision Making for Public Policy		
Theory Type	**SpecificTheory**	**Explanation**
Rational Comprehensive Decision making	**Rational Choice**	is a framework for formally modeling social and economic behavior.
	Public Choice	the use of economic tools to deal with traditional problems of political science"
	New Institutional Economics	emphasize the role of social structures (institutions) in constricting the rationality of individual choices and behaviors.
	Disjointed Incrementalism	*Policy evaluation is not a straightforward process* of rational policy analysis, but rather a political process characterized by fragmentation, conflict, and imperfect knowledge.
		Charles Lindblom developed the theory of administrative incrementalism
		Aaron Wildavsky developed the theory of budgetary incrementalism
Evolutionary Theories	**Evolution and Cognition**	A view of policy making based upon the idea that rationality is not always involved in the process.
	Punctuated Equilibrium	Baumgartner and Jones developed this theory to explain long periods of stasis interrupted by periods dramatic and rapid change
Democratic Theory		Democratic decision making should not be understood as either aggregation or consensus oriented deliberation. It is an inclusive approach that assumes the all actors to be central to decision making.
Governing Policy Networks		The network approach may be considered an alternative to the hierarchical and market models of governance. Policy making and governance take place in networks consisting of various actors (individuals, and coalitions).
Complex Systems	**Complexity**	A complex system consists of a large number of parts with an iteration that is fairly rich. These interactions are nonlinear open systems with a feedback loop.
	Nonlinear Decision Making	Complex systems will sometimes act in ways that vary from the usual sequential processing
	Chaos Theory	An approach to public policy based upon the idea behavior is chaotic, not a type of system

Rational Comprehensive Model of Decision Making

Core Assumptions	Individual decision makers are rational in the sense that they are capable of obtaining full information about the problematic situation they face, and they can make their choices on the sole basis of factual evidence and logical calculations.
	These characteristics of rationality are universal; all decision making can potentially be fully informed, solely factual, and logical, regardless of the historical and cultural context of individual decision makers.
Two Core Assumptions about the Nature of Decision Making:	that they are atomistic entities who are self-interested and whose interests and preferences are set prior to decision making situations
	that they are capable of clearly identifying and rank-ordering their decision criteria (preferences, goals, values) and alternative courses of action and are able to predict the outcomes of their actions with certainty.
Closest Supporters	In *neoclassical economic theory* (public choice) actors are independent, goods exchanged are private, tastes are fixed, there are not barriers to inhibit information exchange, and there are no interdependencies among actors.
	Institutional rational choice theorists (Ostrom) emphasize the role of social structures (institutions) in constricting the rationality of individual choices and behaviors.
Critiques	*Behavioral cognitive psychologists* say that: Humans are "biased" in decision making. These biases affect their decision making styles and capabilities. Biases may occur in the acquisition and processing of information. In the acquisition phase, the *important factors are*: **(1)** the "availability" of information for human perception, **(2)** the "selectivity" of perceivers, **(3)** the ease in perceiving absolute frequencies. Information processing is also biased.
	Simon's theorized that the human mind was only "*intendedly and boundedly rational*" because of its limitations. His model of "*bounded rationality*" describes a process in which decision makers engage only in a limited search for alternatives within the dynamics of their personal problem spaces. Decision makers "*saticfice*" *not optimize*, in their selection of choices: They select the first satisfying choice, rather than comparing all possible choices.
	"*Subjective expected utility*"- says that the rational actor may not be able to pick the best possible decision alternative because of the uncertainties in predicting future states of affairs.
	Zey says that, decision makers do not make decisions independent of their environment, decision making is context dependent. People are not born with preferences; preferences are shaped by family, friends, religious institutions, and larger communities.

Rational Choice Theory

Rational choice theory, also known as **choice theory** or **rational action theory**, is a framework for formally modeling social and economic behavior. Rationality, is defined by "wanting more rather than less of a good." Normally, people make decisions about how to act by comparing the costs and benefits of different courses of action. In general, people will choose the object that provides the greatest reward at the lowest cost.

Individual Preference for Action	**Completeness**	all actions can be ranked in an order of preference
	Transitivity	if action a_1 is preferred to a_2, and action a_2 is preferred to a_3, then a_1 is preferred to a₃. In other words, all actions can be compared with other actions.
	Independence of Irrelevant Alternatives	If A is preferred to B out of the choice set {A,B}, then introducing a third alternative X, thus expanding the choice set to {A,B,X}, must not make B preferable to A.
Individual preference	**Strict Preference**	occurs when an individual prefers a_1 to a_2, but not a_2 to a_1.
	Weak Preference	can be held in which an individual has a preference for *at least a_j*, similar to the mathematical operator $\leq$.
	Preference Indifference	occurs when an individual does not prefer a_1 to a_2, or a_2 to a_1.
Assumptions about knowledge	**Perfect Information**	An individual has full or perfect information about exactly what will occur due to any choice made.
	Proper Functioning	If an individual is functioning properly, then he can make a good decision if given the cognitive ability and time to weigh every choice against every other choice.

Public Choice

Public Choice involves "the use of economic tools to deal with traditional problems of political science" Its content includes the study of political behavior. Public Choice models voters, politicians, and bureaucrats as mainly self-interested. In particular, it studies agents and their interactions in the social system either as such or under alternative constitutional rules. These can be represented in a number of ways, including standard constrained utility maximization, game theory, or decision theory. Public choice analysis has roots in normative purposes, to identify a problem or suggest how a system could be improved by changes in constitutional rules, the subject of constitutional economics.

Principle-Agent Problem	Because of information asymmetry, agents may not act in accordance with the desires of their principle	**Principle-** one who hires another to fulfill a specific purpose
		Agent- one who is employed to fulfill the purposes of the principle
Politicians	An elected official who is the agent of the citizens who voted for them. Because they are vote maximizing, they may not actually fulfill their mandates.	Politicians are agents for the voter and principles for bureaucrats.
Bureaucracy	An organization of public servants that seeks to perform a specific governmental function. Bureaucrats are budget maximizing rational beings. Governmental bureaucracies have a monopoly market structure. As such, they are very inefficient.	These are the agents of the elected officials. They may act contrary to the desires of the elected official and the voter.
Voters	Citizens who vote in accordance with their policy desires. They are rational and utility maximizing agents.	Citizens are principles for the politicians that they vote for.
Analytical Tools	**Game Theory**	A method to determine the optimal strategy for two or more people who are seeking to maximize their utility
	Decision Theory	is concerned with identifying the values, uncertainties and other issues relevant in a coming to an optimal decision.

Policy Making through Disjointed Incrementalism

According to Charles Lindblom, policy makers gain experience with existing policies over time, building up a reservoir of knowledge. *Policy evaluation is not a straightforward process* of rational policy analysis, but rather a political process characterized by fragmentation, conflict, and imperfect knowledge.

The Breakdown of Rationality		**(1)** Policy makers perceive and accurately define public problems.
		(2) The model requires agreement on objectives.
		(3) Rational analysis presumes a capacity to estimate accurately the consequences of all alternatives.
Incrementalism		*Incrementalism* requires neither perfect information nor agreement among policy makers on objectives. **Incrementalism** permits action where the rational ideal is paralyzed. *Incrementalism* focuses on concrete problems to be solved rather than on abstract ideals to be attained. Ends and means are typically considered simultaneously.
Elements	**The Dominant Institution**	issues form policy communities, consisting of legislative committees with jurisdiction over the issue, executive agencies with responsibility for administering laws within the issue areas, and clientele groups with a stake in the policies developed by these policy communities.
	Policy Outcomes	will normally be incremental, representing fairly small changes from existing policy.
	Dramaturgical Incrementalsim	is necessary to account for cases, where public arousal creates real pressure on policy makers to take dramatic action without producing the conditions for rational policy making. Within the policy community, both **conflictual objectives** and **conflictual knowledge** characterize the process, thereby making **incremetalism** inevitable.
Life Cycle of Issues.	**1st stage "breakthrough policies".**	Legislative actions by policy makers establish new programs.
	2nd stage "incremental rationalizing policies"	Policy communities develop around these new programs. More is learned over time how these programs work. Rationalizing policies tend to exhibit the characteristics of normal **incrementalism** for many years, due to the combination of **conflictual objectives and conflictual knowledge.**
	3rd stage	Workable solutions to problems may emerge after many years.

Disjointed Incrementalism: Policy Worldviews

Incrementalism advances three different empirical proposition for policy process:
1- Policymaking involves bargaining among a multiplicity of actors who possess different information, personal or institutional interests and views about public interests.
2- Participants typically build on past policies, focusing on alternatives that only slightly differs from the existing ones.
3- Because the alternatives under consideration are incremental and because there needs to be compromise the outcome will also be incremental.

Utopian visionaries	• They have utopian visions about economic and social justice • They are impatient with incrementalism – because they don't want institutions enforce their beliefs and preference they are unwilling to settle for one piece at a time. • They place premium on flexibility. • Policymakers must have overriding power over laws that impede their version of progress. • UK's system and delegating powers to bureaucrats are two ways to achieve this vision.
Adaptive conservatives	• They want to find a way to restore tradition and apply it to a new situation. • They must be at same time both persistence and reactionary. • They cannot continue appealing to the past.
Nostalgic Conservative	• They don't want to adapt and seek to go back to the values of another era. • They believe in an absolute truth that was once known and somewhere along the way was lost. • This absolute truth (scripture, history etc.) must be restored. • Often times in modern days the truth is not religious it is economic. They want to go back to an earlier economic era where the federal government did not play a great role in the economy. • Checks and balances impede change thus serving the interests of this group.
Meliorative Liberals	• They want social reform • They perceive mankind as fallible and knowledge as incomplete. • Unlike conservatives they view political institutions as product of fallible people and thus always subject to question. • They view incrementalism as the best course of action. • Unlike utopians who view government as being capable of solving all problems meliorative liberals believe that the government can only ameliorate problems by systematic rationality.

Disjointed Incrementalism: Typology of Policy Worldviews

	Meliorative: Pragmatists Process Oriented	Utopian: Ideologues End or Solution Oriented
Progressive vision: Reformers Forward looking reformers	**Meliorative Liberals:** Pragmatic reformers who view change as desirable but best achieved through incremental or piecemeal social engineering	**Utopian visionaries:** Ideological innovators who seek to impose a common purpose on society in accordance with an ideological vision they have formulated (Hayek's rationalists)
Nostalgic vision: Preservers Backward looking conservers	**Adaptive conservatives:** Seek to preserve cherished institutions; accept the need for some reforms to preserve what is truly precious from the past (Hayek's anti-rationalists)	**Nostalgic conservatives:** Restorers who seek to return to a way of life shown to be desirable by past experiences or revelation

Triangle Theory

Iron Triangles	An unbreakable triad of congress, bureaucracies and special interest groups. They produce a narrow group of benefits for the few at the expense of the public interest.	
Ernest S. Griffith (1939)	Political scientists should study "whirlpools of interest," rather than governmental institutions to understand policy formation.	
J.L. Freeman (1965)	Policy subsystems are a unit of analysis in the study of policy formation through the use of case studies.	
Hugh Heclo (1977, 78)	studies of the iron triangle are incomplete because they can't account for the decentralization and change in the policy process	
	Issue Networks	Consists of individuals with highly active citizens with specialized policy knowledge who are drawn to the group for noneconomic benefits
		Organized around technical expertise and ideology
	Technopols	Those within the issue network who have technical knowledge of the policy at hand. They tend to wield the most power

Advocacy Coalition Framework

Invented by Paul Sabatier and *The Advocacy Coalition Framework*- focuses on the interaction of advocacy coalitions- each consisting of actors from a variety of institutions who share a set of policy beliefs- within a subsystem. Policy change is a function of both competition within the subsystem and events outside the subsystem. The iron triangle of politics is highly permeable and unpredictable

Assumptions	1- belief systems are more important than institutional affiliations 2- actors may be pursuing a wide variety of objectives, that can be measured empirically 3- one must add researchers and journalists to the set of potentially important actors
Process	Policy process and policy change are best characterized by a slew of policy subsystems interacting throughout the policy process.
Advocacy Coalitions	Similar to issue networks. They consist of legislators, interest groups, public agencies, policy researchers, journalists and others. All members of the coalition agree on core policy beliefs
The Importance of ACF	1. It explains both stability and rapid change 2. It moves scholars away from the notion that the policy process is linear or based on purely economic benefits

Punctuated Equilibrium

Baumgartner and Jones developed this theory to explain long periods of stasis interrupted by periods dramatic and rapid change. Incrementalism is not sufficient to explain the nonlinear movement within the policy process. They adopted this idea from zoologist, Stephen Jay Gould. Gould developed punctuated equilibrium to explain gaps in the evolutionary record.

Assumptions	**Bounded Rationality**	Because one does not have complete information, he must make the best decision that he can. Hence, his decisions are less than fully rational.
	Description	Punctuated equilibrium is a great descriptive theory
	Prescription	Punctuated equilibrium does little to predict when change will occur
Policy Monopoly	A set of structural arrangements that keep the policy process in the hands of only a few policy actors	
Venue Shopping	Policy groups can challenge a monopoly in one venue by going to another. For example, one can move from a legislative to an executive or court venue.	
Feedback	**Positive**	The process by which a change in policy image based on criticism results in a new point of stability
	Negative	

Garbage Can Model

John Kingdon developed this model to explain the policy process. Both problems and solutions are dumped into the policy making garbage can. The process is not linear nor does it always move incrementally.

The garbage can model is an organized anarchy composed of	(1) problematic preference,
	(2) fluid participation
	(3) unclear technology

Policy Images	The way a policy is understood via an emotional symbol or theme. It is used to mobilize broad groups interested in the policy issue.
Policy Venue	An institution within a society that has the authority to make a decision on a policy.
Pre-decisions	Decisions made by relevant actors that affect whether an issue reaches the government agenda
Policy Entrepreneurs	Policy actors who learn by trial and error

3 streams		
	Problems	The political problem that must be solved
	Policies	Approaches to solving a political problem
	Politics	The participants in the policy process. Some are visible and others are invisible.

Policy Window	A short opportunity for rapid change created when the three streams converge.

Public Policy Think Tanks

Think tanks began as a product of the progressive era. There is no one universally accepted definition of a think tank. Most public policy work is being done in a think. The number of think tanks around the world is increasing.	

James McGann	"Think tanks are public policy research analysis and engagement organizations that generate policy- oriented research, analysis and advice on domestic and international issues, thereby enabling policymakers and the public to make informed decisions about public policy."
John Goodman	Think tanks are not the same as advocacy groups.
	Think tanks are not the same as universities
	Think tanks are not the same as market actors
	Think tanks are not the same as political interest groups or an agent of the state.
	He recommends geographic separation from Washington D.C.
	A good policy expert is an intellectual entrepreneur.
Andrew Rich	"independent, non- interest based, nonprofit organizations that produce and principally rely on expertise and ideas to obtain support and to influence the policy- making process."
Thomas Medvetz	term "think tank" is not clearly defined.
	Think tanks link political and intellectual practice in American life.
	Think tanks have collectively developed their own social forms, conventions, norms and hierarchies.
	Think tanks occupy a sub- space located at the crossroads of the academic, political, economic, and media.

The Nature of Think Tanks		
Elitist View	**C. Mills Wright**	think tanks are instruments deployed strategically in the service of a ruling class political agenda.
	G.William Domhoff	that the purpose of think tanks is to assist in the business of top down policy making.
Pluralist View	Think tanks are one of many things that compete to shape public policy	
	Pluralists refuse to assign a particular role or character to think tanks	
Institutionalist View	The institutional approach focuses on the rules and constraints within which think tanks are embedded and the personnel networks they coordinate.	
	Think tanks comprise a heterogeneous array of organizations with a wide range of possible effects.	
	Think tank affiliated policy experts are members of an "epistemic community"- or a network of policy oriented actors whose members share a certain brand of expertise, such as legal or scientific knowledge.	
	Multiple epistemic communities may coexist within the world of think tanks	

Think Tank Affiliations

Category	Description
Autonomous and independent	Independence from any one interest group or donor
Quasi-independent	Autonomous from government, but controlled by an interest group or donor
Government Affiliated	A part of the forma structure of government
University Affiliated	Located at a university
Political Party Affiliated	Formally affiliated with a political party
Corporate Affiliated (for Profit)	Affiliated with a corporation or merely operating on a for profit basis

Think Tank Organizational Structure

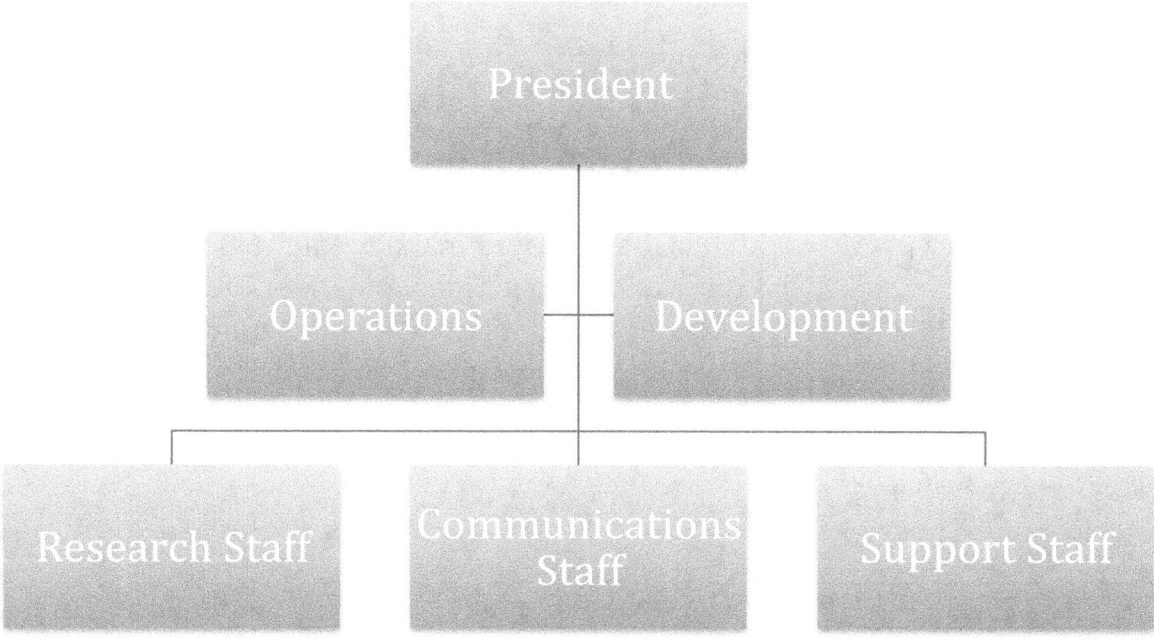

President	The president sets the general direction and takes the lead in fund raising by speaking and writing publicly
Administrative Staff	This is the senior staff of the think tank. This includes those involved in operations, finance and development.
Research Staff	According to Thomas Medvetz, think tanks often hire policy experts with career backgrounds in multiple occupational settings. Even the organizations with the most scholarly reputations, such as Brookings and Hoover, tend to hire ex- academic scholars who have also established some experience in politics, business, or the media. The number of researchers determine the number of other employees. Small think tanks have 10 or fewer researchers.
Communications Staff	The communications staff make sure that the think tank research is disseminated to influence public policy
Support Staff	This includes information technology, human resources, etc.

International Relations Theory		
	Normative	**Epistemology**
Modern Positivist 1. Realism 2. Idealism 3. Liberalism 4. Neo- liberalism 45 Regime Theory	The Goal is not to make the world a better place, because international relations should be studied in a value free way.	International Relations should be like the natural sciences.
Modern Post- Positivist 1. International Society Theory (The English School) 2. Social Constructivism 3. Marxism	The goal is to make the world a better place. All experience is value – laden.	International relations should not be like the natural sciences
Post-modern Post-structuralism	International Relations should be based around the study of values	International Relations should not be like the natural sciences, but its knowledge should be based around the use of narrative and a perspectival perspective

International Relations Definitions

Realism	Is primarily concerned with national security. All states are self- interested, rational and maximize their utility through power acquisition and maintenance It assumes that the international political system is anarchic
	Classical realists believe that human nature is the source of conflict
	Neo- realists believe that conflict results from the anarchic state system
	Neoclassical Realists argue that conflict results from both human nature and the anarchic state system
Liberalism	Individuals are basically good and capable of meaningful cooperation. As such, states depend upon each other multinational corporations and international institutions.
Idealism	Argues that a state should make its internal political philosophy the goal of its foreign policy. This is a pre- cursor to **Liberal** international relations.
Neo- liberalism	Assumes that states are still the primary actors in international relations, but acknowledges the non state actors and inter- governmental organizations cannot be ignored.
Regime Theory	International regimes or institutions affect the behavior of states or other international actors.
International Society Theory (The English School)	Assumes that the shared norms and values of the states regulates international relations. Examples of such norms include diplomacy, order and international law.
Social Contructivism	States have a social, rather than material nature. Consequently, it is their social interactions shape the interests and identities of states.
Marxism	This is ia structural theory like neorealism, but it focuses on the economic sector instead of the political one. It assumes that capitalism defines the unjust political institutions and state relations

Levels of Analysis in International Relations	
Systemic Level	The systemic level of international relations is concerned with broad concepts that affect the international situation. This includes concepts such as: sovereignty, power, national interest, non- state actors, power blocks, polarity, interdependence.
Unit Level	This level is concerned with the state rather than the international system. This includes concepts, such as: regime type, religion, revisionism/ status quo.
Sub- Unit Level	This level focuses on individuals and the factors that explain their behavior in international relations.
	Psychological factors
	Bureaucratic politics
	Religious and ethnic groups
	Science and technology
	International Political Economy
	International Political Culturology
	Personal relations between leaders

Contemporary Sociology

Middle Range Theory	developed by Robert K. Merton, is an approach to sociological theorizing aimed at integrating theory and empirical research. It is currently the de facto dominant approach to sociological theory construction especially in the United States.
	starts with an empirical phenomenon and abstracts from it to create general statements that can be verified by data. This approach stands in contrast to the earlier "grand" theorizing of social theory, such as functionalism and many conflict theories.
Analytic Sociology	a strategy for understanding the social world. It is concerned with explaining important macro-level facts such as the diffusion of various social practices, patterns of segregation, network structures, typical beliefs, and common ways of acting.
	It explains such facts by detailing in clear and precise ways the mechanisms through which they were brought about. This is accomplished by a detailed focus on individuals' actions and interactions, and the use of state-of-the-art simulation techniques to derive the macro-level outcomes that such actions and interactions are likely to bring about.
	Analytical sociology can be seen as contemporary incarnation of Robert K. Merton's well-known notion of middle-range theory.

Stratification in Society		
	Structural Functionalism	**Conflict Theory**
People	Talcott Parsons	Frankfurt School
Assumptions	Society is a meritocracy	Society is all about class warfare
Explanation	is a framework for building theory that sees society as a complex system whose parts work together to promote solidarity and stability. Functionalism addresses society as a whole in terms of the function of its constituent elements; namely norms, customs, traditions, and institutions	Society reflects the conflict between the bourgeouisie (owners of capital) and the proletariat (working class). The bourgeoisie does everything to oppress the proletariat. They employ morality, religion, education, and the family to maintain power and oppress the proletariat.
Societal Change	After equilibrium is reached, change happens slowly	Societal change happens quickly and violently

Structural Functionalism

Emile Durkhiem	Student of August Comte. The father of sociology and advocate of structural functionalism
Talcott Parsons	is a framework for building theory that sees society as a complex system whose parts work together to promote solidarity and stability. This approach looks at society through a macro-level orientation, which is a broad focus on the social structures that shape society as a whole, and believes that society has evolved like organisms. This approach looks at both social structure and social functions. Functionalism addresses society as a whole in terms of the function of its constituent elements; namely norms, customs, traditions, and institutions
Kingsley Davis and Wilbert E. Moore	gave an argument for social stratification based on the idea of "functional necessity" (also known as the Davis-Moore hypothesis). They argue that the most difficult jobs in any society have the highest incomes in order to motivate individuals to fill the roles needed by the division of labour. Thus inequality serves social stability
Robert Merton	theory of deviance derived from Durkheim's idea of **anomie**. It is central in explaining how internal changes can occur in a system. For Merton, anomie means a discontinuity between cultural goals and the accepted methods available for reaching them.
	5 situations facing an actor: • **Conformity** occurs when an individual has the means and desire to achieve the cultural goals socialised into him. • **Innovation** occurs when an individual strives to attain the accepted cultural goals but chooses to do so in novel or unaccepted method. • **Ritualism** occurs when an individual continues to do things as proscribed by society but forfeits the achievement of the goals. • **Retreatism** is the rejection of both the means and the goals of society. • **Rebellion** is a combination of the rejection of societal goals and means and a substitution of other goals and means. as the innovation or rebellion builds momentum, society will eventually adapt or face dissolution.

Marxist Sociological Approaches

Conflict Theory	**People**	Max Horkheimer · Theodor Adorno Herbert Marcuse · Walter Benjamin Erich Fromm · Friedrich Pollock Leo Löwenthal · Jürgen Habermas
	Assumptions	Karl Marx was right
	Distinctives	In philosophy, the term *critical theory* describes the neo-Marxist philosophy of the Frankfurt School, which was developed in Germany in the 1930's. Frankfurt theorists drew on the critical methods of Karl Marx and Sigmund Freud. Critical theory maintains that ideology is the principal obstacle to human liberation
Growth Machine Theory	**People**	**Harvey Luskin Molotch**
	Assumptions	The Marxist revolution has not happened
	Distinctives	land parcels were not empty fields awaiting human action, but were associated with specific interests—commercial, sentimental, and psychological. Especially important in shaping cities were the real estate interests of those whose properties gain value when growth takes place. These actors make up what Molotch termed "the local growth machine" -- a term now standard in the urban studies lexicon. From this perspective, cities need to be studied (and compared) in terms of the organization, lobbying, manipulating, and structuring carried out by these actors. The outcome—the shape of cities and the distribution of their peoples— is thus not due to an interpersonal market or geographic necessities, but to social actions, including opportunistic dealing.

Urban Sociology

Chicago School	**People**	Frederick Clements
	Distinctives	The city is viewed as an organism. It is orderly and predictable. It grows via linear evolution
		Concentric Zone Model 1. Central business district 2. Transitional- lower income 3. Lower class residential area 4. Residential zone Commuter zone- highest income
		The city is a laboratory, so ethnographic methods are used for observations. A positivistic- value free approach to observation is employed. They focused on individual choices and then aggregates
LA School	**Distinctives**	Cities are chaotic, random and non-linear
		They employ a polycentric model for a city
		Edge cities – growth of business areas at the intersection of freeways, and developments have no relation to each other
		Cities are the intersection of the global with the local
		Postmodernist
		Post fordist- movement from industrial to service industry and more flexible

Race In the Urban Environment

William Julius Wilson	**The Truly Disadvantaged** **When Work Disappears** **The Declining Significance of Race**	Wilson has concluded that, as racial barriers have dissolved, the continued poverty of urban blacks is less a product of racial prejudice than a result of the changing economic landscape. His prescription for breaking this cycle of doom involves "race neutral" government-backed jobs and health programs. "Affirmative action," he writes, "has to be combined with a broader program of social reform that would emphasize social rights: the right to employment, the right to education, the right to good health."
Massey and Denton	*American Apartheid*	The black ghetto was created by whites during the first half of the twentieth century in order to isolate growing urban black populations. Despite the Fair Housing Act of 1968, segregation is perpetuated today through an interlocking set of individual actions, institutional practices, and governmental policies.
		As ghetto residents adapt to this increasingly harsh environment under a climate of racial isolation, they evolve attitudes, behaviors, and practices that further marginalize their neighborhoods and undermine their chances of success in mainstream American society.

Sociology of Poverty	
The *concept of poor*	can direct attention to any array of "linked problems such as unemployment, discrimination, poor skills, low income, poor housing, high crime, bad health and family breakdown"
The *poor and their advocates*	will have *limited power* in the political world, stemming from their systematic social disadvantage in capitalist societies and liberal political system.
Three types of theoretical approaches	encompass much of the scholarship on urban politics and the poor:
	1. The role of politics in shaping the prospects for the poor
	2. The role of economy
	Problem-centered lens, considering how multiple macro-and micro – level political, economic and social forces simultaneously produce a particular kind of urban problem

Poverty: Politics First

"Politics first" approaches to the place of the poor in urban politics focuses on political relationships and regimes that govern policy-making and implementation in cities and mobilization of poor people through strategies such as community organization.

Pluralist Approach	the fragmentation of policy arenas within the city, and the observation that no group is permanently excluded, nor has inequalities that cumulate across policy arenas, led to the assertion that the poor could influence particular policy arenas at particular points in time
	rejects the idea of ruling elites who influenced all spheres of decision making
Regime Theory	In US context, resources needed to support the needs of the poor are not typically present
	In his typology of regimes **Stone** includes "lower class opportunity expansion regime" focused on "enriched education and job training, improved transportation access, and enlarged opportunities for business and home ownership"
	Stone's and colleagues' work focuses on identifying and understanding governing regimes where steps toward this ideal have been attempted and in some cases, where there is evidence of modest success.
	The study of regimes directs attention to regime membership and posits that regime priorities will vary depending on who takes part, with that resources.
Community Organizing	Represents an important and commonly used strategy through which low-income people and their advocates pursue policy changes and influence at City Hall
	Increasing *fragmentation* of the civic sector also makes mobilization and coalition-building more difficult
	Ferman's work on neighborhood politics in Chicago and Pittsburgh speaks to this problem by pointing to the importance of institutionalizing progressive neighborhood agendas
	He suggests that elected officials do not always take steps to institutionalize change, but that when they do, neighborhood voice can be incorporated into city governance
	Institutionalization occurs for a narrow band of reforms-unidimensionally around local economic development, rather than for a broad set of progressive measures across multiple policy issues

Poverty: Economics First

Elite theories	and related political economy and Marxist approaches such as "growth machine" and "city trenches" are pessimistic about the future of poor.
	each asserts that a business dominated local elite exercises power to advance its interests, at expense of the poor
Logan & Molotch	- develop the concept of a local growth machine, analyzing which elite actors take part, and how their actions privilege the exchange values of land rather than the use values held by lower income renters
Katznelson's	study echoes the depiction of subordinated working- and lower-class groups in the city, but identities a somewhat different mechanism of exclusion.
	A. Conflict is limited to the scale of the neighborhood, where groups fight for influence and control of local resources
	A. He implied that neighborhood control merely diverted the attention of the working classes and racial minorities from broader inequalities, recent work examines local and neighborhood institutions as mechanisms for effectuating broader change
	B. Altering a locality's relations to capital is a precondition for political equality
Williamson-	presents an array of "community-centered place-stabilizing policies" originating at the international, national, state and local level, that they argue would invigorate community democracy
DeFilipps	- focuses on the collective ownership of work, housing and money: he examines cases of worker cooperatives, mutual housing associations, cooperative housing, land trust, community- based financial institutions and credit unions
	He argues for careful assessments of such projects' strengths and weaknesses; over- promising to solve poverty risks generating a backlash that can erode support for partially successful programs.

Social Movements

According to George Yancey, social movements are shaped by the institutions that they confront. These institutions also help to determine the type of tactics employed by the social movement. Social movements are not based upon a rational perception of the situation. Rather, social movements meet important social and psychological needs that are not in the realm of rationality.

Theory	Theorists	Explanation
Resource Mobilization Theory	**Economic** John McCarthy Mayer Zald	Social movements are successful when those movements are able to take control of sufficient economic and social resources and employ them wisely
	Political Charles Tilly Doug McAdams	The intensity of grassroots activism is an essential aspect of a movement's success
Relative Deprivation Theory	Robert K. Merton Walter Runchman	Subcultures that feel deprived are likely to mobilize and become social movements.
Emergent Norms	Turner and Killian 1987	Norms help to define a group and allows them to construct goals and methods to correct perceived injustice.
Collective Action Frames	Taylor and Whittier 1995 Snow and Benford 1992	Extends the theories of emergent norms. Events are "framed" to attach an advantageous interpretation to them, thereby advancing the cause of the social movement
Collective Identity Theory	Gamson 1992	When the identity and goals of a group are threatened, individuals in the group also feel threatened. Collective identity helps to produce commitment to the group through solidarity with the other members of the group. This is the most important task of any social movement that desires to make major social changes, because it binds people together to take some kind of action. Collective identity results in a new culture for those involved

Philosophy of Law

Theories of Justice	**Retributive**	Ensures that those who violate the laws of society receive the punishment that they are due.
	Distributive	The fair arrangement of goods, benefits and responsibilities of a society
Legal theory	**Natural law**	The classical view of natural law is based upon metaphysical presuppositions that asserts that there is a higher law that serves as a basis for civil law. The contemporary views of natural law are contrasted with legal positivism. Contemporary natural law theory asserts that there is a moral aspect to every law that should show the validity of that law. Natural rights are based upon the idea of natural law.
	Legal positivism	An idea of the nineteenth century that asserts that laws are only social constructs of a given society. They also assert that there is no connection between law and morality.
	Law and economics	Asserts that economic principles apply to every legal problem. This includes such things as family law, criminal law, and tort law
	Postmodernism	This is concerned with how lawyers use language and how language relates to truth. This includes the study of feminism and the law, deconstruction and pragmatism.
Areas of law	**Business law**	Includes such things as; property law, contract law, and tort law
	Criminal Law	Is concerned with crime and punishment
	Constitutional law	Is concerned with whether a given law is consistent with the constitution of a country.
	International law	is concerned with the resolving disputes of the laws of one country to another.

Legal Theory

Theory	Metaphysics	Ethics
Natural Law	Realism	Teleological/ Virtue ethics
Legal Positivism	Nominalism	Deontological/ utilitarianism
Legal Realism	Nominalism	Deontology
Law and Economics	Nominalism	Deontological/ Utilitarianism
Critical Legal Theory	Nominalism	Deontology

Plato's Legal Philosophy

General Terminology	**Nomos**	designates positive laws as well as customs. Plato notes that these are commonly unwritten. This term derives from the verb *nemo-* which explains the concept of lawgiver as shepherd.
	Thesmos (or *Themis*)-	connects morality to divinity.
	Psephisma-	for measures that a political body decides to adopt in determinate circumstances and by vote, in decisions that are immediately branded as being of human origin.
	Eunomia	is like divine order.
	Divine law	was not revealed by the gods but was rather the right of humans to establish with the gods a system of predictable relations.
Plato *The Laws*	**Theology**	Many Greeks believed that the god Cronus placed humanity under the care of divinities (*daimon*).
		The political is the imperfect substitute for the divinities in the government of men.
		The political becomes secularized when the law (*nomos*) replaces the divine shepherd (*nomeus*)
		The divine exercises its influence over a city through an intermediary, who is an inspired (*theia moira*) political figure. Nonetheless, priests must be kept from power.
	Penal Theology	The reduction of impiety is achieved by asserting the existence of the gods, their providence and their moral incorruptibility.
		There are three levels of impiety 1. Believing that there are no gods. 2. Believing that gods exist, but care nothing for men. 3. Believing that the gods exist and care about men, but that they can be swayed by prayers and sacrifices.
	Other Key ideas	A judge must study the letter of the law to become a better judge since the law is divine.
		There is a close connection between the law (*nomos*) and the intellect (*nous*).
		The city that is based upon the law is a divine regime (*theia politeia*).
		Legislators and judges must persuade the citizens that the laws are legitimate because man is no longer immediately tied to the divine.

Aristotle, the Stoics and Epicureans

Aristotle	"He therefore that recommends that the law (*nomos*) shall govern seems to recommend that God and reason (*nous*) alone shall govern, but he that would have man govern adds a wild animal also."
	The natural law is established by the gods **The natural law is like the physical laws of nature** **The natural law exists everywhere** **To act in accordance with the natural law is to act in accordance with reason** **The moral virtues are based upon natural law** **The emotions are tied to natural law**
Stoics	**The universe is a vast *polis* constituted by right reason or the law of nature** **The law of nature is mediated by the *Logos* the divinely given universal law of nature stands over against the positive laws of the various human states.**
Epicureans	The epicureans subscribed to a law of nature The law of nature is in accordance with reason

Judeo- Christian Views on Natural Law

Markus Boeckmuehl, *Jewish Laws in Gentile Churches* is an excellent source of information on this topic

- Broadly speaking, universal ethics in ancient Jewish thought can be discussed under two headings: positive law and 'natural law'.
- The former category is generally captured by the moral commands of the law and the prophets

2nd Temple Judaism	- 1.Law that carries authority is never "natural" in the sense ob being anything other than divine in origin. - 2. The law of nature is in keeping with the Law of God - 3. The Law of God is in keeping with the law of nature. - 4. The idea of a law according to nature is well established except in Palestinian scribal circles. - 5. The idea of a law according to nature is well established prior to Philo

Philo	Philo was a Jewish Hellenistic author of the first century. He thought that the Greeks stole these ideas from the Hebrews. The Torah's laws are but copies of the law of nature.	The laws of nature include first of all the subordination of creation under the Creator, but beyond that also several of the commandments of the decalogue. The law of nature is synonymous with the Law of God. Philo depended upon the writings of Antiochus of Ascalon, the head of the Academy in the early first century, who devoted much of his energy to a reinterpretation of Stoic ethics Bockmuehl, 107-109.

The Early Church	- 1.Early Christianity agrees substantially with Jewish wisdom and to some extent with Stoic moral teaching. - 2. At the same time, the created world is also fundamentally in need of redemption… Natural law is never simply identical with revelation, and can never substitute for it. - 3. The moral theatre of redemption is nothing less than the world that God has loved. Creational givens are at once relativized, embraced and redeemed in the light of Christ's resurrection, and of the renewal of creation that he promises.

Thomas Aquinas

Subject	Explanation
Types of Law	**Eternal Law**-The laws of God. This includes both the revealed and unrevealed laws. This includes the laws of science
	Divine Law-The old law and the new law. The Old and New Testaments
	Natural Law- The aspect of general revelation made available to all men by reason. It is consistent with the created order and conscience is tied to it.
	Civil (or Positive) Law- The laws of men. These laws are good only to the extent that they are consistent with the natural law
Natural law and Eternal law	**The natural law is part of the eternal law (God's law)**
Natural Law and Divine law	**The natural law is consistent with the divine law (the Old and New Testaments)**
prudentia)	**The natural law is known by reason**
(synderesis)	**The natural law is written in our hearts**

	***Synderesis*- Self-evident, naturally known principles of practical reason by which we know the natural law**
	     ***Synderesis* provides general principles, like do good and avoid evil, do no harm**
	     ***Synderesis* provides more direction so that we can live in accordance with reason**
	     ▪ ***Synderesis* tells us what we should be, how it is good, and reasonable for us to act**

Virtue	*Arete*- that which makes one excellent or good. Virtue is in accordance with the natural law
	Cardinal virtues are natural virtues that everyone can attain. These are Justice, wisdom, courage and temperance.
	Theological Virtues are gifts of the Holy Spirit that give the believer the power to live righteously. These gifts are Faith, Hope, and Love (*caritas*)
Character	Mature character is developed by acting in accordance with the virtues and the natural law
***Eudaimonia* (Greek) or *Felicitas* (Latin)**	A natural happiness or flourishing that comes from acting in accordance with the natural law and virtue. A happiness that comes

Protestant Reformers and Natural Law

All Protestant confessions uphold natural law. *Sola Scriptura* does not eliminate need for tradition or the natural law. There is no tension between original sin and natural law

Three uses of the law:	1.To convict of sin 2. To maintain order 3. To exhort believers to obedience and gratitude	
Martin Luther	He acknowledged natural law, but did not base his ethics or political theory on it. He was a divine command theorist. He held to deontology because of William of Occam,	
John Calvin	▪ acknowledged natural law, but he did not do much with it either	
	John Calvin's students	Peter Martyr Vermigli
		Jerome Zanchi
Peter Martyr Vermigli (student of Calvin, 1499-1562)	2 reasons for natural law:	To take away excuses
		To motivate us to do right and avoid wrong
Jerome Zanchi (student of Calvin, 1516-1590)	three reasons for natural law:	Self- preservation
		Procreation and education
		Worship God and do justice to neighbor

Modern Natural Law

Francisco Suarez	He wrote *Tractatus de legibus ac deo legislatore* Human beings, argued Suárez, have a natural social nature bestowed upon them by God, and this includes the potential to make laws. But when a political society is formed, the authority of the state is not of divine but of human origin; therefore, its nature is chosen by the people involved, and their natural legislative power is given to the ruler	all legislative as well as all paternal power is derived from God, and that the authority of every law resolves itself into His. Suárez refutes the patriarchal theory of government and the divine right of kings founded upon it. He argued against the sort of social-contract theory that became dominant among early-modern political philosophers
Hugo Grotius		Hugo Grotius made the connection between the natural law and international law
Samuel Pufendorf (January 8, 1632 – October 13, 1694)	German jurist, political philosopher, economist, statesman, and historian. In the *De jure naturae et gentium* Pufendorf took up in great measure the theories of Grotius and sought to complete them by means of the doctrines of Hobbes and of his own ideas.	natural law does not extend beyond the limits of this life and that it confines itself to regulating external acts. He disputed Hobbes's conception of the state of nature and concluded that the state of nature is not one of war but of peace. But this peace is feeble and insecure, and if something else does not come to its aid it can do very little for the preservation of mankind.

John Locke	based natural rights upon the natural law. All men have these rights (in opposition to the divine right of kings)	Natural rights are based upon natural law
		Natural rights include the right to:
		  ▫ Life
		  ▫ Liberty
		  ▫ Property
		It is wrong for the government to interfere with these rights

William Blackstone	William Blackstone argued for natural law in his *Commentaries on the Law of England* volume 1, section 2.	He argued that law and morality rests upon a God who set everything in order.

Positive Law		
Jeremy Bentham	Jeremy Bentham attacked Blackstone's *Commentaries on the Laws of England.*	He referred to what happened in English courts as "dog law"
		He advocated the separation of law from morality
John Austin	Austin was greatly influenced in his utilitarian approach to law by Jeremy Bentham.	best known for his work developing the theory of legal positivism. He attempted to clearly separate moral rules from "positive law."
		he viewed the law as commands from a sovereign that are backed by a threat of sanction. In determining 'a sovereign', Austin recognized it as one who society obeys habitually
Law and Economics One important trend has been the application of game theory to legal problems. Other developments have been the incorporation of behavioral economics into economic analysis of law, and the increasing use of statistical and econometrics techniques. Within the legal academy, the term socio-economics has been applied to economic approaches that are self-consciously broader than the neoclassical tradition.	**Positive Law and Economics**	uses economic analysis to predict the effects of various legal rules. Positive law and economics has been used to explain the development of legal rules, for example the common law of torts, in terms of their economic efficiency.
	Normative Law and Economics	makes policy recommendations based on the economic consequences of various policies. The key concept for normative economic analysis is efficiency, in particular, allocative efficiency.

Legal Realism

- Began in American schools of law
- It is closer to positivism than it is to natural law
- There is no single outlook shared by all of the realists
- Based on the pragmatism of Charles Sanders Peirce
- It has a pragmatic conception of the law which undermines the plausibility of orthodox legal positivism and natural law

Oliver Wendell Holmes	Holmes espoused a form of moral skepticism and opposed the doctrine of natural law, marking a significant shift in American jurisprudence.	In *Abrams v. United States* (1919), he regarded the United States Constitution as "an experiment, as all life is an experiment" and believed that as a consequence "we should be eternally vigilant against attempts to check the expression of opinions that we loathe and believe to be fraught with death."
Critical Legal Theory Many founding American Critical Legal Theory scholars were profoundly influenced by the experiences of the civil rights movement, women's rights movement, and the anti-war movement of the 1960s and 1970s.	It is a critical stance towards the dominant legal ideology of modern Western society.	**Feminist Legal Theory**
		Black Legal Theory
		Queer Legal Theory
	Sociology of Law consists of various sociological approaches to the study of law in society.	These approaches empirically examine and theorize the interaction between law and legal institutions, on the one hand, and other (non-legal) social institutions and social factors, on the other

Law and Economics

- Economic concepts are used to explain the effects of laws, to assess which legal rules are economically efficient, and to predict which legal rules will be promulgated.
- Because of the overlap between legal systems and political systems, some of the issues in law and economics are also raised in political economy, constitutional economics and political science.
- Most formal academic work done in law and economics is broadly within the Neoclassical tradition
- Economics is not everything. Other considerations like morality are important

Positive Law	uses economic analysis to predict the effects of various legal rules. So, for example, a positive economic analysis of tort law would predict the effects of a strict liability rule as opposed to the effects of a negligence rule. Positive law and economics has also at times purported to explain the development of legal rules, for example the common law of torts, in terms of their economic efficiency.
Normative Law	*Normative law and economics* goes one step further and makes policy recommendations based on the economic consequences of various policies. The key concept for normative economic analysis is efficiency, in particular, allocative efficiency.
Pareto Efficiency	A legal rule is Pareto efficient if it could not be changed so as to make one person better off without making another person worse off. A weaker conception of efficiency is Kaldor-Hicks efficiency. A legal rule is Kaldor-Hicks efficient if it could be made Pareto efficient by some parties compensating others as to offset their loss.
Socio-Economics	One important trend has been the application of game theory to legal problems. Other developments have been the incorporation of behavioral economics into economic analysis of law, and the increasing use of statistical and econometrics techniques. Within the legal academy, the term socio-economics has been applied to economic approaches that are self-consciously broader than the neoclassical tradition.

American Legal Ethics

The source of the technical legal terms "matter of fact" and "matter of law" and the usage of "guilty" and "not guilty" (rather than "innocent") in legal terminology		
Ethical Theory	Legal ethics are inherently **deontological**- rule based	whether any particular action on the part of an officer of the court is ethical is dependent on competing obligations that that officer may have
	Legal ethics are internally consistent, but not necessarily consistent with a metaphysical realist conception of morality.	
Theory of Truth the goal of the American adversarial system is justice rather than truth: **Example**- John commits a robbery and is arrested and tried for the robbery, but at trial, a jury acquits John. John did actually commit the robbery, so he is guilty of robbery as a matter of fact, but a jury found him to be not guilty so as a matter of law, John is not guilty.	**Correspondence theory of truth**	-The statement "John is guilty of robbery" is true when the correspondence theory of truth is applied to his circumstance. (He is guilty as a matter of fact.)
	Coherence Theory of Truth	-While not innocent, "John is not guilty of robbery" is true when a coherence theory of truth is applied to his circumstance. (The statement is coherent with its context: He is not guilty as a matter of law.)
Due Process	a concept to insure a level playing field for all who come before the court	

Business Law: Property Rights	
Natural Law	Property rights are conferred from natural laws
Positive Law	Rights are a legal fiction
Legal Realism	Property rights are not sancrosanct
Law and Economics	Property rights are essential

Business Law: Contracts	
Types of Law	**Consequences**
Natural Law	Contracts are rooted in the right of self-determination. Enforceable because of natural rights
Legal Positivism	Contracts are private law because the source of the la.ws are private individuals. Enforceable as long as it does not transgress public law
Legal Realism	Contracts are private law because the source of the laws are private individuals. Enforceable outside of the legal system
Law and Economics	Contracts are private law because the source of the laws are private individuals. . Enforceable as long as it does not transgress public law

Business Law: Corporations	
Type of Law	**Consequences**
Natural Law	Corporate law is rooted in partnership, which flows out of contract law
Positive Law	Corporations are legal fictions designed to shield owners from personal liability
Legal Realism	Corporations are legal fictions that may or may not exist in reality irrespective of the law. Corporations do have legal personhood.
Law and Economics	Corporations are aggregates of contracts so a corporation has no legal personhood.

Business Law	
Types of Law	**Consequences**
Natural Law	Tort liability comes from transgressing the natural rights of another
Positive Law	Liability arises from transgressing the civil rights of another
Legal Realism	Liability arises from committing a wrong against another
Law and Economics	Liability arises from transgressing the civil rights of another

Business/ Environmental Law	
Types of Law	**Consequences**
Natural Law	**Pigouvian taxation and regulation** moves the equilibrium to the social optimal position **Coasian bargaining** reduces transaction costs and respects property rights
Positive Law	**Pigouvian taxation and regulation** moves the equilibrium to the social optimal position
Legal Realism	**Pigouvian taxation and regulation** moves the equilibrium to the social optimal position
Law and Economics	**Coasian bargaining** reduces transaction costs and respects property rights

Sociology of Religion

Secularization is sometimes credited both to the cultural shifts in society following the enlightenment and the development of science. As the responsibility for education has moved from the family and community to the state, two consequences have arisen:

- *Collective conscience* as defined by Emile Durkheim is diminished
- Fragmentation of communal activities leads to religion becoming more a matter of individual choice rather than an observed social obligation.

A major issue in the study of secularization is the extent to which certain trends such as decreased attendance at places of worship indicate a decrease in religiosity or simply a privatization of religious belief, where religious beliefs no longer play a dominant role in public life or in other aspects of decision making.

Max Weber	Author of The Protestant Work Ethic and the Spirit of Capitalism	called secularization the "disenchantment of the world"—and to the changes made by religious institutions to compensate.
Peter Berger	Professor at Boston University Author of **The Sacred Canopy**	Berger believes that modernization does not require secularization theory, but does involve pluralization theory
Charles Taylor	Professor at Harvard University Author of **The Secular Age**	Major proponent of secularization theory- it suggests that modernity would result in a decline in religion Secularization theory did not pass the test of time.
Jose Casanova	Professor at Georgetown University	He argues that modernity results in privatization- religion becomes a private matter. Modernity does not result in a decline in religious belief or practice
Grace Davies	Professor at University of Exeter	She views the church as a public utility. She developed the concept of **Vicarious Religion-** people who are not involved in a church still want the church there. She thinks that pluralization leads to relativization

Sociology of Religion Concepts

According to Peter Berger Revival of Religion	
Today every religion in the world is experiencing revival. Evangelical Protestantism and Islam are the two biggest religions experiencing revival. Evangelical Protestantism is changing the world, the most significant part is Pentecostalism. There are possible 130 million Christians in China- around 10%	
A Nation State versus religion	
A nation is a language with an army. The exception is Switzerland with four languages. China views Christianity as good because it is productive and bad because it leads to democracy. Only the U.S.A. has church/ state separation	
Pluralization results in:	
• 1st in freedom • 2nd relativism- all we have is our own narrative- all are supposedly equal • 3rd Fundamentalism- any organized attempt to return to the certainty of doctrine	
Fundamentalism	**Reconquista**	re-establish ideas on the whole society – Requires totalitarianism – Very difficult in the modern world
	Sectarian or sub-cultural	only on sub-culture within society – i.e. Amish, Mennonites
Social Consequences of Revival	**Islam**	women in general are put into socially inferior position
	Protestantism	women are emancipated and men are domesticated by their wives – There is no Protestant equivalent to Sharia law
	The Roman Catholic Church	is still very influential
Religious Freedom	• Reduces violence • Is a universal human right • Brings with it bundled commodities – Freedom of the press – Economic freedom – Freedom for women – Better healthcare	

Sociology of Religion Concepts Continued

Secularism and Atheism	<ul><li>In the Czech Republic, Estonia, and East Germany secularism is the cultural norm.</li><li>Only communist governments endorse atheism</li><li>State enforced secularism always fails.</li><li>Secularism is a point of view, not an empirical fact. It is a sociological/ political ideology</li><li>Atheism is a worldview</li></ul>	
Religion and Conflict	<ul><li>Every trouble spot in the world today has a religious component</li><li>Religious social movements can be deadly because they have cosmological significance</li><li>Religion does not cause conflict, but it makes it much worse. It makes conflict much more violent and deadly</li></ul>	
Exceptions to Religious Revival	**Cultural Elites**	these are a thin class of people who are highly educated in the humanities. They are intellectuals who control the media, education and law. They have influence far greater than their numbers
	Europe	much less religious than the rest of the world
	Turkey	was once modeled after France. As they became more democratic they have become more Islamic
	Israel	the founders of modern Israel were secular. Secular Jews do not have kids, while religious Jews have kids and vote
	India	The founders of the Indian state were secular. Most people are religious. The country is democratic.
	U.S.	has a Swedish elite with an Indian population. Democratic party is the home for the Swedes while the Republican party is the home for the Indians

Cultural Elites	
The Narrow elite	• Their jobs directly affect the nation's culture, economy, and politics • Includes top executives in the nation's largest corporations and financial institutions, legislators, lawyers, judges, journalists/ media • Fewer than 100,000
The Broad Elite	• Those who are successful within a city or region • Includes businessmen, doctors, lawyers, college faculty, media/ journalists • Top 5% economically
Characteristic of the Elite	• They are educated at elite universities: Columbia, Harvard, Princeton, Yale, Stanford, Duke, MIT, and the other ivy league schools • They are wealthier • They are healthier • They do not divorce • They plan everything for their children • They live in their own communities

Adam Smith on Economics of Religion

Wealth of Nations bk. 5, CH. 1, PT. 3, ART. 3
Of the Expense of the Institutions for the Instruction of People of all Ages

Factors of Production	**Capital**	• Tithes • Gifts • Offerings • Buildings • Equipment
	Labor	• Church staff • Church members/ workers
Entrepreneurs	Clergymen work harder when they are paid by their congregation	
	Clergymen will act rationally and will attempt to maximize their utility	
	Clergymen desire monopoly and will seek the aid of politicians to get it.	
Firms	Churches can be viewed as firms and they participate in a religious market structure	
Market Structure	With religious monopoly clergymen become lazy and immoral	
	With freedom of religion, there is a perfect competition model and pators are forced to be more flexible and creative	

Economics of Religion: Market Structure

Economics		Religion	
Perfect Competition Model	• Many buyers and sellers • Homogenous goods • Firms have ease of entry and exit • Everyone is a price taker • No spillover effects • Perfect information	**Religious Pluralism**	• Many religions: pluralism • All offer salvation • Easy to start a religion • Examples include: USA after 1963 • Spillover effects are positive externalities
Monopolistic Competition	• many firms • Firms produce differentiated goods • Everyone is a price taker • Firms have ease of entry and exit • No spillover effects • Perfect information	**Semi Pluralistic**	• Examples include: America before 1963 with Roman Catholic, Protestant and Jewish religions • Spillover effects are positive externalities
Oligopoly	• Only a few firms • Everyone is a price taker • Danger of collusion or cartels	**Semi-pluralistic**	• Examples include: Post Reformation Europe with Roman Catholic, Protestant and Jewish religions • Positive externalities • Negative externalities include religious war/conflict
Monopoly	• Only one firm • Firms have barriers to entry • The government gives a single firm the exclusive right to produce some good or service • Firm is a price maker • A single firm can produce output at a lower cost than can a larger number of firms	**Official State religion**	• Only one religion sanctioned • Very difficult to establish other religions • Religious adherence has high cost • Clergy is unresponsive • Examples: most Islamic countries, • Can produce negative externalities like lower economic growth

Religious Marketplace in the USA

U.S. Constitution	Congress shall make no law respecting an establishment of religion, or prohibiting the free exercise thereof; or abridging the freedom of speech, or of the press; or the right of the people peaceably to assemble, and to petition the Government for a redress of grievances.
The Entrepreneur	Pastors and especially church planters are social entrepreneurs. Pastors must continually seek to grow their congregations and or plant new churches
Creative Destruction	Pastors must be wise and efficient with their capital (finances, facilities, equipment) and labor (church staff, and church members) or they will lose them to other Churches who will be.
History	In the beginning, The USA had a religious market structure that was largely a monopoly of protestant denominations
	Beginning in the 1800s, there was a large immigration from Europe with many Roman Catholics. The religious market structure, became more of a monopolistic competition.
	Until 1963, the religious market structure in the USA was monopolistic competition. This was because there were mai

University of Chicago School of Economics on Religion	
Jacob Viner and Frank Knight were the founders of the University of Chicago's School of Economics.	
Jacob Viner	***The Role of Providence in the Social Order*** The essays in this book were originally presented by Professor Viner as the 1966 Jayne Lectures of the American Philosophical Society. The relationship between religious doctrines and economic theory and behavior had long interested Professor Viner, and the conclusions he disc ussed represented years of thoughtful study. They focus in particular on the way in which providence was used to justify existing economic and social conditions.
	Providence, as an intelligent being, external to nature but governing nature, is an idea common to most religions. The term, or its equivalent in various languages, is often used also to signify the pattern in which that supernatural being conducts his operations (4)
	The generalist framework of providentialist doctrine was thus set initially largely in terms of the relation of God to the physical order of the cosmos he had created, and on the path to immortal life he had established for mankind. (5)
	There is no logical conflict between a socially oriented teleology and individualism if the individual either has conscious social ends without having adopted them as his own ultimate objective. (60).
	Adam Smith thought that man's "psychological apparatus is providential; it is designed by God for the benefit of mankind, and it is presumptuous for man, even if he be a moral philosopher, or especially if he be a moral philosopher, to find flaws in it." (81)
	Providence favors trade among peoples in order to promote universal brotherhood; providence also creates social inequality because it is part of the Divine plan. Providence designed a world in which commerce was necessary, in which good business benefited not only the individual but all of mankind, in which inequality in rank and income was part of the scheme of things.

University of Chicago School of Economics on Religion (Continued)

Frank Knight	*The Economic Order and Religion* (Knight and Merriam [1945] 1979
	As the old saying went at Chicago, "there is no God, but Frank Knight is his prophet." Knight did not consider himself a Christian—indeed, he was famous for his antagonism to traditional religion (Kern 1988). When the time came to deliver his presidential address to the American Economic Association in 1950, Knight self-consciously labeled it his "sermon" to the profession (Knight 1951). In teaching his economics courses, Knight was, as Patinkin observed, prone to engage in "long digressions on the nature of man and society—and God" (1981, 46). The core social and economic problem in Knight's view was one of "discovery and definition of values—a moral, not to say a religious, problem," which stood in great contrast to progressive aspira- tions to the "value-free" scientific management of society (Knight 1936, 52).

Economics of Religion: Political Economy and Religiosity	
Robert Barro and Rachel McCleary: Religion and Political Economy in an International Panel, 2002. They investigated the way that economic and political developments affect religiosity and vice versa. In this study, they used data gathered over a twenty year period for fifty-nine different countries.	
State Religion	State religion promotes monopoly and therefore, poor service and low rates of church attendance."
	State religion results in a low degree of religious pluralism.
Religious Belief	An increase in religious beliefs (at least belief in heaven) or a decrease in church attendance tends to stimulate economic growth."
Religiosity	The measures of religiosity are positively related to education and negatively to urbanization.
Church Attendance	Enhanced life expectancy and reduced fertility are inversely related to church attendance but have weak associations with religious beliefs."

Barro and McCleary: Religion and Economic Growth, 2003

Focused on the relationship between religion and economic growth. They used data from 87 countries. They sought to "determine how church attendance and beliefs co-vary with per capita GDP, education, and urbanization, while holding fixed other measures of economic development and the other independent variables."

Economic Growth	Economic growth responds positively with religious beliefs, notably those in heaven and hell, but negatively to church attendance.
	There is a weak correlation with economic growth when church attendance and religious beliefs "move together."
	Roman Catholicism and Muslim religious services was higher than for other religions. The same is true for belief in heaven and hell.
	Higher religious beliefs stimulate growth because they help to sustain aspects of individual behavior that enhance productivity.
	Higher church attendance is accompanied by lower economic growth because of a larger use of resources by the religion sector. In other words, the social capital associated with higher church attendance is expensive.
Religiosity	Increases in GDP result in decreased religiosity.
	There is a causal relationship between GDP and religiosity. The more the economic growth a country experiences, the less religious the people become.
	The existence of a state religion increases religiosity. This is the result of government subsidies to the state religion.
	Government regulation of the religious marketplace reduces religiosity.
	Religiosity is positively related to education and the presence of children and negatively related to urbanization

Religion and Society

Faith and Economics, Number 55, Spring 2010

Love thy Neighbor as thyself: Community Formation and the Church

Authored by Thomas Deliere, Thomas Jeitschko, Seamus O'Connell, Rowena A. Pecchenino

A **secular equilibrium** is always in existence that is based upon the state and culture.	

If secular equilibrium is unbalanced by **Religious Equilibrium** then society may unravel. Men are inherently moral creatures and the church provides moral norms that ensure a civil society. A **Religious Equilibrium** exists when a minimum level of religious devotion exists and a minimum level of financial resources

Moral Authority of the Church	An equilibrium in which agents sustain religious participation does not exist if the Church lacks sufficient moral authority
Church Membership	In the religious equilibrium, an increase in Church membership yields higher religious participation by individual members and results in higher levels of spirituality and over-all wellbeing
Church Doctrine and Leadership	In religious equilibrium, a strengthening of Church doctrine and an improvement of the quality of Church leadership yields higher religious participation by members and results in higher levels of spirituality and over-all wellbeing.
Financial Resources	In the religious equilibrium, an increase in the financial resources available to the Church yields higher religious participation by members and results in higher levels of spirituality and over-all wellbeing
Leisure	In the religious equilibrium, an increase in the socially minimal requirements on time spent at leisurely activities yields diminished religious participation by members and results in lower levels of spirituality and overall wellbeing.

Separation of Church and State	
Separation of Church and state is a modern idea that developed over a long period of time. It is similar to, but quite different from religious liberty. The two go hand in hand. The Treaty of Westphalia (1648 AD) resulted in the formation of the modern nation- state. This meant that every country has its own territory and could determine its own state religion.	
William of Ockham 1287- 1347	Ockham made a theological argument for separation of church and state. He was motivated to do so because of a heretical pope (John XXII and his successors).
Jean Bodin 1530- 1596	Bodin was influenced by philosophical Judaism, but it is not clear what his religious convictions were. He created the concept of the divine right of kings. This divine right does not mean that the state has a requirement to enforce religious doctrine. Consequently, he argued against the use of compulsion in religious matters. In his *Colloquium of the Seven* (1588), it is clear that he is also an early advocate of religious liberty.
Thomas Jefferson 1743- 1826	In 1777 he drafted the Virginia Statute for Religious Freedom. He later interpreted the first amendment in the Bill of Rights to mean that there is "a wall of separation between church and state." He was motivated to do this by Baptists (Isaac Backus and others from the Danbury Connecticut Baptist Association). They feared the power and problems of state churches.

Religious Liberty

Name	Book	Description
Thomas Helwys, 1575 (?) – 1616	***A Short Declaration on the Mystery of Inquity***	He states that Scripture demonstrates that the first and second beasts of the Great Tribulation ought to be identified with the Roman Catholic Pope and Anglican Church hierarchy respectively. Due to their demands upon the people to believe and obey their own word or face punishment, these two dishonor Christ by assuming honor due only to Him.
John Milton, 1608–1674	***Areopagitica***	Milton wrote *Areopagitica* in 1644 in an effort to demonstrate that truth prevails no matter what temporary victories lies and half-truths might enjoy. *Areopagitica* was an answer to the 1643 Order of Parliament that forbade the publication of unlicensed works. Why, according to Milton, should the state or the church attempt to interfere with the dissemination of ideas for fear that those ideas might be false and thus lead people astray? Truth will prevail on its own and needs no help from the state or the church to triumph over falsehood. *Areopagitica* is a treatise defending freedom of speech
Roger Williams, 1603–1683	***The Bloody Tenant of Persecution***	Williams' entire work defends the freedom of every person to follow the religious dictates of his conscience, and that the church and the state have distinct jurisdictions. Williams did not restrict his views of religious freedom to the various sects of Christianity, but to people of all faiths, which makes his position on religious liberty quite unique

Name	Book	Description
John Locke, 1632–1704	***Letter Concerning Toleration***	Locke wrote *A Letter Concerning Toleration* as a self-professed Christian, and based his convictions regarding religious freedom largely on Christ's example. Locke wrote that the civil government had no jurisdiction in religion. Second, civil government enforces temporal laws through the compulsion of physical force, while the truths of religion are practiced and adhered to through the persuasion of the mind. Third, if soul-care were within the jurisdiction of the civil power, then salvation would be tied solely to citizenship within the state which possessed the true religion. For Locke, this was absurd.
William Penn - 1644-1718	***The Great Case of Liberty of Conscience***	*The Great Case* was written "to the Supreme Authority of England," *The Great Case* is nothing less than a plea for toleration, on the basis that liberty of conscience is a matter of faith, that only God can compel religious belief, and to violate one's conscience on matters pertaining to faith is sin. Violations of liberty perpetuated by the state upon the population are contrary to the Christian faith in general practice, contrary to Scripture, contrary to reason, contrary to the nature of government, and contrary to history. Furthermore, they are thoroughly hypocritical. Protestants in the

Henri Bergson on the Nature of Society		
Human Nature	Change is deeply grounded in human nature. Consequently, societies generally become more open over time	
Religion	Arises as a kind of mental habit that binds human intelligence to the instinctive drive for solidarity and continuity. All types of religion points people beyond themselves and causes them to carry conviction.	
	Static Religion	The call of instinct. An essential aspect of a closed society
	Dynamic Religion	Calls people towards an open society. It can take many forms. Mysticism (especially Roman Catholic) is often a driving force for an open society. An essential part of an open society
Closed Society	Based on tradition and archaic rules. Static religion is an essential aspect of a closed society.	
Open Society	The type of society in which the human drive for change can be fulfilled. It is based on ideals and aspirations. Dynamic religion is an essential aspect of an open society.	
Every Society	Every society has open and closed elements. Most attempts at open societies fail. In the best cases, some of these attempts at an open society achieve a partial success over time.	

Chapter 4: Public Administration

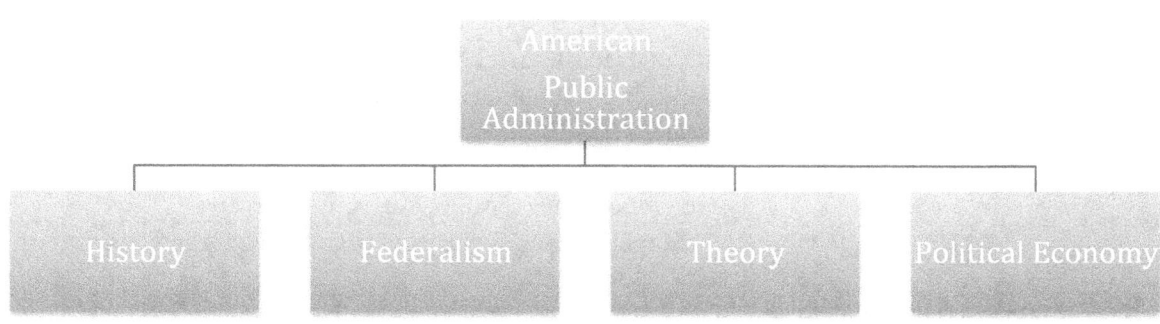

John Stuart Mill:
Considerations on Representative Government

According to Beth E. Warner, "John Stuart Mill is reported to have been one of the prime "democratic theorists because of his work toward inclusion and his emphasis on public participation in government."

First Governing Elite	Interested voters who make the effort to take part in public affairs, to be informed, and to conscientiously cast the best possible vote for the public good
	These provide an enlightened tone to the electorate
The Wise Representative	Chosen from among the people who have intellect, education, experience and dedication to governing
	Have a moral duty to govern according to their own wisdom
	Must be responsible to the voters
	Charged only with the task of legislating
	Is strictly limited from interfering with the bureaucracy
Third Governing Elite Bureaucrats are the actual governors	Assigned the task of administering
	Have skill, experience and practical knowledge
	Is responsible for providing public policy feedback to representatives and citizens to make better choices
	Problems include, control, accountability and responsibility
Good Government	Has the principles of competence and citizen participation
	Is measured by "the degree to which it tends to increase the sum of good qualities in the governed
	The degree of perfection with which they organize the moral, intellectual and active worth already existing, so as to operate with the greatest effect on public affairs
Private Citizens	Should receive moral instruction
	Are responsible for choosing good governors
	Participation in government gives the citizen a feeling of self- esteem and belonging
	Citizen participation improves both citizens and government
Representative Government	Prescribed for the dangers of democracy
	The best form of government in both practice and theory because it combines complete popular control over public affairs with the greatest attainable perfection of skilled agency.
	Diverse interests are represented
	One of several mechanisms that improves the intellectual level of the citizenry

"Bureaucracy" by Max Weber			
Part 1 Characteristics of Bureaucracy	I.	There is the principle of fixed and official jurisdictional areas, which are generally ordered by rules, that is laws or administrative regulations	
	II.	The principles of office hierarchy and of levels of graded authority mean a firmly ordered system of super and subordination in which there is a supervision of the lower offices by the higher ones	
	I.	The management of the modern office is based upon written documents, which are preserved in their original or draught form.	
	II.	Office management, at least all specialized office management and such management is distinctly modern- usually presupposes thorough and expert training.	
	III.	When the office is fully developed, official activity demands the full working capacity of the official, irrespective of the fact that his obligatory time in the bureau may be firmly delimited.	
	IV.	The management of the office follows general rules, which are more or less stable, more or less exhaustive, and which can be learned.	
Part 2 The Position of the Official	I.	Office holding is a vocation	
	II.	The personal position of the official is patterned in the following way:	1. The modern official always enjoys a distinct social esteem as compared with the governed
			2. The pure type of bureaucratic official is appointed by a superior authority.
			3. Normally, the position of the official is held for life, at least in public bureaucracies
			4. The official receives the compensation of a normally fixed salary and the old age security provided by a pension.

Types of Public Administration based on the Founding Fathers			
	Alexander Hamilton	**James Madison**	**Thomas Jefferson**
Party	Federalist-Whig Republican	Federalist-Whig Republican	Anti-Federalist, Democrat
Presidency	Wanted the president to be like a king		Wanted the president to be like a common man
Public Administration Dichotomy	Energetic president able to control day to day operations of the government	General distrust of administrative power	Elected legislature exercising direct and heavy control over the president
Bureaucracy Government should be kept small to protect individual liberties	Desired government to be activist and under the control of a strong executive.	Emphasized the separation of powers.	Emphasized strong state rights
Economics	The architect of U.S. political economy. His system was designed to use financial means for achieving political, economic and social ends.	Public Choice-Agent Theory is consistent with Madison's beliefs	
	Influenced by Adam Smith and free markets	Had no well-formed thought of political economy	Influenced by the French physiocrats
	Wanted a strong national economy.	Wanted a strong national economy.	Emphasized small agrarian economy based on local communities
	Established the first Bank of the United States to establish public credit. He thought that this would result in a strong and stable government		

Basic Principles of Various Government Models

Confederal System	1. League of equal and sovereign members 2. Abstinence on part of central government from internal administration or governance 3. Member units only effect people directly 4. Equal suffrage of member units
Unitary System	1. All power resides in central government 2. Central government only operates directly on people 3. Member units serve as administrative arms of central government 4. Central government can alter or abolish member units
Federal System	1. Constitutional division (or sharing) of governmental powers 2. Each government supreme in its own sphere 3. Both governments act directly over people 4. Both derive their power from the constitution 5. neither dependent upon the other for its existence

The Articles of Confederation

Based upon the Iroquois Confederacy, which had existed since the 14th or 15th century. Known as the "Great Law of Peace" which describes a federal union of five (and later six) Indian nations. Benjamin Franklin was greatly influenced by this model of government. He followed the advice of Canassatego (speaker of the Onandaga) that the colonies form a similar government. The Articles of the Confederation were agreed to by Congress November 15, 1777, ratified in force, March 1, 1781.

Article	Explanation
Preamble	To all to whom these presents shall come, we the undersigned Delegates of the states affixed to our names send greeting.
1	The style of this Confederacy shall be "The United States of America"
2	Each state retains its sovereignty, freedom and independence
3	The said states enter into a firm **league of friendship** for their common defense, the security of their liberties and their mutual and general welfare
4	Laws of other states to be abided by, including extradition. Full faith and credit shall be given in each of these states to the records, acts and judicial proceedings of the courts and magistrates of every other state
5	For the general interests of the United States, delegates shall be annually appointed as the legislatures of each state shall direct. The states retain the power to recall those delegates. Each state shall have one vote.
6	Rights denied the states the right to establish their own embassies or to establish treaties, allies, etc. with other countries without the express consent of the United States
7	Appointment of military officers by the states for the common defense limits their rank to colonel.
8	All costs of war shall be paid out of a common treasury. The Congress shall determine how much and how long the states will have to pay taxes to pay for such costs.
9	The Congress of the United States has the express privilege of determining war or peace.
10	The committee of the states
11	Canada may join the United States
12	Assumption of Debt
13	Every state shall abide by the determination of the United States Congress on all questions which by their confederation are submitted to them. The union is perpetual and no changes are allowed without agreement.

Vices of the Political System of the United States By James Madison

Written by James Madison in April 1787. This provided fodder for the Constitutional Convention later that year.

Article	Explanation
1	Failure of the States to comply with the Constitutional requisitions
2	Encroachments by the States on the Federal authority
3	Violations of the law and of treaties
4	Trespasses of the States on the rights of each other
5	Want of concert in matters where the common interest requires it
6	Want of gauranty to the States of their Constitutions and laws against internal violence
7	Want of sanction to the laws, and of coercion in the government of the Confederacy
8	Want of ratification by the people of the articles of Confederation
9	Multiplicity of laws in the several States
10	Mutability of the laws of the States
11	Injustice in the laws of the States
Causes	The representative States
	The People themselves — Representatives are sought from motives of 1.ambition, 2. personal interest, and 3 public good. Most come from 1 and 2
	The different factions of the people themselves who vie for power and take advantage of the others

Montesquieu vs. Madison			
	size	government	powers
Montesquieu	Small societies	Federal republic (confederacy)	Separation of powers
Madison	Large society (empire)	Compound republic (federalism)	Separation of powers

Federalism and Public Policy

Advantages	Policy experimentation and innovation	"It is one of the happy incidents of the federal system that a single state may, if its citizens choose, serve as a laboratory, and try novel social and economic experiments without risk to the rest of the country." Louis Brandeis
		Unemployment compensation- Wisconsin
		Child labor laws- Massachusetts
		Progressive income tax- Wisconsin
		Minimum wage- Oregon
		Suffrage for women- Colorado
		Direct election of senators
	Customized or tailored policy making	
	Multiple points of access	
Disadvantages	**Achieving national goals and objectives**	
	Local abuses of power	
	Inequities in resources and services	

Federalism and Public Opinion

Health of Federalism	Regional Equity	Each region is treated the same
	Balance of trust within levels	Each member of every level trusts one another
	Federal Political Culture	See below
Federal Political Culture	Tolerance of cultural, racial and ethnic differences	Strife is minimized
	Willingness to compromise	Members need to both give, take, and work with each other
	Values Consensus	If the members work together and will seek to make the greater number happier
	Values broad participation in decision- making	Every member is requested to help make decisions
	Values decentralized decision- making and local units	No one member makes decisions for the rest

The History of American Federalism

Over time, the federal government and the states have had a changing relationship.

Nation Centered Federalism 1787-1860s	1. National government is free to expand authority unless specifically prohibited by the constitution 2. When states and national government are in dispute, the states must give way 3. National government can judge acts of Congress and of the states as constitutional
State Centered Federalism 1787-1860s	1. National government has delegated powers only 2. National government has no right to judge constitutionality of state actions 3. States have right to nullify actions within their boundaries
Dual Federalism 1860-1930s "layer cake philosophy"	1. Separate spheres of legitimate authority 2. Spheres should not encroach upon one another 3. Role of the courts to referee in case of conflicts 4. Court rulings are generally friendly to the states 5. Beginning of grants in aid

Cooperative Federalism 1930-1970s "marble cake philosophy"	**The New Deal 1930s -1960s**	1. Shared federal/ state activities 2. Court rulings generally favorable to the national government 3. Growth of grants in aid
	The Great Society 1960s- 1970s	1. Explosion of grants in aid 2. Direct federal aid to city programs 3. Strong emphasis on nationally set priorities and goals 4. Functional shift in grants from "bricks and mortar" to social needs

Coercive Federalism 1970-2000s	1. Increasing use of federal mandates and preemptions 2. Court decisions favorable to the national government
Rediscovered Federalism 2000-present	1. Increasing state challenges to federal legislation 2. Increasing policy activism at state level 3. state friendly court decisions

Landmark Supreme Court Decisions

Marbury vs Madison 1803	Established the Supreme court as the final arbiter of the Constitution
Green vs Biddle 1823	Concerned the "necessary and Proper" clause as well as the "national supremacy." The national government is supreme
Gibbons vs Ogden 1824	Recognizes the U.S. Supreme Court authority to declare a state law unconstitutional.
Massachusetts vs Mellon 1923	States cannot interfere with interstate commerce
Wickard vs Filburn 1942	Upheld as constitutional distribution of federal aid to the states
Garcia vs San Antonio 1985	Congress can use interstate commerce powers to regulate local activity. Roosevelt threatened to stack the court and limit the age of Supreme Court justices to 70. This resulted in the court deciding this way.
South Dakota vs Dole 1987	Local governments must adhere to minimum wage standards set by Congress
United states vs Lopez 1995	Invalidated the 1990 federal Gun-Free School Zones Act. Thus limiting the reach of the federal governments use of the interstate commerce clause.
U.S. vs Morrison 2000	Struck down the 1994 Violence Against Women act, which permitted victims of crimes "motivated by gender" to sue in federal court.
Gonzales vs Raich 2005	Congress can criminalize the production of home grown cannabis, even when states approve its use for medical purposes.
Arizona vs U.S. 2012	Struck down parts of Arizona's immigration law and affirmed national supremacy in such matters.
U.S. Department of Health and Human Services vs Florida	Upheld major portions of Obamacare

Federal Grant in Aid Programs		
Categorical specific, well defined by the federal government	**Formula-**	distributed based on formula
	Project-	competitive
Block Grants	Favored by republicans, state and local governments TANF is an example	
Grants in Aid: Pro	Cheap money	
	Expands state/ local opportunities and service options	
	Equalizes resources	
Grants in Aid: Con	Skews state spending	
	Costly, because they require matching funds	
	Creates constituents dependent on programs	

History of Federal Grants
to State and Local Governments

Date	Name	Explanation
1785	**Articles of Confederation**	Land grants to townships for public schools
1817		Land grant to Hartfiord Deaf and Dumb Asylum in Connecticut
1836	**Surplus Distribution Act**	Returned 28 million to states based on representation in Congress
Pre 1860		Numerous grants of land to states as well as private developers for railroad expansion, roads, highways and etc.
1862	**Morrill Act**	Land grants to establish universities
1879		Grants to states for distribution of educational materials for blind students
1913	**16ᵗʰ Amendment**	Federal income tax
1916	**Federal Aid to Highways Act**	This is the first "modern" grant
1923	**Massachusetts vs Mellon**	Supreme Court upheld the constitutionality of grants to states
1930s	**Roosevelt's New Deal**	
1960-1970	**LBJ's Great Society**	More than doubled the number and dollar amount of all previous grants. Grants are made directly to cities for the first time.
1970s-1980s	**General Revenue Sharing and Block Grants**	
1987	**South Dakota vs Dole**	Courts approves use of sanctions. The condition is merely a "pressure and not a compulsion."

Horizontal Federalism

This can also be called federalism without Washington D.C. or governmental communication

Coordination/ Fragmentation	**Positive Features**	Freedom of choice for individuals
		Competition drives governments to economize and be more efficient
	Negative Features	Coordination of service delivery and adequacy of service provision
		Efficient and effective use of scarce resources
		Equity of problem and resource distribution
Solutions (article IV)	**Full faith and credit**	Full faith and credit shall be given to each state in public acts records and proceedings of every other state
	Privileges and immunities	The citizens of each state shall be entitled to all privileges and immunities of citizens in the several states
	Extradition	A person charged in any state with treason, felony, or other crime, who shall flee from justice, and be found in another state, shall on demand of the executive authority at the state from which he fled, be delivered up, to be removed to the state having jurisdiction of the crime.
	Interstate Compacts	No state shall, without the consent of congress enter into any compact with any other state.
		Once enacted states may not be unilaterally renounced, except as provided by the compact itself.
		Unlike treaties, compacts are not solely dependent upon the good will of the parties
		Congress and the courts can compel compliance with the terms of interstate compacts
	Uniform state laws	Seeks adoption of identical or similar laws by all of the states

Interstate Compacts: Advantages and Disadvantages		
Advantages	Flexible and enforceable	
	Interstate uniformity without federal intervention	
	States maintain collective sovereignty	
	Alternative to federal pre-emption	
Disadvantages	Lengthy and challenging process	
	Lack of familiarity with mechanism among state government officials and the public	
	Perceived loss of individual state sovereignty	
	Delegation of state regulatory authority to an interstate agency	

States and City Governmental Relations

Four dimensions of regional governance:

1. The state and the constituent local governments
2. The relationships among the local governments
3. Collaboration between local governments and organizations in nonprofit and private sectors
4. Local governments and the regional institutions like the Metropolitan Planning Organization

Dillon's Rule	Cities are creatures of the state. Hence, cities can only do what states allow.
Home Rule	Some states grant cities a certain amount of latitude.

Solutions	**City-county consolidation**	• Incentives to consolidate are small • The extent to which money is saved in a merger depends on the design of the new government
		Types of consolidation include: 1. Full 2. Two- tier or federal approach is not total consolidation 3. Regional or unitary
		Confederal
	Councils of Government	**COGs do not:** 1. Raise taxes 2. Legislate 3. Deliver services
		COGs do: 1. Serve as a form for regional discussion 2. Gather and disseminate region-wide data 3. Serves as a regional training center 4. Review and approve federal funding for regional projects

States and City Governmental Relations
Continued

Solutions	**Special Districts**	**Advantages:** 1. Easily formed 2. Cross jurisdictional boundaries 3. Circumvent taxing limitations **Disadvantages:** 1. Tend to be invisible to voters 2. Multiplication of government units Characteristics: 1. Perform a single function 2. Taxing 3. May cross boundaries of other jurisdictions 4. Government boards may be elected or appointed
	Interlocal Contracting	**Types of interlocal contracts:** 1. Fee for service 2. Joint enterprise agreements 3. Stand by arrangements to provide service under certain conditions
	Annexation	Motivations for annexation: 1. Increase tax base for city 2. Growth management 3. Pressure by developers 4. Possibility of vote dilution
	Consolidation	

Cities in the U.S. Federal System

When the U.S Constitution was formed, the country was largely rural. Only 30, 000 people lived in NYC at the time of ratification. Consequently, there is no mention of cities in the U.S. Constitution. There is no federal "Department of City Affairs. " Cities do not have representation in the Senate. The Great Society represented a dramatic change in federal/ city relations because grants were made directly to cities (often with strings attached).

The U.S. had the first federal system of government, but it was followed by many others. Constitutions in other countries with federal systems of government will normally include the federal government, states and municipalities.

Dillon's Rule	**1868 case:** "Municipal corporations owe their origin to, and derive their powers and rights wholly from, the legislature. It breathes into them the breath of life, without which they cannot exist. As it creates, so it may destroy. If it may destroy, it may abridge and control." **The city is a creature of the state.**
	1872 case: (Municipal Corporations) Dillon explained that in contrast to the powers of the states, which are unlimited but for express restrictions under the state or federal constitution, municipalities only have the poers that are expressly granted to them. This formulation of the scope of municipal power came to be known as the "Dillon Rule." Any ambiguities in the legislative grant of power should be resolved against the municipality so that its powers are narrowly construed.
Home Rule	**Home rule** is the power of a constituent part) of a state to exercise such of the state's powers of governance within its own administration area that have been decentralized to it by the central government
	a devolved home rule system of government is created by ordinary legislation and can be reformed, or even abolished, by repeal or amendment of that ordinary legislation.. A state legislation may, for example, create home rule for a county or parish, so that a county commission orboard of supervisors may have jurisdiction over its unincorporated areas, including important issues like zoning. Without this, a U.S. county is simply an extension of state government. The legislature can also establish or eliminate municpal corporations, which have home rule within town or city limits through the city council. The state government could also abolish counties/townships, or their governments, according to the state constitution and state laws.
	Home Rule Charters- Missouri was the first state to grant Home Rule Charters in 1875. Other states soon followed by making constitutional amendments for home rule. These charters may not contain any provision that is inconsistent with the state constitution or statutes. Home Rule Charters in Texas are stronger than cities in any other state according to the **Advisory Commission on Intergovernmental Relations**
Forms of city Government	**Council- manager**
	Mayor-Council
	Commission

History of U. S. Public Administration

Date	Event	Explanation
	Iriquois nations	This document unites 6 different Indian nations and served as an example for the Articles of Confederation.
1776	Articles of Confederation	First document that establishes a United states. It fails because the states have all of the power.
1787	U.S. Constitution	Madison was the primary author. Used the ideas of Montesquieu. Emphasized the separation of powers to prevent tyranny
1835/ 40	Alexis de Tocqueville	He explains that there is no public administration in the U.S.
1861	John Stuart Mill	*Considerations on Representative Government* This is a work on public administration.
1865	Civil War	Strengthened the federal Government. The states do not have the right to secede. Contra Calhoun, the Constitution is not a compact between the states.
1883	Pendleton Act	First rules for federal employees.
1887	Woodrow Wilson	Writes article about public administration. Explains the politic- administration dichotomy
	Interstate Commerce Act	Industrialization and urbanization
1913	16th Ammendment	The income tax instituted. The federal government grows because of the increase in revenue
	Federal Reserve System	The U.S. gets a strong central bank
1921	Budgeting and Accounting Act	The line item budget comes into existence for the federal government
1934		Control over foreign immigration
1979	Inspector General's Act	A system to root out corruption

"The Study of Administration" by Woodrow Wilson

Woodrow Wilson played a significant role in the development of American public administration. As a professor of jurisprudence and political economy at Princeton University, he was a strong advocate of public administration rather than political philosophy

Part I **What Others** **have said**	Wilson notes that the study of public administration is of recent vintage. Instead of administration, political writers set their focus only on the constitution of government. Wilson explains that "The functions of government were simple, because life itself was simple. Government went about imperatively and compelled men, without thought of consulting their wishes. There was no complex system of public revenues and public debts to puzzle financiers; there were, consequently, no financiers to be puzzled (Wilson, 1887, 23)." With the coming of the American democratic republic politics obviously became much more complex. American democracy requires for the government to consider the thoughts and feeling of the voters. There are so many types of complications that did not exist until Wilson's time that the invention of public administration was relatively late in its coming to America.
Part II **What is the** **subject matter**	Wilson understood that public administration is a hybrid creature which must be properly developed and learned. Wilson believed that "there should be a science of administration which shall seek to straighten the paths of government, to make its business less "unbusinesslike," to strengthen and purify its organization, and to crown its dutifulness (Wilson, 1887, 24)." He realized that what had passed for public administration in this country was not sufficient to meet the needs of the new age. Efficiency, reliability, and consistency were obviously not the order of government in his day. He later explains that administration "is a field of business (28)." At the same time, Wilson acknowledges that administration "is closely connected with the study of the proper distribution of constitutional authority(29)."
Part III **Best methods to** **develop public** **administration**	Wilson thought that all countries have the same desire in public administration (32). Consequently, one must look at Europe for a good model of public administration which could be Americanized. He also understood that one cannot apply everything from one government to another because of the differences in constitutions. Wilson understood that the federalist type of government that America has was still very new and requires the public officer to serve both his superiors and the community (34)."

The History of the
Political- Administration Dichotomy

Explanation- Begins in Woodrow Wilson's article, "The Study of Administration." It is based on the fact- value dichotomy. Politics relates to value and administration is related to facts.

Dates	Figure	Explanation
1887	**Woodrow Wilson**	Establishes politics- administration dichotomy. Politics should not meddle in administration and administration should not meddle in politics.
1946	**Dwight Waldo**	Emphasized that administration is value laden. Consequently, there is no dichotomy.
1947	**Herbert Simon**	Logical positivist who emphasizes the empirical approach to public administration. Values have no place in public administration. Consequently, there is no dichotomy.
1950s-1970s	**WWII**	The rapid growth of government required a suspension of the argument. Consequently, There was no dichotomy.
1980s	**Control of bureaucracy**	1. Politics- administration dichotomy re- emerges. 2. The significance of control of bureaucracy. theory is that it provides for the analysis of public administration by making distinctions between political and administrative acts or actions and/ or between political and administrative actors. 3. Requires that elected officials control the actions of appointed officials

The Waldo-Simon Debate on the Political-Administrative Dichotomy

By 1952, Dwight Waldo and Herbert Simon were already two preeminent theorists on the study of public administration and organizational behavior (Harmon, 1989). These two titans engaged in an exchange of words via the journal, *American Political Science Quarterly* in that year, initiated by Waldo's essay, "Development of the Theory of Public Administration." The occasion for Waldo's essay was to attack what he saw as poisonous to the democratic system of America in holding efficiency in administrative affairs as value-neutral (Waldo, 1952).

	Dwight Waldo He taught at the University of California at Berkeley and at the University of Syracuse	**Herbert Simon** He taught at the University of Chicago and at Carnegie Mellon University. He was awarded the Nobel Prize in Economics in 1978.
Books	*The Administrative State* **1946**	*Administrative Behavior* **1947**
Philosophical Presuppositions	Empiricism Pragmatism	Empiricism Logical Positivism Scientism
The Political Administration Dichotomy	This dichotomy is invalid because there is no separation of fact from value.	This dichotomy is invalid because science is only concerned with facts and there is no place for value judgments.
Conclusions	Public Administration is a part of political science, so value is inherent throughout the discipline. Science is not the one true road for doing public administration. Science should be balanced with morality	The true problem in the study of administration, noting that empirical methods allow for logical premises to overcome weak metaphor and philosophizing that are themselves detrimental to the administrative decision-making process (Simon, 1952).

Dwight Waldo
The Administrative State

It was Waldo's intent to explain "public administration movement from the viewpoint of political theory and the history of ideas (Waldo, 1948, XXIII)." He explains in the preface that this book was a refinement of his PhD dissertation at Yale University.

Part I **The Rise of Public administration**	Waldo seeks to provide a historical overview of public administration.. He focuses on people and motifs. He also addresses the use of scientific management in public administration.
Part II **The Problems of Political Philosophy**	"The object of this and the four following chapters is a more intensive review of that part of the literature of public administration that bears upon five problems in political philosophy. Each of the chapters in this part address a different problem in political philosophy. The "Good Society" that public administrators embraced is one that has made science as an ideal (66). Waldo asserts that public administrators are heavily influenced by positivism. Consequently, the criteria for action that public administrators use are "principles of public administration" as well as the twin standard of economy and efficiency (88).
Part III **Some Fundamental Concepts: A Critique**	Waldo's criticism of principles in public administration. He explains that the belief in principles is related to the belief in higher laws (162). Waldo wrote, "It would be impossible to prove, beyond question, that 'principles' in public administration in recent times have been higher law concepts (Waldo, 162)." He shows how a scientific view of administration is problematic. Waldo also explains that the other standard employed by many public administrators, efficiency and economy, are "intimately bound up with values or valuing (195."
Conclusions	Waldo believes that the future of public administration will require the development of a more substantial philosophy and ethics than existed in his day. Pragmatism is the philosophy that he thinks might fill this void. Waldo also asserts that the successful study and practice of administrative duties and policy-making alike cannot occur without a balance between both fact-based empiricism and value decisions (Waldo 1952). Making a decision means selecting from two or more alternatives, and that selection cannot occur in the absence of values (Waldo, 1952). Waldo concludes his essay by inserting a reference to Herbert Simon as an example of those leading the forces against value-decisions in public administration

Herbert Simon: *Administrative Behavior*

According Herbert Simon, *Administrative Behavior* belongs to perhaps the second generation of modern studies of organizations, following so called classical theory represented by Frederick Taylor, Fayol, and Gulick and Urwick

Chapter I	General introduction, summary and commentary	Concerned with the process of choice which leads to action.
Chapter II and III	Lays out some conceptual issues that are basic to the structure of human choice	**Chapter II:** The existing principles of administration are subjected to critical analysis to show their inadequacy and need for development
		Chapter III is concerned with the fact/ value dichotomy as it is related to administrative decision making.
Chapters IV and V	Constructs a theory that describes and explains the realities of human decision making, essential for understanding the influences that come to bear upon decision- making in an organization environment	**Chapter IV** provides a description of the conceptual apparatus that will be used throughout the rest of the volume for the description and analysis of social behavior systems, including behavior in administrative organizations
		Chapter V considers the psychology of the individual in the organization and the ways in which the organization modifies his behavior
Chapter VI	Provides a motivational link between the individual and the organization- explaining why organizational influences, and particularly the influence of authority are such effective forces in molding human behavior.	The organization will be viewed as a system of individuals whose behavior maintains some sort of equilibrium.
Chapters VII- X	Examine the main organizational influence processes- authority, communication, efficiency, and organizational loyalty- in detail in order to explain how organization affects the decision- making process	**Chapter VII** analyzes the role of authority and vertical specialization within an organization
		Chapter VIII is concerned with the process of communication whereby organizational influences are transmitted.
		Chapter IX the concept of efficiency is examined
		Chapter X considers organizational loyalty
Chapter XI	Applies the analysis to questions of organizational structure	Provides a survey of the structure of administrative organizations and a discussion of the problems faced by research in administrative theory.

The Waldo Simon Debate: II		
Philosophical Presuppositions	**Pragmatism**	**Logical Positivism**
What replaces science?	Common sense and prudence should replace science	Abstract concepts should be replaced by **operational definitions**
Is a science of public administration possible?	**No.** Pragmatism does not reject science, but science assumes a kind of metaphysical realism that principles are based upon.	**Yes.** Logical positivism leads to scientism. Decision theory and rational choice form the basis of an administrative science.
Are principles of public administration possible?	**No.** just as people are different, so are organizations. Context determines everything.	**Yes.** Administrative science is possible.
Most important criteria for public administration	**Democracy/ social equity**	**Efficiency**
Is there a single approach to public administration?	**No.** Different types of governmental organizations have different goals and purposes. The approach should change in accordance with the purpose of the organization.	**No.** Scientific methods still allow for more than one way to accomplish goals.
Is a new synthesis possible for public administration?	**No.** There is no one way to do public administration	**Yes.** A science of public administration is a possibility.

Models of Politics- Administration Relationships		
According to James Svara		
Policy-administration dichotomy	Policy	Classic council- manager form of local government
	Bureaucracy	
Mixture in policy	Administrators exercise discretion in policy making and deliverance of service	Politics and administration is about the distribution of values, costs and benefits. Politicians and bureaucrats both participate in value distribution.
		Has plenty of empirical warrant
Mixture in administration	Elected officials are involved in day to day conduct of government administration	Micromanagement and political meddling. Can result in corruption
Elected official-administrator as co-equals in policy	New Public Administration	Public administrators have an ethical obligation to protect the interests of the underrepresented.
		They are agents for the citizens.
		They act in accordance with the law, direction from elected officials and bureaucratic standards of efficiency and fairness.

New Public Administration

New Public Administration resulted from the Minnowbrook Conference at Syracuse University in the late 1960s. NPA is a postmodern approach to public administration. Modern public administration based on the Enlightenment is misguided. NPA emphasizes the application of interpretation or action theory rather than a rational decision theory. It allows for feminist and other critical perspectives on public administration.

Core Ideas	1. Public administrators and agencies are not and cannot be neutral or objective 2. Technology is often dehumanizing 3. Bureaucratic hierarchy is often ineffective 4. Bureaucracies tend toward goal. Displacement and survival 5. Cooperation, consensus, and democratic administration are more likely than the simple exercise of administrative authority to result in organizational effectiveness. 6. Modern concepts of public administration must be built on post-behavioral and post-positivist logic- more democratic, more adaptable, more responsive to changing social, economic, and political circumstances	
NPA Rejects	Particularism	
	Scientism	The idea that only science provides true knowledge
	Technologism	The attempt to base everything upon new technology
	Enterprise	Markets are not the only or best way to solve problems
NPA Embraces	Relevance	Everything should relate to social problems
	Values	Every experience is value laden. Consequently morality and beauty matter.
	Social Equity	The desire to see that no on is in need and that all needs are taken care of.
	Change	The status quo is not good enough
	Client Focus	Each person matters

The Blacksburg Manifesto	
Blacksburg Manifesto is described as an example of high modernism, beyond the functionalist paradigm, because although the central commitment is to reason and progress, the classic forms of administrative rationality are surpassed. It is classified as high modernism because the agency perspective, as articulated in the Manifesto, calls for a dialogue that evokes reason through process in the tradition of Mary Parker Follett.	
The **Center for Public Administration and Policy**	is an academic department focused on public administration at Virginia Tech in Blacksburg, Virginia. It is known for strong advocacy of an agential and moral perspective on government.
	CPAP is known for producing public administration theorists who assert that government is a positive force in society.
Refounding Public Administration (1990)	is a noted text in the public administration field that formulated a multi-faceted argument that government is properly an agential and active servant of the public good. It is among a very few books that have been pivotal in defining public administration as a distinct field from political science with its own theory and raison d'etre. The work was edited by Gary Walmsley, who contributed a classic essay on bureaucratic agency, and also includes works by Charkles, goodsell, John Rohr, Cammilla Stivers, Orion White, Phillip Kronenberg, James Wolf and others
Scholars	Well-known scholars associated with the program like Charles Goodsell, Gary Walmsley, and John Rohr have been instrumental in creating an important scholarly.

Friedrich- Finer Debate

This debate concerns the need for accountability and the need for discretion in the execution of public policy. It is concerned with laws, regulations and the democratic control of public administration. This debate actually begins with Plato and Aristotle concerning discretion amongst judges.. Plato argued that courts and judges have no discretion, but must rule solely based upon the law. Aristotle, on the other hand, believed that every application of a law requires an elaboration of that law. From Woodrow Wilson to New Public Administration, there have been advocates of social equity as a third pillar in public administration along with economy and efficiency.

Carl Joachim Friedrich was a German-American professor and political theorist. His writings on Law and Constitutionalism made him one the world's leading political scientists in the post-World War II period. **Herman Finer** was a Bessarabian born British political scientist and Fabian Socialist. He taught for many years at the University of Chicago.

	Carl Friedrich 1940	Herman Finer 1941
Platonic/ Aristotelian	**Aristotelian** People should not choose between perfection and stability. Instead they should focus on the various ways of approximating justice in society. Justice is the goal.	**Platonic** One encounters the problem of integrity to the general law and the application of justice in a particular case.
Presuppositions	Democratic government requires some level of expertise which requires latitude.	Democratic control of bureaucracy
Social Equity	Allows for more social equity	Inhibits social equity
Position	Public servants must have discretion in the execution of public policy	Public servants must have correction and discipline. They must have no discretion in the execution of public policy

Governance	
Governance is not a simple concept. Some think that governance is synonymous with public administration. The following are a number of explanations given by leaders in the field of public administration.	
Frederickson	Governance is concerned with understanding the process by which public policy is created, implemented, and managed. Its explanatory goal is to identify the actors and their role in this process, and to illuminate how their behavior and interrelationships shape public service provision. Governance connects policy makers to citizens.
Laurence Lynn	governance is made up of separate but interrelated parts. Their definition of governance includes "regimes of laws, administrative rules, judicial rulings, and practices that constrain, prescribe, and enable government activity, where such activity is broadly defined as the production and delivery of publicly supported goods and services
	Government at every level is far more complicated than in the past. Our goal was to suggest a way to evaluate governmental effectiveness systematically with quantitative research that would be useful to both scholars and practitioners," He asserts that theory-based empirical research, when well conceived and executed, can be a primary source of fundamental, durable knowledge about governance and policy management.
Donald Kettl	"**New Managerialism**", "characterizes a global public management reform movement that has redefined the relationships between government and society"
Peters and Pierre	Governance is different from NPM, but although NPM emerges as a sharply defined public management model (albeit one sporting clear ideological stripes), the same cannot be said of governance. Governance is more encompassing, is less hostile to orthodox models of public administration, and is wedded to no particular point of the ideological spectrum, but as a theory it is left rather vague

Governance Theory

Governance theory is the combination of administrative conjunction, institutionalism and network theory, is important because it is closely tied to the big issues of democratic government.

Institutionalism	Includes core ideas of contemporary public administration – results, performance, outcomes, and purposefulness; institutionalism could be said to account for both how institutions behave and how they perform. Institutionalism is particularly useful in the world of the disarticulated state because its assumptions do not rest primarily on sovereignty and authority, but rest instead on the patterns of politics, order, and shared meaning found in both governmental as well as nongovernmental institutions.
Public Sector Networks	Structures of interdependence that exhibit both formal and informal linkages that include exchange or reciprocal relations, common interests, and bonds of shared beliefs and professional perspectives. Network theory accounts for an increasing percentage of the activities of public programs. Network theory is thought of in organizational sociology and in parts of academic business administration as that which is situated between hierarchies and markets. Examples would include theories of federalism, intergovernmental relations, and policy implementation.
Administrative Conjunction	the networking of public administration across jurisdictional borders. These conjunctions are not formalized and tend to weaken due to the characteristics of the actors involved or because of large distances. These are major drawbacks. This focus on the process of cooperation contrasts greatly with NPM.

New Public Management

New Public Management labels a series of innovations occurring domestically and abroad." She goes on to add that this subject is heavily influenced by economics. More specifically, it focuses on public choice, principal agent theory and New Institutional Economics.		
New Public Administration resulted from the triumph of the global free market He also asserts that it also resulted from the triumph of democracy and the rule of law over authoritarianism and statism. A direct consequence of all this is command and control bureaucracy must come to an end. Consistent with this state of affairs is the belief that governmental planners should have a reduced role in the shaping of the world.		
New Public Management Endorses	**Normativity**	New Public Management has "an explicitly normative model of public managers."
	Public Policy	New Public Management advocates point out "that while civil servants are not supposed to make policy, they often do." These advocates of New Public Management both accept and endorse this state of affairs.
	Quality	- an emphasis on quality and continuous improvement, devolution and expansion of managerial autonomy, a commitment to customer satisfaction
New Public Management Rejects	**Command and Control**	This results in an inefficient and unresponsive bureaucracy that fails to meet the needs of the client/ citizens
	Governmental Planners	Planners often do not take into account the needs and desires of their citizen/ clients

The Intellectual Crisis in Public Administration

Vincent Ostrom, PhD is a public choice theorist and professor at the University of Indiana.

1.	**The Crisis of Confidence**	the intellectual crisis in American public administration has turned out following the political scandals such as Watergate.
2.	**The Mainstream in American Public Administration**	Bureaucratic administration which originated with Weber and Wilson is associated with a system of "good" administration. This is hierarchically ordered in a system of graded ranks subject to political direction by heads of departments at the center of government. The bureaucratic administration is assumed to produce efficient results and also makes the government responsible, as opposed to fragmented authority.
3.	**The Work of the Contemporary Political Economists**	The centralization of power does not always produce "efficient" results, because "efficiency" changes from one situation to another. This centralization of power is interested only in "supply side" at the expense and ignorance of "demand side". Each decision structure has advantages and disadvantages. Consequently, when determining one of the decision structures we must weigh these advantages and disadvantages.
4.	**A Theory of Democratic Administration: The Rejected Alternative**	Democratic administration is associated with fragmentation of authority and overlapping jurisdictions, and represents the opposite of bureaucratic administration based on unitary command of authority. Democratic administration, indulging fragmented authority and overlapping jurisdictions, is that what founding fathers of the United States deliberately envisioned.
5.	**The Choice of Alternative Futures**	the alternative to bureaucratic administration is "public choice" under the name of democratic administration.
6.	**The Continuing Crises in American Government**	The Wilsonian paradigm of bureaucratic administration has changed the nature of American public administration by numerous reforms aimed at strengthening the President and by overcoming "fragmented authority and overlapping jurisdictions" with the promise to "make the government more responsible and efficient. Further, the centralization of power in the Executive branch created unfortunate problems that have consumed the trust of citizens in government. This distrust divulges itself in the fact that half of the registered voters don't bother to voting any longer.
7.	**Intellectual Crises and Beyond**	Here are guidelines that will "help" determine the appropriate decision structures under specific circumstances.

Rationale for the Public Sector

Wagner's law- (1880s) economic development creates opportunities for new activities that government alone can perform

Externalities	Spillover that affects a third party	**Positive-** benefits third party
		Negative- costs third party
Asymmetrical Information	When both sides do not have the same information	**Adverse Selection-** market failure resulting from choosing a bad customer
		Moral hazard- market failure resulting from continuing a bad customer.
Pure Public Goods	Two requirements: goods must be non- rival in consumption and non-excludable	**Efficiency rule for Public Goods-** because all individuals consume a pure public good simultaneously, the marginal costs to society should equal the sum of the marginal benefits of all consumers, which is the marginal social benefit
		Samuelson's Rule- public goods equilibrium happens when the marginal cost to society is equal to the sum of the marginal benefits. Marginal costs to society includes all of the costs to society, including opportunity costs generated by production.
		Aggregate Marginal Benefit Function- the individual's marginal benefits are added vertically
Partial Public Goods	Only some degree of the two requirements for pure public goods	**Example:** toll roads
Merit Goods	A benefit given that positively affects everyone	**Examples include:** Free vaccinations

Reasons for the Growth of the Public Sector

The size of government always relates to both government revenues and expenditures. The size of government is determined in a political context involving the executive and legislative branches. The context can change at the local, state, and federal levels.

Value Questions	Those who want to preserve freedom and liberty will desire to keep government small. Those who desire more public goods and services will prefer a larger government. These views are antithetical, so one cannot have more of one without less of the other.
Demographic Changes	Significant changes in population (but particularly growth) can result in an increase in the size of government
Changes in Living Patterns	As people move from urban to suburban settings there are associated changes in government that can cause it to grow. There is generally a need for more roads, schools, etc. All of this leads to an increase of government.
Economic Hardships	Activists governments will respond to recessions or depressions with a growth in government goods and services.
High Risk Situations	There are many situations in which the private sector is not willing to risk its resources.
Technological Changes	The government can provide support when there is new technology. Airports, Spaceports, the internet, radio, and television are examples of this type of support.

Monopoly Models of Fiscal Choice

Median Voter Theory	**Median Voter Theorem-** if the choice to be made by voting is represented along a single continuum, the choice selected by majority vote is the median of the desired outcomes	
	Assumptions	Single peak preferences- utility always decreases past a certain point.
Theorists	William Niskanen- 1968	
	Thomas Romer- 1979	
	Howard Rosenthal- 1979	
Monopoly Models	Government Officials Seek to	Maximize the amount of government spending and remain in office
		Know the preferences of the residents of their communities
	Amount of government spending	Is selected by a majority vote of the residents. Options for the vote are determined by government officials
	If the majority of voters rejects all of the options	Government spending reverts to a predetermined amount

Charles Tiebout Hypothesis

Paul Samuelson assumed that people do not reveal their preferences for a mix of public goods at the national level.

Tiebout's Assumptions	Charles Tiebout assumed that people do reveal their preferences for a mix of public goods at the local level.
	The city manager is analogous to a plant manager
	Single peak preferences- utility always increases and then decreases past a certain point.
	The perfect competition model can be applied to government at a local level
	The optimal size of a community for a basket of public goods is determined by the lowest average cost for that set of goods

This is a model of local government expenditures, which will yield the same optimal allocation that a private market would

1. Consumers are mobile and will move their residences to the communities that best satisfy their preferences
2. Consumers have perfect information about differences in tax/ service packages among communities
3. There are many communities to choose from
5. There are no restrictions or limitations on consumer mobility due to employment opportunities
6. There are no spillovers of public service benefits or taxes among communities
7. Each community, directed by a manger, attempts to attract the right size population to take advantage of scale economies

Types of Tiebout Communities

	Government Spending	
Housing Type	High	Low
Big	Big: High (highest incomes)	Big: Low (next highest)
Small	Small: High (next lowest)	Small: Low (lowest incomes)

New Public Management Versus Governance		
	New Public Management	**Governance**
Explanation	An ideology for a model to more effectively deliver public goods and services	A concept that relates government to society and concerns both the public and private sectors
Theory	An organization theory	A theory of politics
Focus	Output	Process
Serves	Clients/ Customers	Citizens
Methods	Institutionalism, public choice	Networks
Goal	Wants to radically change the public sector	Wants to make the public sector work better

Types of Goods

	Rival	Non- Rival
Excludability	**Private goods** Apples, cars, computers	**Club goods** Movie theaters, cable television
Non- Excludable	**Common resources** Fish in rivers, unclaimed land, resources that everyone uses, but no one owns	**Public goods** National defense, public works, judicial system

Efficiency Rules for Public Goods

Social Optimum	The best price and quantity combination for all of society. It is reached by eliminating externalities.
Marginal Social Costs (MSC)	Is the change in society's total cost brought about by the production of an additional unit of a good or service. It includes both the marginal private cost and the marginal external cost.
Marginal Social Benefit (MSB)	Is the change in society's total benefit brought about by the production of an additional unit of a good or service.
Efficiency Rule for Public Goods	the marginal costs to society should equal the marginal social benefits
Samuelson Rule	the marginal cost includes all of the costs to the society, which includes the opportunity costs generated by production (such as pollution)
Lindahl Equilibrium	the consumer's marginal costs reflect their marginal benefits, then the efficient amount of public good will be demanded

Types of Public Goods

Public goods are a type of market failure because no public good can be paid for by an individual consumer. Consequently, the government must intervene by requiring all to pay taxes to pay for the good that a nation, state, or locality may require. National defense, public safety, or clean air are examples of pure public goods. There are a number of type of public goods that must be considered

Pure Public Goods	Willingness to pay. Non-rival in consumption And non-excludable
Partial Public Goods	Willingness to pay, non- rival or non- excludable
Merit Goods	Individual or societal need. These goods are under produced and under consumed in a free market economy. These goods provide positive externalities.
Demerit Goods	These are not public goods, but they result in government intervention. Government is likely to tax these goods because they provide a negative externality. These goods are over produced and over consumed in a free market economy.

Government Intervention in Private Markets

Government intervention into the market comes largely as a result of market failure. Market failure results from either information asymmetry or externalities.

Information Asymmetry	**Adverse Selection-** results when one party enters into an arrangement without knowing the liabilities of the other party
	Moral Hazard- results when one party supports the other after they have already demonstrated that they will behave in a wreckless manner.
Externalities	**Positive Externality-** occurs when the **marginal social benefit** of a transaction is exceeded by its **marginal social cost.**
	Negative Externality- occurs when the **marginal social cost** exceeds the **marginal social benefit** in a given transaction
Direct Intervention	The govern could directly provide goods and services

Incentives	The government could create incentives to alter economic decisions through the use of taxes and subsidies.	
	Pigouvian Taxes	A government response to producer of a good or service when there is a negative externality to alter their behavior. It results in a lower quantity of the good being produced at a higher cost.
Regulation	The government could regulate private economic activity. This results in a lower quantity of the good being produced at a higher price.	

Public Budgeting

According to Irene Rubin, public budgeting is political, because:

- Budgets reflect choices about what government will and will not do
- Budgets reflect priorities and citizens preferences
- Budgets provide a tool for accountability
- Budgets reflect the relative power of different individuals and organizations to influence outcomes

Budgetary Actors	**Bureau Chiefs**	Many administrators desire to increase the size of their budget. Other administrators desire autonomy more than an increased budget.
	Executive Budget Office	Normally, these officials are concerned with the scrutiny of agency budgets. They avoid deficits and manage cash flow.
	Chief Executive Officers	Each city, state and federal office is different and so are the responsibilities of the CEO. In general, they must approve of the budget and the process.
	Legislators	Because they represent different constituencies, they will hold different positions on each part of the budget.
	Interest Groups	In general, these groups seek to influence legislators to achieve whatever their interest is.
	Individual Citizens	For the most part, individual citizens can only vote for the CEO and/ or the legislators, with the goal of moving the budget I their desired direction.
	The Courts	The courts become involved in the budgetary process only when one of the actors brings a legal case against one of the others.
Budgetary Process	**Constraints**	Various factors can constrain a budget
	Decision Making	Once constraints are understood and priorities are set decisions can be made
	Implementation	Occurs after the budget is approved

Key Concepts in Federal Public Budgeting

Terms	Explanation	
Revenue	Government funding from taxation	
Expenditures	Government spending	
	Entitlements	Refers to programs that are automatically set by the legislature and by eligible recipients.
	Discretionary	Spending set by annual appropriation levels
Government Debt	The amount that government owes to others who have loaned it money	
Government Deficit	The amount of spending that exceeds its revenues in a given year	
Standardized Budget Deficit	This reflects longer- term trends in the federal government's fiscal position. This is computed by the Congressional Budget Office (**CBO**)	
Cyclically Adjusted Budget Deficit	This takes into account the effect of the business cycle upon the deficit. This approach attempts to estimate how much revenue is lost and how much spending increases are needed due to the economy's deviation from its full potential GDP.	
Cash Accounting	Measures the deficit solely as the difference between current spending and current revenues.	
Capital Accounting	An approach that takes into account the change in the value of the government's net asset holdings.	
Static Scoring	A method used by budget modelers that assumes that government policy changes only the distribution of total resources, not the amount of total resources.	
Dynamic Scoring	A method used by budget modelers that attempts to model the effect of government policy on both the distribution of total resources and the amount of total resources.	
Real Prices	Prices stated in some constant year's dollars	
Nominal prices	Prices stated in today's dollars	

Federal Public Budgeting Reforms

Budget Idea	Explanation	Emphasis
Line Item Budgeting	(early 1900s) Listed categories or objects of expenditure which could be collapsed into broad categories	Control
Executive Budgeting	(1920s- 1940s) Placed budget making responsibility in the executive.	Control
Performance Budget	(1950s) Emphasizes what government does rather than what it buys	Economy and Efficiency
Program Planning and Budgeting System (PPBS)	(1965- 1969) Involved long range planning, quantitative analysis and performance analysis	Planning Evaluation Effectiveness
Zero Based Budgeting (ZBB) (TBB) (BBB)	(1977- 1981) ZBB can be viewed as a component of PPBS. It builds the budget from the ground up. Variations of ZBB include Target Based Budgeting and Below base Budgeting.	Planning Prioritization and Budget Reduction
New Performance Budget	(1993- This version of Performance Budgeting is focused on outcomes or results	Accountability Efficiency and Economy

Federal Budgeting Acts

Date	Act	Explanation
1910- 12	Taft Commission on Economy and Efficiency	They reported on the need for a national budget. They wanted agency budget requests to be based on agency performance.
1921	Budget and Accounting Act	Required the president to submit a budget for the executive branch to Congress. It also gave the president a budget office.
1939	Reorganization Plan 1	Established the new Executive Office of the President and transferred the Bureau of the Budget from the Treasury
1949	First Hoover Commission	Wanted agency budget requests to be based on agency performance
1949	National Security Act Amendments	Recommended changes to the administration of the federal government. It put the idea of performance budgeting into practice at the federal level
1950	Budget and Accounting Procedures Act	Recommended changes to the administration of the federal government. It put the idea of performance budgeting into practice at the federal level
1955	Second Hoover Commission	It continued to make recommendations and checked the progress made by the first commission.
1970	Office of Management and Budget	Replaced the Bureau of the Budget
1974	Budget Reform Act	The Congressional Budget Office helped Congress to understand and assess the President's budget.
1985	Balanced Budget Emergency Control Act	Also known as the Gramm- Rudman – Hollings Deficit Reduction Act. This act set mandatory annual targets for reducing the federal deficit.

Federal Budgeting Acts Continued

1990	Budget Enforcement Act	This gave Congress some control over the federal budget. This act was aimed at restraining government growth by setting caps on discretionary spending.
1993	Government Performance and Results Act	Focused attention on results and performance budgeting. It required federal Agencies to prepare annual reports to the President and that compare plans to actual performance.

Urban Economics

Urban economics began as a separate field in the early 1960s. The discipline of urban economics is defined by the intersection of geography and economics. Cities are formed by the location decisions of firms, households and governmental bodies. Urban economics also identifies inefficiencies in location choices and examines alternative public policies to promote efficient choices.

Agglomeration Economy	Cost reductions occur because economic activities are located in one place.
Topics in Urban Economics	1. Market forces in the development of cities 2. Land use within cities. 3. Urban transportation. 4. Crime and public policy 5. Housing and public policy 6. Local government expenditures and taxes

Five Axioms in Urban Economics	1. Prices adjust to achieve locational equilibrium
	2. Self- reinforcing effects generate extreme outcomes
	3. Externalities cause inefficiency
	4. Production is subject to economies of scale
	   • **Individual inputs-** a small operation has the same indivisible inputs as a large operation
	   • **Factor specialization-** a specialized worker is the master of one task
	5. Competition generates zero economic profit. (Economic profit equals the excess of total revenue over total economic cost, where the economic costs include the opportunity costs of all inputs).

Economic Actors	**Households**	Households are utility maximizing
	Firms	Firms are profit maximizing
	Governments	Governments provide public goods and public services by taxing firms and households.

Urban Economics: Cities

According to Arthur O'Sullivan, "cities exist because of the benefits of centralized exchange and centralized production. The industrial revolution resulted in massive urbanization because of its innovations in agriculture, transportation and production. Changes in energy technology altered the location decisions of firms. Spatial competition among firms generates a market area for each firm and a system of cities.

Types of Cities	Trading City	A **trading city** develops when comparative advantage is combined with economies of scale in exchange.
	Factory City	A **factory city** develops when there are scale economies in production.
Census Definitions	**Urban Population**	**Urbanized Area-** a densely settled core of census block groups and surrounding census blocks that meet minimum population density requirements
		Urban Clusters- a scaled down version of an urban area
		Urban Population—all people living in urbanized areas and urban clusters
	Statistical Areas	**Metropolitan Area-** at least one urbanized area with at least 50,000 people
		Micropolitan Area- at least one urban cluster of between 10,000 and 50,000 people
	Principal City	The largest municipality in each metropolitan or micropolitan statistical area
City Model	**Monocentric City Model**	A model that assumes that the city revolves around a single center
	Central Business District	The center of a monocentric city
Urban Growth	**The city grows with employment opportunities and quality of life**	Dependent upon city innovation, human capital and employment growth
Urban Social Problems	Poverty	Poverty has numerous causes
	Crime	Criminals are rational, utility-maximizing individuals who will commit crime if the benefit exceeds the cost

Urban Economics: Households

One aspect of urban economics is households. In a market economy households are rational and utility maximizing agents. Households rent or buy homes to live in. Housing is different from other products because:

1. Housing stock is heterogeneous
2. Housing is durable but can deteriorate over time
3. The cost of moving is prohibitive so consumers do not make rapid adjustments in their housing consumption.

Price of a Dwelling	**Base Price**	The sum of these factors together determines the price of a dwelling
	Access price	
	Size	
	Roof Age	
	Air Quality	
	Schools	
Housing Policy	**Middle Income Americans**	are encouraged to own their homes. The federal income tax deduction and the federal mortgage insurance were set up to do so.
	Low income Americans	Are not encouraged to buy houses. When banks lower their lending standards, either adverse selection or moral hazard may result.
	Abandonment	Abandoned houses are an externality because they decrease the attractiveness of the neighborhood and they contribute to crime.
Zoning	Zoning can have deleterious effects, by preventing many from entering this part of the real estate market.	
Home Ownership	Home ownership is dependent upon the price and the ability of the purchaser to pay for a home. The government often offers incentives to qualified buyers to purchase a home through taxation and other means	
Renting	People will rent a dwelling for a number of reasons. In many cases renting is a short term option. In other cases, renting is a necessity for lack of income.	
Real Estate Markets	**Short Run Equilibrium**	Net rent and the number of occupied and vacant dwellings are functions of the total inventory
	Long Run Equilibrium	Net rent is a function of the cost of capital for occupied and vacant dwellings

Urban Economics: Firms

Urban economics explores the location decisions of profit maximizing firms, and it shows how these decisions cause the formation of cities of different size and shape. Urban economics also identifies inefficiencies in location choices and examines alternative public policies to promote efficient choices.

Static Agglomeration Economies (according to Bertil Ohlin)	**Single Location**	Economy of scale internal to a firm's operation
	Localization Economies	External to the individual firm. Arises from the size of the local industry
	Urbanization Economies	External to the local industry. Arises from the size of the local economy
	Inter-industry	Arises from transportation cost savings in purchases of intermediate inputs
	Dynamic	Important for the growth of an urban area
Dimensions of Agglomeration Economies (according to Rosenthal and Strange)	**Industry**	Varies from localization economies within a single industry up to urbanization economies
	Geographic	When the effect is attenuated by distance between two establishments
	Temporal	When the effect takes place over time
	Organization of Industry	When the level of competitiveness has a positive effect on productivity
Types of Firms	**Market Oriented Firm-** located in a city where consumers are	
	Input Oriented Firm- located in a city where the inputs are	
Inputs for Firms	**Capital-**	Every firm needs capital
	Labor Costs-	Every firm needs labor
	Energy Costs-	Some firms are energy intensive
	Land Costs-	Some firms need plenty of land or facilities
	Intermediate Inputs	Goods needed by the firm to produce
		Services needed by the firm to produce
	Knowledge Inputs-	For firms that specialize in intellectual property
Government	**Public Goods and Services**	Includes public infrastructure, fire and police services. These expenses must be paid for.
	Taxes	Property taxes are the primary form of taxation for local economies
	Subsidies	Some activities are subsidized to achieve the social optimum

Urban Economics: Government

In a market economy, local government's role is limited to resource allocation. More specifically, local government is responsible for providing goods and services. This includes, but is not limited to: education, highways, police and fire protection, parks and sewers.

Local Public Goods and Services	Characteristics	Non- rival-
		Non- excludable
		Benefits are limited to a small geographical area
Tiebout Model	Municipal Choice	A household chooses the municipality that provides the ideal level of public goods
	Perfect Information and Mobility	All citizens have access to relevant information about alternative municipalities and moving is costless.
	No Inter-jurisdictional Spillovers	There are no externalities associated with local public goods. All the benefits from local public goods accrue only to citizens within the municipality
	No Scale Economies	The average cost of production is independent of output.
	Head Taxes	A municipality pays for its public goods and services with a head tax: if you have a head, then you pay the tax.
Lindahl Model	Taxes are proportional to the willingness to pay for public goods. The government allocates the cost of the public good to its citizens based on their willingness to pay.	
Median Voter	Definition	The median voter prefers a quantity less than the optimum, so government acquires an inefficient amount of the good or service.
	Assumptions	Since politicians only care about winning elections, they will act in accordance with voter preference
		If there are several election issues, candidates will offer package deals to voters
		All citizens vote
Local Government Revenue	Property Tax	Paid by land owners, owners of capital, and consumers
	Inter-governmental Grants	Grants in aid from the federal government

Urban Economics: Infrastructure

The larger the urban area, the more public infrastructure that there is. States and localities should determine what infrastructure is needed and invest on a case by case basis. Traditional infrastructure systems must be tended to even as newer infrastructure systems are built. Infrastructure costs and benefits should be evaluated in the light of their short run and long run effects. In general, infrastructure makes small contributions to economic productivity.

Transportation	**Roads**	Includes highways, and bridges
	Railroad systems	Includes both freight and mass transit systems
	Airports	Regional, county, and municipal airports
	Waterways	River systems
Utilities	**Water**	Used for drinking, industrial, commercial and agricultural needs.
	Electricity	Nuclear, hydrodynamic, and coal fired systems
	Natural Gas	These systems are still being developed
Tele-communications	**Telephone**	Cell phone and land lines
	Telegraph	These systems are simple, but still important
	Radio Systems	Radio communication systems are important for police and fire departments
	Internet	There is more need for these service to provide information to the public and for public servants to gain information.
Public Buildings	**Offices, warehouses, sport stadiums, schools**	These facilities should be designed to maximize capacity, reduce energy costs, and last as long as possible.
Waste Management	**Disposal and Recycling**	Includes sewer systems, wastewater treatment facilities and landfills
	Stormwater Management	There is always a need for more in the suburbs

Chapter 5: Political Economy

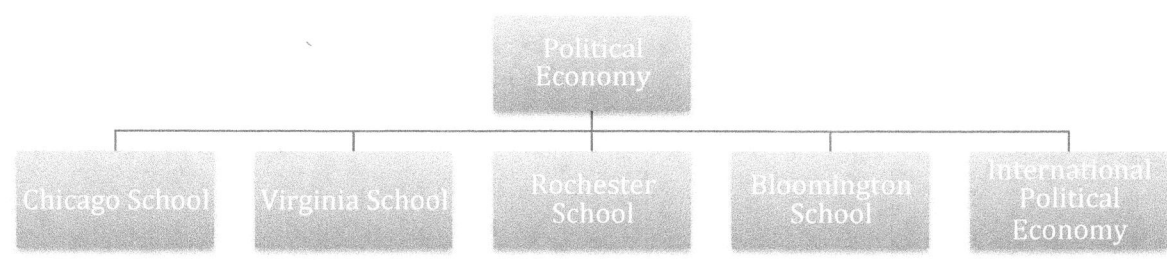

Schools of Political Economy	
These are contemporary approaches to political economy based upon neo-classical economic theory.	
Chicago School of Political Economy	Based on the University of Chicago. Ronald Coase and Oliver Williamson laid down the foundations of New institutional Economics. This approach is based upon the reduction of transaction costs.
Virginia School of Political Economy	Based on the work of James Buchanan and Gordon Tullock at the University of Virginia, Virginia Tech, and George Mason University. This approach is based upon public choice theory. It is not concerned with transaction costs.
Rochester School of Political Economy	Started by William Riker and others at the University of Rochester (NY). A positivistic approach to political science that employs social choice theory, game theory and public choice theory. It is not primarily concerned with transaction costs.
Bloomington School of Political Economy	Based on the work of Elinor and Vincent Ostrom. At the University of Indiana. It combines, New Institutional Economics and Public Choice theory to deal with the problems in public administration. Transaction costs are an important concept for New Public Management.

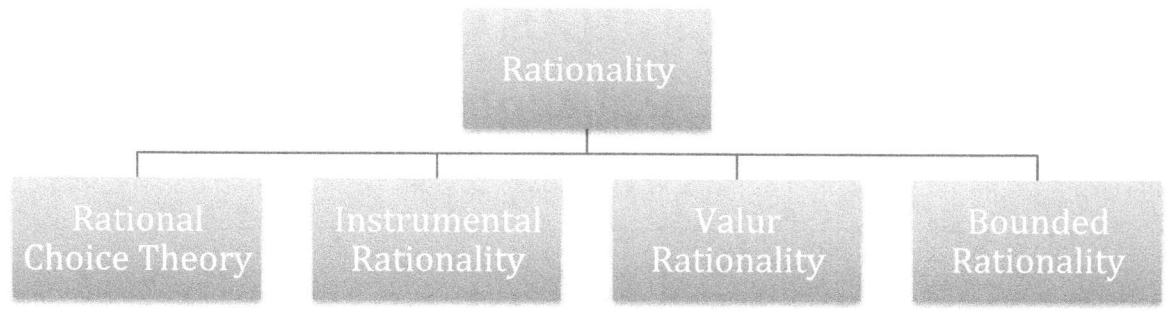

Reason and Political Economy	
Theory	**Explanation**
Rational Choice	A model of human decision making emphasized by Gary Becker at the University of Chicago. He argued that people are rational, self- interested and utility maximizing
Instrumental Rationality	A model of human decision making by Max Weber. Decisions are determined by expectations as to the behavior of objects in the environment and of other human beings. These expectations are used as means to achieve the actor's own rationally pursued and calculated ends.
Value Rationality	A model of human decision making by Max Weber. Decisions are determined by a conscious belief in the value for its own sake of some ethical, aesthetic, religious or other end
Bounded Rationality	A model of decision making conceived of by Herbert Simon at the University of Chicago. He asserts that people experience limits in solving problems and in processing information. This should modify the RCT

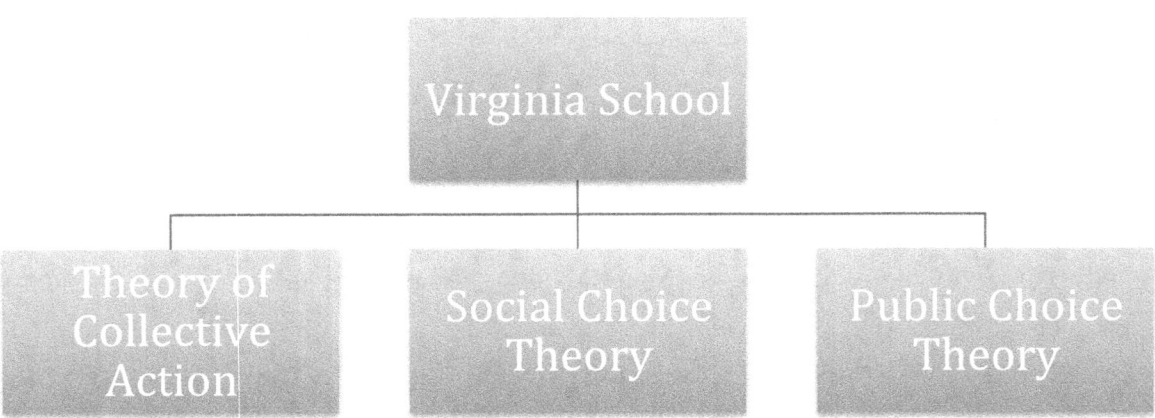

The Virginia School of Political Economy	
James Buchanan	One working in the area of public choice must first cover the works of James Buchanan. It was his work that led the way in this field. In 1975, Buchanan wrote *The Limits of Liberty*. In this work Buchanan takes a contractarian approach to political economy. In many ways this work set the course for public choice. As a result of this work, Buchanan became one of the leading political theorists in the 20th century.
Gordon Tullock	Gordon Tullock is the premeire student of James Buchanan. As a result, he co- wrote multiple books with Buchanan. He has also written a number of books on his own.

Bureaucracy and Public Economics

William Niskanen Jr, PhD was chairman of the Cato Institute

Part I **Introduction**	Niskanen argues that bureaucrats have personal objectives - that differ from those of both their political supervisors and the general public - which they further by use of their monopoly power. He develops his argument to contend that government budgets have become too large and should be curtailed.
Part II **Critical Elements of a Theory as Supply by Bureaus**	Characteristics of Bureaus
	Bureaus and their Environment
	The Bureaucrat's Maximand
Part III **The Basic Model**	Budget and output behavior
	Production Behavior
	Comparison of Organizational Forms
	Effect of Changes in Demand and Cost Conditions
Part IV **Variations on the Basic Model**	Non Profit Organizations
	The Mixed Bureau
	The Multi- Service Bureau
Part V **The Government Market for a Bureau's Services**	The Behavior of Collective Organizations
	A Model of the Review Process in Representative Government
	Bureaucratic Behavior in a Competitive Environment
	An Aggregative Model of Public Services in the United States
Part VI **The Alternatives**	Normative Judgments
	Bureaucratic Alternatives
	Market Alternatives
	Political Alternatives
Part VII **Conclusion**	He believed that we have only started to converge on a simple model of bureaus and political markets

Constitutional Political Economy

Constitutional Political Economy is an aspect of public choice theory. It does two things. One provides an analysis of the economic interests of those who vote for a constitution. The other aspect is an analysis of economic freedom and growth that results from a given constitution.

Economic Interpretation of the Constitution	**Charles Beard** *Economic interpretation of the Constitution*	argues that the constitution was framed based on the economic interests of those who wrote the constitution. Beard presents his argument from the standpoint of class warfare. This is a progressivist interpretation of U.S. history.
	Robert E. Brown *Charles Beard and the Constitution: A Critical Analysis.*	Brown applies the fruits of modern historical scholarship toward an understanding of Beard's work. With a perspective of forty years, Brown separates the valid from the invalid in this work. Thus he displays the problems associated with Beard's arguments.
	Forest MacDonald *We the People: Economic origins of the Constitution*	refutes Beards arguments by examining the actual financial records of the men who wrote and voted to approve the constitution.
Economic Freedom and Growth	**James Buchanan and Gordon Tullock**	Buchanan gave a technical definition of constitutional economics as the research program directed at the rules of institutions in which individuals make choices, along with the process of creating these rules. While ordinary economic inquiry focuses on the choices within the rules or the constraints imposed on the individuals, constitutional economics aims at the actual rules themselves, the choice among constraints. Individuals agree to place constraints on themselves in exchange for anticipated benefits, a similar to a social contract view of government. Just as a market transaction occurs through voluntary, mutually beneficial exchange, so with political "exchanges" of rights and authority

Constitutional Political Economy:
Economic Growth and Freedom

Positive Constitutional Economics	Positive constitutional economics employs comparative institutional analysis	examines how certain constitutional rules arose and what factors caused the rules to be developed as a result of aggregated individual inputs.
		Examines rules from the perspective of their individual and collective factors
		considers the effects of further constitutional (or rules) change for their effects on efficiency and equity.
		examines the economic effects of developed or modified change to rules.
Normative Constitutional Economics	focuses on legitimizing the state and its actions as the best means of maximum efficiency and utility,	
	judging conditions or rules that are efficient, and discerning and studying the political systems to maximize efficiency, where the outcome of collective choices are considered "fair", "just", or "efficient"	
Constitutional Law and Economics	examines the interrelationship between constitution law and the economic growth.	
	"economics may provide insight into questions that bear on the proper legal interpretation."	

Public Choice Overview

	Society	Rejection of organic conception of the state and societal will. There is no "public good" only many individual goods.
	Methodological Individualism	Society's actions are based on many individual decisions in a democratic process
	Motivation	People are not motivated differently in the public domain
Assumptions	Game Theory	Politicians are power maximizing because they participate in a zero-sum game
		Participants in markets are utility maximizing because it is a non- zero sum game with Nash equilibriums.
	Arrow's Impossibility Theorem	It is impossible to arrive at efficient and optimal outcomes in a democratic system, because while individuals are rational, groups are not.

Level	Motivation	Problem	Theory
Politicians Anthony Downs	Are utility maximizing, consequently, they are also vote maximizing	Asymmetrical information may lead them to act in ways that are contrary to the electorate	Median voter theory
Bureaucrats William Niskanen	Are utility maximizing, consequently, they are also budget maximizing	Asymmetrical information may lead them to act in ways that are contrary to the electorate	Government bureaus should compete with one another
Voters James M. Buchanan and Gordon Tullock Mancur Olson	Are utility maximizing	Each individual has a desire for a different mix of public goods	Rent seeking Log- rolling
			Olson argues that small groups are more likely to be successful at making change

Public Choice
Asymmetrical Information: Voters and Politicians

Voters elect politicians and trust them to represent their desires in public office. If voters are not wise, they may elect a dishonest politician. Dishonest politicians will act contrary to the common good.		Agents	
		Guileless Politician	**Deceitful Politician**
Principal	**Alert Voters**	**Social optimum** Best case scenario	**Less than optimal**
	Careless Voters	**Less than optimal**	Worst case scenario (corruption) **Adverse selection and Moral hazard**

Public Choice
Asymmetrical Information: Politicians and Bureaucrats

Politicians hire and direct the activities of bureaucrats. Politicians make policy, while bureaucrats carry it out. Bureaucrats should not, but sometimes do make policy. Bureaucrats are accountable to and report to politicians. If politicians are careless, this will allow dishonest bureaucrats to carry out their own agenda, contrary to the common good.		**Agent**	
		Honest Bureaucrat	**Dishonest Bureaucrat**
Principal	**Alert Politician**	Social Optimum Best case Scenario	Less than optimal situation
	Careless Politician	Less than optimal situation	Adverse Selection and Moral hazard (corruption) Worst Case Scenario

Stratton and Orchard's Reasons for the Failure of Public Choice Theory

Reason	Explanation	Details
Underlying presuppositions	PCT rests on four faulty assumptions and they are intertwined	Individual self- interest sufficiently motivates most economic behavior
		Economic behavior is understood by neoclassical economic theory
		Individual self- interest also motivates political behavior
		Political behavior is also understood by neoclassical economic theory
Assumptions on bureaucracy	PCT believe that bureaucrats cannot be trusted	Bureaus should compete with each other
		When a bureau wins a contract, its chief should be allowed to pocket a proportion of any budget savings
		Bureau chiefs should get their appointments via competitive bidding
Rent Seeking	Rent- an advantage that one party in a market has over another	Rent seeking- when firms attempt to influence politicians to act in the firm's interest. The social costs are the consumption lost by the winner's inefficient use of resources
Positivist Pretense	PCT are not value free. Their positivism is an illusion.	PCT argue for positivism, while their use of Pareto optimality is value laden
Meanings of Unanimity	PCT use different meanings of unanimity for different purposes.	Strong interpretation- the Pareto test which entitles any citizen to veto any change that threatens his interests
		Weak interpretation- every member of society consents to the rules
Processes and Outcomes	The distinction between processes and outcomes are pretty slippery.	PCT want laws to be as clear as possible and individuals to be as free as possible to determine how to behave within the rules
		To protect established property rights and interests against redistribution
		Reifies the Rawlsian veil of ignorance. The less people know about the effects of their voting, the more unanimously they may vote.
PCT are opponents to democracy	PCT believe that rules need to be put into place that cannot be changed	Rules are needed which specify not only how governments must be elected, but also the substantial things which they may or may not do- and these rules need to be entrenched against alteration by a democratic majority.
Authority and Public Interest	PCT do not believe in the "Public good" or the "public interest."	PCT think that when people speak of public interests or the public good, public choice theorists often accuse them of wanting to impose their beliefs on others
Endowments	PCT explain existing inequalities by	The market distributes income
		The distinction between nature and artifice
		The scientist desire to make social theory as parsimonious and universal as Newton's laws of motion

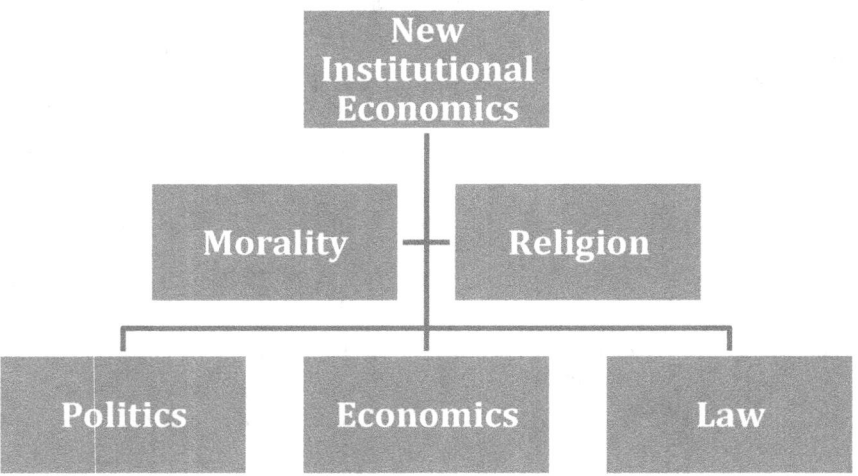

New Institutional Economics	
John R. Commons	Proposed that the transaction be made the unit of analysis.
Ronald Coase	work in this area began with two articles that he wrote. The first of these is "The Nature of the Firm", which was published in 1937. The second article that Coase that relates to transaction costs economics is "The Problem of Social Costs, " which was published in 1960
Oliver Williamson	Williamson coined the term, "New Institutional Economics (NIE)." According to Williamson, "The NIE maintains that (1) institutions matter and (2) institutions are susceptible to analysis. This analysis is done by "focusing on the microanalytics of contract and organization. Elsewhere, Williamson goes on to say: "Most of what I refer to as the New Institutional Economics is located on the efficiency branch of contract. The efficiency branch of contract distinguishes between those approaches in what incentive alignments are emphasized and those which feature economies as transaction costs.
Douglass North	NIE "focuses on the beliefs that humans develop to explain their environment and the institutions (political, economic, and social) that they create to shape that environment."

Economics of Institutions

According to Oliver Williamson

Level	Description	Frequency (years)	Purpose
L1: Social Theory	Embeddedness: informal institutions, customs, traditions, norms and religion	100-1000	Often non-calculative; spontaneous
L2 Economics of property rights/ positive political theory	Institutional environment: formal rules of the game- esp. property (polity, judiciary, bureaucracy)	10-100	Get the institutional environment right. 1st order economizing
L3: Transaction cost economics	Governance: play of the game –esp. contract (aligning governance structures with transactions)	1-10	Get the governance structures right. 2nd order economizing
L4: neoclassical economics/ agency theory	Resource allocation and employment (prices and quantities; incentive alignment)	continuous	Get the marginal conditions right. 3rd order economizing

Levels of New Institutional Economics

Institutional Environment	Rules of the game
Institutions of Governance	Individual transactions, and the realm of organizational economics
The individual Actor	Operates with bounded rationality and opportunism

278

Mancur Lloyd Olson Jr.

(January 22, 1932 – February 19, 1998) From 1967 until his death in 1998 Olson was a Professor of Economics at the University of Maryland, College Park. Among other areas, he made contributions to institutional economics on the role of private property, taxation, public goods, collective action and contract rights in economic development. Olson focused on the logical basis of interest group membership and participation.

***The Logic of Colklective Action* (1965)**	"only a separate and 'selective' incentive will stimulate a rational individual in a latent group to act in a group-oriented way"; that is, members of a large group will not act in the group's common interest unless motivated by personal gains (economic, social, etc.). He specifically distinguishes between large and small groups, the latter of which can act simply on a shared objective. Large groups, however, will not form or work towards a shared objective unless individual members are sufficiently motivated.
The Rise and Decline of Nations (1982)	Small distributional coalitions tend to form over time in countries. Groups like cotton-farmers, steel-producers, and labor unions will have the incentives to form lobby groups and influence policies in their favor. These policies will tend to be protectionist and anti-technology, and will therefore hurt economic growth but since the benefits of these policies are selective incentives concentrated amongst the few coalitions members, while the costs are diffused throughout the whole population, the "Logic" dictates that there will be little public resistance to them. Hence as time goes on, and these distributional coalitions accumulate in greater and greater numbers, the nation burdened by them will fall into economic decline.
Power and Prosperity	Olson distinguished between the economic effects of different types of government, in particular, tyranny, anarchy and democracy. Olson argued that a "roving bandit" (under anarchy) has an incentive only to steal and destroy, whilst a "stationary bandit" (a tyrant) has an incentive to encourage a degree of economic success, since he will expect to be in power long enough to take a share of it. The stationary bandit thereby takes on the primordial function of government - protection of his citizens and property against roving bandits. Olson saw in the move from roving bandits to stationary bandits the seeds of civilization, paving the way for democracy, which improves incentives for good government by more closely aligning it with the wishes of the population.

New Institutional Economics

Problems from the Neoclassical Model			
	There are zero transaction costs.		
	Force is monopolized by the state.		
	Institutional arrangements play an inconsequential role in the economic process.		
	The price system is the only way to coordinate different activities		

Classical Liberal State			
	Constitutional Rules	Private property and property rights	
		Transfer of property rights by consent according to the principle of freedom of contract	
		Individual liability for contractual obligations	
	Problems of Power	A state strong enough to protect property rights and enforce contracts is also strong enough to confiscate the wealth of its citizens	
		Individual inequality of power	Naturally caused asymmetries of power
			Asymmetries of power caused by formation of coalitions
		Pressure groups, monopolies and other things can destroy the principle of freedom of contract	
	Law	The classical liberal state leaves room for the creation of law by private individuals	
		Freedom of contract is the institutional counterpart of the principle of economic decentralization which is presupposed by competitive market models	

Assumptions and Terms from New Institutional Economics		
	Methodological Individualism	People are different with different tastes, goals, and purposes. Consequently, collective entities, like the state should not be confused with individual agents
	The Maximand	People maximize their utility subject to the constraints established by the institutional structures
	Individual Rationality	Rather than employing *perfect individual rationality*, bounded rationality results in people using *imperfect individual rationality.*
	Opportunistic Behavior	Rationality is not the only factor involved in decision making. Some people are dishonest and will take advantage of others as opportunities allow
	Economic Society	Involves individuals and a set of formal and informal rules or norms that assign property rights to citizens
	Governance structure	The system of formal and informal rules and the instruments to enforce the rules
	Institutions	The purpose of an institution is to steer individual behavior in a particular direction. Institutions are characterized by the existence of bounded rationality.

New Institutional Economics Continued

Assumptions and Terms from New Institutional Economics	**Evolution of Institutions**	Institutions come about by collective action and arise either spontaneously or by design
		When institutions arise spontaneously, they are self- enforced, which is more stable than when enforced by third parties.
		An institution is defined as a salient Nash equilibrium of a recurrent super-game which is repeatedly replayed
	Organizations	Institutions with people taking advantage of them
	Social Networks	Consists of actors, relational ties between pairs of actors, and attributes of actors.
		Typical relational ties are economic transactions. Relational ties are any kind of social action that established linkage between a pair of actors
		Typical attributes of actors are sex, race, location, firm.
	Social Capital	Consists of the present value of actor's relationships with other actors.
		Social capital is a relational good, it is owned by the parties in a relationship. No actor has the exclusive rights to social capital
		Social capital concerns the rate of return of an actor's production function.

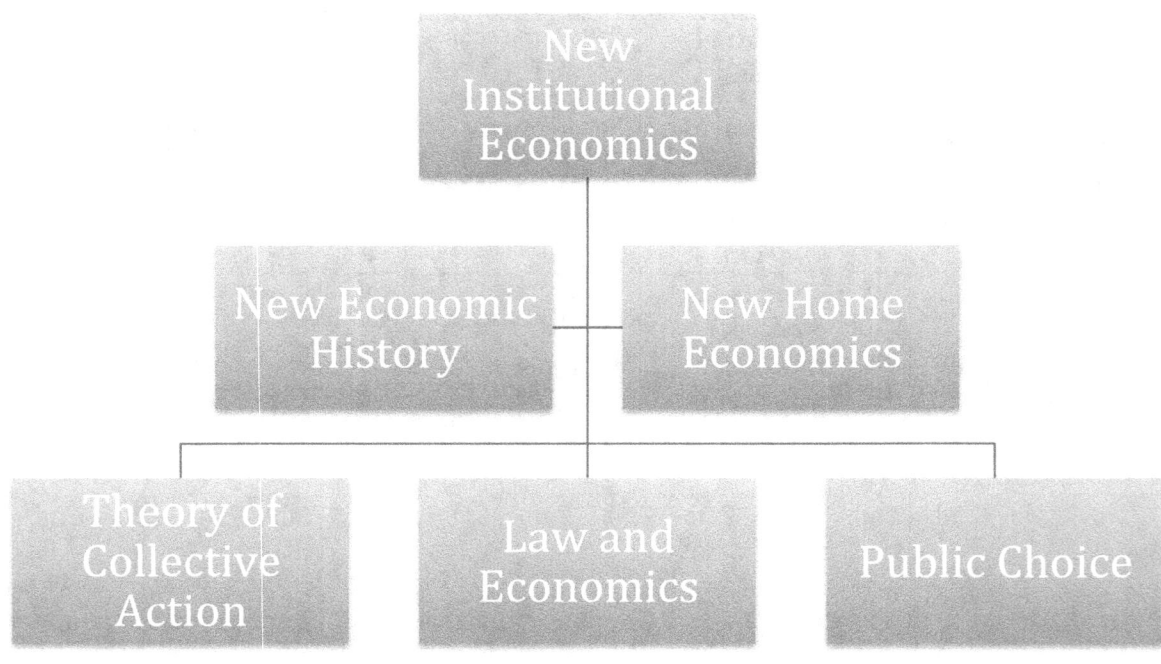

New Institutional Economics and Modern Institutionalism		
Transaction Cost Economics	Transaction costs come with the exchange process These include: search and information, bargaining and decision costs as well as policing and enforcement costs. All of this has an effect on the formation of contracts.	
Property Rights Analysis	Property rights affect human behavior in predictable ways. Property rights provide incentives and affects economic outcomes.	
Economic Theory of Contracts	Deals with incentives and asymmetric information problems	**Agency theory-** concerned with asymmetrical information between contractual parties. Involves either adverse selection or moral hazard
		Relational Contract Theory- asymmetries between those involved in the transaction and third parties
New Economic History	Attempts to explain why some institutions produce poor economic outcomes. It is mostly concerned with the institutions that defined and enforced by the state.	
Historical and Comparative Institutional Analysis	This applies the concept of institutions as an equilibrium of a game approach to deal with the pervasive presence of coercive power in politics.	
Evolutionary Game Theory	Seeks to explain how spontaneous order comes about. It differs from traditional models of game theory by assuming bounded rationality	
Constitutional Economics	Considers the way that laws, and constitutions act as institutions that guide political and economic agents.	
Theory of Collective Action	Is concerned with the supply of public goods and services. It is concerned with collective agreements and how they affect the marketplace. A central problem of this theory is the incentive to be a free rider.	
New Institutionalism in Organization Theory and Sociology	Some approaches reject rational choice models, while others embrace them. They focus on the ways that institutions complicate and constitute the paths by which solutions are sought	
New Institutionalism in Political Science	New Institutional Economics applied to theories of the state, public administration, and international organizations.	**Rational Choice Institutionalism-** a calculus approach that argues that institutions embody something like a Nash equilibrium
		Sociological Institutionalism- explains the persistence of institutions by noting that many conventions cannot be subject to individual choice
		Historic Institutionalism- a combination of the other two methods

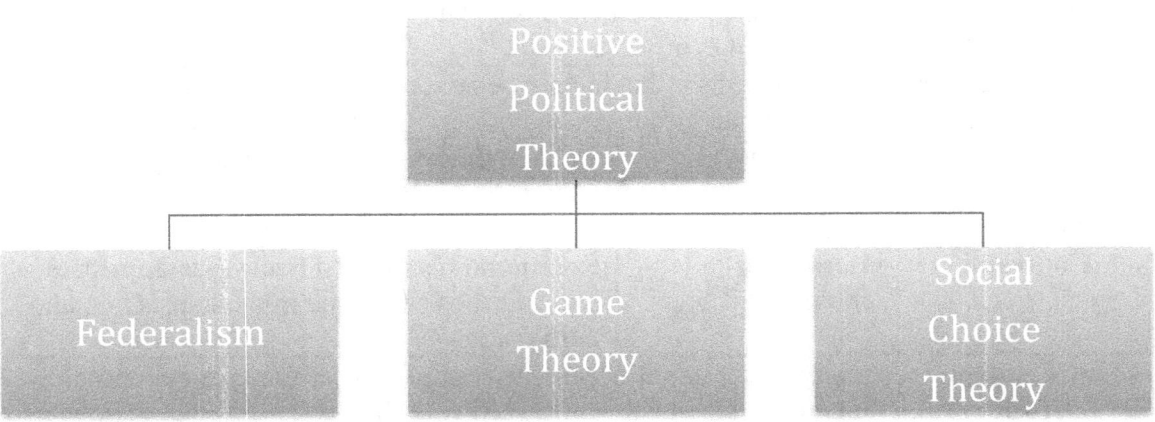

The Rochester School of Political Economy	
Positive Political Theory is now the mainstream approach which moved political science from just a descriptive to a prescriptive study of social interaction.	
William H. Riker	Riker founded the positive approach to political theory. He employed game theory and social choice theory as primary tools to change the discipline into what it is today.
Students, or people influenced by Riker	James Enelow at the University of Texas John Aldrich of Duke university Morris Fiorina at Stanford University Peter Ordershook at Cal Tech Kenneth Shepsle at Harvard University Norman Schofield at Washington University St Louis

Social Choice Theory

Social choice theory combines elements of welfare economics and voting theory.	

Kenneth Arrow's Impossibility theorem implies that the only voting method that is without flaws is in a dictatorship.	• If every voter prefers alternative X over alternative Y, then the group prefers X over Y. • If every voter's preference between X and Y remains unchanged, then the group's preference between X and Y will also remain unchanged (even if voters' preferences between other pairs like X and Z, Y and Z, or Z and W change). • There is no "dictator": no single voter possesses the power to always determine the group's preference.

Duncan Black	A Scottish economist who was taught by Anthony Downs and influenced by Ronald Coase. He established the foundations of social choice theory. He developed the Black electoral system, which employs a Condorcet method. In the absence of a Condorcet winner, the Borda winner is chosen instead. Black is also known as the founding father of public choice theory.	
	Condorcet	is an election method that elects the candidate that would win by majority rule, in all pairings, against the other candidates, whenever one of the candidates meets that goal. A candidate with that property is called a *Condorcet winner*.
	Borda	a consensus-based voting system rather than a majoritarian one

Amartya Sen	Indian economist and morsal philosopher who was awarded the Nobel Prize in Economic Sciences for his work in welfare economics and social choice theory. Sen showed under what conditions Arrow's impossibility theorem applies.

An Economic Theory of Democracy

Anthony Downs wrote among the most influential books in political science. It is concerned with governing of democratic state - by making intelligible the party politics of democracies. His explanations are systematically related to, and deductible from, precisely stated assumptions about the motivations that attend the decisions of voters and parties and the environment in which they act. He is concerned also with the central features of party politics in any democratic state, not with that in the United State or any other single country. Down's most famous innovation is the result that two party competition leads to both parties offering the same platform in order to maximize votes. This formulation is actually the Hotelling spatial competition model applied to elections. Moreover it forms the basis for the median voter theorem.

I. **BASIC** **STRUCTURE** **OF THE MODEL**	1. Introduction
	2. Party Motivation and the Function of Government in Society
	3. The Basic Logic of Voting
	4. The Basic Logic of Government Decision-Making
II. **THE GENERAL** **EFFECTS OF** **UNCERTAINTY**	5. The Meaning of Uncertainty
	6. How Uncertainty Affects Government Decision-Making
	7. The Development of Political Ideologies as Means of Getting Votes
	8. The Statics and Dynamics of Party Ideologies
	9. Problems of Rationality Under Coalition Governments
	10. Government Vote-Maximizing and Individual marginal Equilibrium
III. **SPECIFIC** **EFFECTS OF** **INFORMATION** **COSTS**	11. The Process of Becoming Informed
	12. How Rational Citizens Reduce Information Costs
	13. The Returns From Information and Their Diminution
	14. The Causes and Effects of Rational Abstention
IV. **DERIVATIVE** **IMPLICATIONS** **AND** **HYPOTHESIS**	15. A Comment on Economic Theories of Government Behavior
	16. Testable Prepositions Derived from the Theory

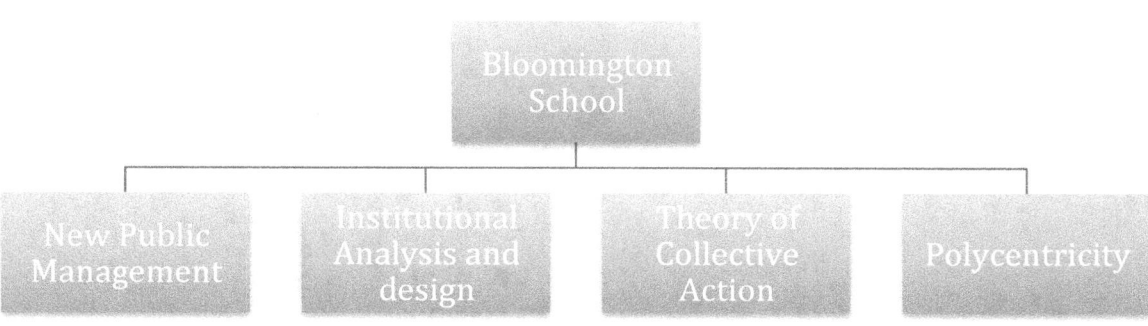

The Bloomington School	
The Ostrom's work on governance created one of the main channels of the transition from public choice to the new institutionalism."	
Vincent Ostrom **(NPM)**	assumed that Public Choice is as aspect of **NIE** because, "The leading contributors to the Public Choice tradition have never confined themselves to a 'core' built on extreme rationality assumptions." He wrote: " In my judgment, the innovative thrust in early **Public Choice** efforts was to bring together concerns about 'methodological individualism', 'the nature of goods', and 'decision making arrangements' (institutions) as distinct elements to be taken into account in addressing market and non market decision making."
Elinor Ostrom **(IAD)**	Institutional analysis has come a long way from the initial reactions to challenges derived from the public choice approach, the debate over the tragedy of the commons, the innovative work of the new institutional economics, and the challenge of behavioral game theory. At the beginning of the twenty-first century, however, strong foundations have been achieved for further research on complex, multitier, institutional arrangements and their consequences. Let the potlatch continue.

NIE Elinor Ostrom's IAD

Elinor Ostrom	Elinor Ostrom was a professor of Public Administration at the University of Indiana along with her husband Vincent Ostrom. She received the Nobel Prize in Economics in 2008 for her work in solving environmental problems with common resources.			
Institutional Analysis and Design	helps integrate work undertaken by those interested in how institutions affect the incentives confronting individuals and their resultant behavior. The essential foundations of her system include: (1) frameworks, (2) theories, and (3) models.			
Frameworks Helps to identify the elements and the relationships among these elements that one needs to consider for institutional analysis.	**Action Arena** A conceptual unit used for analyzing, predicting and explaining behavior within institutional arrangements. An action arena refers to the social space where individuals interact, exchange goods and services, solve problems, dominate one another, feel guilty, or fight.	**Factors affecting the structure of an action arena**	Rules and norms	
			Attributes of the states of the world	
			Structure of the more general community	
		Action Situation	Participants	
			positions	
			outcomes	
			control that participants exercise,	
			information costs and benefits assigned to outcomes	
			action outcome linkages,	
			information	
		Actors	Resources that an actor brings	
			The valuation actors assign to states of the world and to actions	
			The way actors acquire, process, retain, and use knowledge contingencies and information	
			The processes actors use for selection of particular courses of action	
Theories	The particular assumptions made by an analyst about an actor enable one to build a theory of rational choice, a theory of bounded rationality, or a theory of norm driven behavior.			
Rules	Shared understandings about what actions are required, prohibited or permitted. All rules are the result of implicit or explicit efforts to achieve order and predictability among persons. Only some of these are written.			
	Rules in Use	Used by participants to justify their actions		
	Rules of Law	General legal frameworks taken in constitutions, etc.		
	Working Rules	Affect the structure of any repetitive action situation		
		Boundary rules, position rules, scope rules, etc.		

Ostrom's IAD Working Rules

seven groups of working rules can be said to affect the structure of any repetitive action situation, including markets, hierarchies, legislatures, common-property management systems, or competitive sports.	
Boundary Rules	Boundary rules directly affect the number of *participants,* their attributes and resources, whether they can enter freely, and the conditions they face for leaving.
Position Rules	Position rules establish *positions* in the situation.
Scope Rules	Scope rules delimit the *potential outcomes* that can be affected and working backwards, the actions linked to specific outcomes.
Authority Rules	Authority rules assign sets of *actions* that participants in positions at particular nodes must, may, or may not take. Authority rules, combined with the scientific laws about the relevant states of the world being acted upon, determine the shape of the decision tree-the *action-outcome linkages.*
Aggregation Rules	Aggregation rules affect the level of *control* that a participant in a position exercises in the selection of an action at a node.
Information Rules	Information rules affect the *knowledge-contingent information sets* of participants.
Payoff Rules	Payoff rules affect the *benefits and costs* that will be assigned to particular combinations of actions

International Political Economy

The field of international political economy (IPE) is also known as Global Political Economy (GPE). Benjamin Cohen explains that IPE is an effort to bride the gap between international economics and international relations.

Schools	**British School**	IPE is seen as a discipline unto itself. The British school takes a more interpretive approach and searches for grand theories. The state is viewed as just one actor among many. International relations is seen as a part of IPE.
	American School	According to Benjamin Cohen, this is the dominant school of IPE. Priority is given to the scientific method. Analysis is based on the twin principles of positivism and empiricism. The state is viewed as the central actor in IPE. IPE is seen as a part of international relations.
	French School	More emphasis is placed on regulatory issues.
	German School	More emphasis is placed on institutions.
International Relations	**Theory**	Positivist theories
		Post- Positivist theories
		Leadership Theories
		Post- Structuralist Theories
	Institutions	General Insitutions
		Economic Institutions
		Legal Institutions
International Economics	**International Finance**	Based on macroeconomic theory. It is concerned with balance of payments, and currency trading.
	International Trade	Based on microeconomic theory. Concerned with economic geography intellectual property rights.

International Political Economy

Globalization is a key concept in IPE. The big question in IPE concerns whether it is economics that drives global change or is it politics?

Governance	Hegemonic stability organizes international politics and economics. It results in a prosperous world system.
Public Policy	It is concerned with a systematic understanding of how political institutions and public policies operate in world affairs.
International Development	Is concerned with the level of development on an international scale. Countries are classified as: developed, developing and least developed.

Positions in IPE

Constructivist	Liberal	Mercantilist
This is a globalist approach to IPE. It takes a Marxist approach to economics.	This is a middle position that accepts globalism and or regionalism. It takes a Keynesian approach to macroeconomics.	It rejects globalism in favor of the nation-state. It takes a free market approach to economics. It also takes a realist position from international relations

International Monetary Relations	
Regimes in International Monetary Relations	**Classical Gold Standards** based on fixed exchange rates (1870s-1914)
	The Interwar Period (1918-1944)
	The Bretton Woods System (1944- 1973)
	Fixed Exchange Rates (1973- present)
Bretton Woods	After World War II, the economies of most nations were destroyed. Because the United States was protected by the Atlantic and Pacific Oceans, it was the sole economic world power. At this conference, the economists established a new gold exchange standard in which each country's currency was pegged to either gold or the U.S. dollar.
International Monetary Fund	Its primary purpose is to ensure the stability of the international monetary system- the system of exchange rates and international payments that enables countries(and their citizens) to transact with each other. The IMF's mandate was updated in 2012 to include all macroeconomic and financial sector issues that bear on global stability.
World Bank	An internal financial institution that provides loans to countries of the world for capital programs. It comprises two institutions: the **International Bank for Reconstruction and Development (IBRD)** and the **International Development Association (IDA)**. The World bank is a component of the **World Bank Group**, which is part of the **United Nations System**.

International Trade Relations	
Before World War II, states would shift their positions from trade liberalization and protectionism. Both globalism and regionalism have proven to be significant forces in international trade since the post war period began.	
General Agreement on Tariffs and Trade	**GATT** resulted from a desire to create an **International Trade Organization** that would join the other two Bretton Woods Institutions: The **World Bank** and the **International Monetary Fund**. From 148- 1994 **GATT** provided the rules for much of world trade and presided over periods that saw some of the highest growth rates in international commerce.
World Trade Organization	Is concerned with the global rules of trade between nations. It's main function is to ensure that trade flows smoothly and predictably. All decisions are made by member governments and the rules are the outcome of negotiations among members. It was established in 1995 by the work of the **General Agreement on Tariffs and Trade.**

Regional Trade Agreements

There is disagreement over the reasons for regionalism. At the same time, there is no disagreement that regionalism is at odds with globalism

Mercantilism	RTAs are a response to security and power relationships
Liberalism	RTAs are formed to increase regional peace and provide a larger market for members goods. RTAs are formed because of pressure from domestic groups and they also increase foreign investment.
Materialism	RTAs are formed as a result of **Multinational Corporations (MNC)** that desire to move into a country and then trade with member nations. These MNCs also seek to benefit from lower taxes, wages and environmental regulation within the RTA.

Types of RTAs

Free Trade Area	Member states eliminate tariffs and other restrictions of trade with each other.. At the same time, each member can retain its own trade policies with non- member states.
Customs Union	Like a **Free Trade Area**, but with a common external tariff for non- member states.
Common Market	Like a **Common Union**, but it includes the free mobility of capital and labor among member states.
Economic Union	Like an **Common Market** which harmonizes the members industrial, regional, transport, fiscal, and monetary policies. It also includes a common currency.
Political Union	Like a Economic union, but it also harmonizes the members foreign and defense policies. It is more like a federal political system than an agreement among sovereign states.